First Citizen

First Citizen
The Industrious Life of Joseph G. Butler, Jr.

Joseph Lambert, Jr., and Rick Shale

McFarland & Company, Inc., Publishers
Jefferson, North Carolina

ISBN (print) 978-1-4766-9040-7
ISBN (ebook) 978-1-4766-4829-3

LIBRARY OF CONGRESS AND BRITISH LIBRARY
CATALOGUING DATA ARE AVAILABLE

Library of Congress Control Number 2022047026

© 2022 Joseph Lambert, Jr. All rights reserved

No part of this book may be reproduced or transmitted in any form or by any means, electronic or mechanical, including photocopying or recording, or by any information storage and retrieval system, without permission in writing from the publisher.

Front cover image: portrait of J.G. Butler, Jr., 1920, by Ivan Gregorovitch Olinsky. Oil (The Butler Institute of American Art, Youngstown, Ohio; gift of Jonathan Warner, 1920. This painting was conserved by Mr. and Mrs. James Miller. © Ivan Gregorovitch Olinsky or Estate).

Printed in the United States of America

McFarland & Company, Inc., Publishers
Box 611, Jefferson, North Carolina 28640
www.mcfarlandpub.com

Joseph Lambert, Jr.:
To my wife, Tracy, and my children:
Sidney, Alexandra, and Matthew Lambert.

In memory of Rick Shale.

Table of Contents

Preface	1
Introduction	5
ONE. A Family Tree Full of Ironmasters	9
TWO. Going to Work for James Ward	17
THREE. Ironman	28
FOUR. The Onward March	38
FIVE. Taking Hold at Brier Hill	51
SIX. Iron's Demise and the Promise of Steel	62
SEVEN. First Steel in Youngstown	74
EIGHT. The Original McKinley Man	87
NINE. Big Steel	98
TEN. The Western Adventures	107
ELEVEN. The Gary Dinners	115
TWELVE. "The Youngest Old Man We Know"	128
THIRTEEN. The National McKinley Birthplace Memorial	142
FOURTEEN. A Journey to France and the Great War	154
FIFTEEN. Pro Bono Publico	167
SIXTEEN. Writing the Final Chapters	179
Epilogue	191
Chapter Notes	195
Bibliography	217
Index	225

Preface

UNDER AN AUTUMN SKY in September 1920, a large crowd gathered for the dedication of the Butler Art Institute, known today as the Butler Institute of American Art. The museum's founder and namesake, Joseph G. Butler, Jr., nearing his 80th birthday, and in delicate health, was on hand to present the new museum and its fine art collection to the people of Youngstown, Ohio. It was Butler's greatest visual offering to his beloved community and the culmination of an industrious life devoted to the advancement of the iron and steel industry, American art, and other philanthropic causes in which he was lifelong engaged.

As far as turn of the century industrialists turned philanthropists are concerned, Butler stands out for several reasons. Amassing his fortune in the iron and steel industry in Ohio's Mahoning Valley, Butler helped shape the local economy like no other figure as he led the industry's transition from iron to steel. Because of his foresight, vision, and ability to bring people together for a common cause, he helped position the local economy for unprecedented growth.

His experience in the iron and steel industry began at the early age of 13 as an unskilled laborer. He rose quickly in the ranks while still at a young age to management positions and in due course to owner status. Eventually, his success brought him into the highest and most influential circles in the industry where he routinely encountered powerful business leaders and prominent politicians.

In some ways, Butler was like most businessmen of the era because he possessed the necessary attributes for business success, namely, determination, a drive to succeed, and an inherent understanding of the market. Yet, unlike most, he often directed his energies toward community enrichment projects as much as he did toward his business interests. And despite the accumulation of wealth, influence, and prestige, Butler's roots and devotion remained firmly planted in Youngstown and the Mahoning Valley where he acquired a reputation as an energetic and benevolent figure who worked tirelessly for a variety of civic causes.

Within his community, he led important campaigns to build and furnish libraries, hospitals, the local historical society and art societies, and he was involved in animal welfare projects, railroad crossing safety, school reunions, parades, memorials, and his art museum. He even made time to serve on the city council and head the local chamber of commerce. Aside from business and art, his other passion was politics, and he worked enthusiastically for the Republican party in local, state, and national campaigns where he enjoyed the personal friendships with senators, governors, and presidents. And he used those relationships for practical ends, like seeking protection for the iron and steel industry, and for any advantage he could acquire for his hometown.

Undoubtedly, there were no pious successful businessmen during the Gilded Age. It was not a time of innocence. To be sure, Joseph G. Butler, Jr., was as aggressive and competitive as any young capitalist on the rise in the 19th century. And in most instances, his dogged determination usually brought him the prize he sought. Joseph G. Butler, Jr., was as surely a self-made man as any who achieved success during this period. But what makes Butler stand out more than others is that he became known as a civic-minded citizen while in the throes of his multifaceted business career. And he didn't wait to act until after his wealth was secured. He had already been busy serving his community.

His efforts also made him an endearing figure among his business associates. One observed of Butler, "While some of us are dreaming, Mr. Butler is doing, and when we wake up we find our dreams realities, for he is always wide awake and always finds something good to do."

His junior colleagues affectionately referred to him as "Uncle Joe," and they admired him for his wise counsel and guidance. Charles Schwab once saluted Butler when he declared, "When I am as old as Uncle Joe, I shall indeed be proud if my career leaves me with a record as clean and as good as his."[1]

By the time of his 70th birthday celebration, Butler's reputation as a benevolent community leader had already been established. But more was yet to come. For the next 17 years, Joseph G. Butler, Jr., devoted the remaining years of his life to his adoring family and to his beloved iron and steel industry, nation, and community. And they admired him all the same, rallying around his leadership for a variety of causes. For his efforts, his boyhood town of Niles, Ohio, once held Joe Butler Day in his honor.

Today, his name lives on because of the beautiful art gallery he gave to his city, the Butler Institute of American Art. Yet so little is known of him or his life. The marble façade of the museum bears his name but not his story. Joseph G. Butler, Jr., lived a purposeful life. His story is as interesting and multifaceted as any who lived during that era and makes for an exciting story.

Preface

This book could not have been completed without the assistance of so many. My late co-author Rick Shale and I are indebted first to the late distinguished historian Professor Frederick J. Blue. His constructive input, guidance, and support during the manuscript's early development was invaluable. The support and encouragement of friends is always gratifying. James Marling accompanied me on a memorable road trip to locate Butler's birthplace. He also read portions of the manuscript and offered invaluable input. Dan O'Brien also reviewed several chapters and provided critical advice. Their faith over the years helped to get the project across the finish line.

My wife Tracy deserves special mention. She read every page of every chapter without fail and helped to transform an idea into this finished product. Her encouragement and support never failed and helped to see this project through.

Many local institutions and their staffs graciously opened their doors and assisted our research efforts including the Youngstown Historical Center of Labor and Industry, Pat Finan and the McKinley Memorial Library, the Youngstown Chamber of Commerce, the Niles Historical Society, Youngstown State University's Maag Library, and the Public Library of Youngstown and Mahoning County. Much gratitude is extended to the Butler Institute of American Art and its director, Lou Zona. His staff, especially Patrick McCormick and Alison Begala, were extremely helpful. McCormick discovered a collection of Butler's letters and correspondence between McKim, Mead, White and J. Massey Rhind. Likewise, the archival staff at the Mahoning Valley Historical Society under archivist Pam Speis was always accommodating as we pored over a plethora of Butler's letters, notes and scrapbooks and his vast collection of ephemera.

The bulk of the research relied upon Butler's personal correspondence, memoirs, numerous books and published articles, newspapers, and numerous published and unpublished secondary sources.

Special thanks are given to Sidney Lambert, Alexandra Lambert, and Matthew Lambert for their faith and support. They all have grown up hearing about Mr. Butler.

I would also like to thank Malorie Eagle and Steffanie Kolovich who provided research assistance.

Of course, the authors are grateful to McFarland and their supportive staff for helping this project see the light of day. We are responsible for the content and hope that errors are minimal.

My co-author Rick Shale passed away in February 2022. His passion and dedication to this project knew no bounds. He liked to say enthusiastically, "I think we have a good book here." We hope you agree.

Introduction

THE MOST VISIBLE REMINDER of the life of Joseph G. Butler, Jr., is the art museum in Youngstown, Ohio, that bears his name. Butler gave the Butler Art Institute to his city in 1920. It was the first museum in the country to collect and display works strictly by American artists. Although it was not his only cultural contribution, it is by far the one for which he is most remembered. The second most visible contribution is the National McKinley Birthplace Memorial in Niles, Ohio. As a childhood friend of William McKinley, the nation's 25th president, Butler almost single-handedly saw to the construction of the assassinated president's memorial. These two landmarks are synonymous with Butler's name and his philanthropic legacy and continue to attract art and history enthusiasts. The art museum bears his name; however, few know little if anything about the life of the successful iron and steel industrialist for whom it was named.

Born to parents of indefatigable character in 1840, Butler did not come from a wealthy family. His own arduous struggles were not unlike the personal experiences of those who later worked in his mills. He was nothing but a bright, upstart teenager when he got his first job in the iron industry where he proved to be a highly motivated and self-conscious young man. From this well-timed opportunity he eagerly embraced fortuitous possibilities that led him down a successful career path. What followed was a truly American self-made success story. One recent historian reminds us that while Butler was active in his career, among his colleagues, he was regarded as "one of the finest minds in the iron and steel industry."[1] Later on, he was deferentially referred to by his younger colleagues as "Uncle Joe" because of the paternal guidance he offered to the next generation of iron and steel men. That endearing title was also taken up by the local citizens who warmly embraced his philanthropic work on their behalf. His rise in status and accumulation of wealth was not without casualties, however.

Butler did not attain the unimaginable wealth of a Vanderbilt, Morgan, Carnegie, or Frick. But make no mistake, Joseph G. Butler, Jr., was a wealthy man when he died. During his career, he was an aggressive businessman who thrived on spirited competition, a characteristic of other successful business leaders of the era. Opportunities were everywhere during the mid–19th century, and if one didn't grasp them, someone else would. Joseph Butler grabbed with both hands.

The growth of 19th-century industry required unskilled labor, great quantities of it. In Youngstown, the booming iron industry demanded thousands of unskilled hands to work the furnaces and mills constructed in the Mahoning River Valley. Attracted by the promise of a fresh start and economic independence, European immigrants and African Americans from the South were lured to emerging manufacturing centers like Youngstown where they arrived in waves. This influx brought with it great strains upon livable conditions including clean and affordable housing and healthcare.[2] The cheap and plentiful masses of unskilled labor meant low wages for workers and increased profits for operators.

Owner-operators focused on production and profit, not wages. Both owners and workers living in the Mahoning Valley depended on production. The flow of molten iron was the life blood of the business. For decades, generations of men continued to seek work in the Mahoning Valley to scratch out a living to support their families. Without the mills running, there was no work, and Butler and his co-owners did everything in their power to ensure that the mills kept on running for all involved. Without the financial investment, foresight, and methods of the owners, the mills could not function. And without the sweat and back-breaking labor of the workers, the owners would know no wealth. The relationship between owners and labor was a precarious one. Prior to the organization of unskilled labor, owners maintained the upper hand.[3]

This Gilded Age saw an explosion of new millionaires in the United States. They were guided by a philosophy of fierce competition.[4] And Joseph G. Butler, Jr., was as aggressive and competitive as any capitalist in the latter half of the 19th century. In most instances, his determination brought him success. He was surely as self-assured as any during this period. While Butler helped to lead the industry's transition from iron to steel, his success earned him a position in the highest and most powerful circles in the industry. Once there, he used his influence with politicians to gain protection for the industry. With his increased stature, he became one of the most recognizable figures at the national level where he was constantly in the mix of the most pressing issues affecting industry and politics. By 1920, he was one of a handful of well-known iron and steel executives that called Youngstown home, and he was easily the most recognizable of any of the region's industrial leaders. Andrew Carnegie, Andrew Mellon, John D. Rockefeller, and Henry Frick were the leading philanthropists in terms of monetary donations, but Butler was more often in the mix of the common citizen serving on the town council or chairing fundraising causes.

Before he attained his wealth, Butler split his attention between business and community improvements. He was known to work for a variety of civic causes like leading campaigns to build libraries, hospitals, memorials, and museums, and lesser causes like organizing the local historical society, school reunions, parades, art societies, and historic preservation. His passion for worthwhile causes appeared limitless. And he often sought support from his fellow business colleagues. There was no one of means, including presidents, safe from Butler's relentless solicitations for financial or political support for some endeavor. These efforts and more made him an endearing figure among the local citizens.

Butler was supported throughout his life by his loving and beautiful wife, Harriet. They shared the same level of intellect, a love of travel, and an appreciation for culture and refinement. They also raised three children together, each of whom provided loving and doting grandchildren. Butler's children and their offspring revered him. But it was his only son, Henry, upon whom he grew extremely dependent. The son was groomed to take over his father's many business and charitable concerns.

Butler was feted in 1910 by one local leader as "the leading citizen of our town" who, as head of the Chamber of Commerce, was in the process of "securing an adequate water supply for the city and has worked hard to have grade crossings eliminated in our principal streets." James Campbell concluded, "No worthy charitable proposition has ever been turned down by him."[5] But more was yet to come. For the next 17 years, Joseph G. Butler, Jr., devoted the remaining years of his life to his adoring family, his beloved iron and steel industry, his nation, and his community.

This period of United States history is full of success stories like Butler's. For as much wealth as Butler attained, it did not come close to that accumulated by the real Titans of the Age who were either looked upon admirably as the great Captains of Industry or derisively as devilish Robber Barons. The former propelled the might of American industry and the influence of the United States on the international scene; the latter trampled upon the rights of the laboring class while they themselves climbed the ladder of success.[6] In the twilight of their careers, for a variety of reasons, many decided to donate portions of their wealth to charity, some, it was said, to make amends for their sinful gains. The most famous effort was that of Carnegie who pledged to give away his fortune—all of it—before he died.

Aside from the iron and steel industry, art was Butler's one true passion, first aroused as a young boy. With wealth, he began to build a personal collection of art that became one of the most respected private collections in the country. His ultimate desire was to share this with the public because he believed an appreciation of art was universal and offered something of value for everyone. Butler took the lead and built his own art museum for all to enjoy. What benefit a laboring mill worker providing for his family would gain from such an offering was questionable, but, to his credit, Butler took steps to lay the welcome mat at the door for the lower socio-economic class.

Butler's impact on the iron and steel industry, his contributions to the art world, his philanthropic endeavors, and his accomplishments as an author and historian were uncommon for his era. Many of his larger-than-life contemporaries surrounded themselves with art and beauty and lived lavishly. Butler lived well, to be sure, but he, more than any other, lent his personal efforts to bring about positive change in his community, a community that he did not grow weary of, for he remained a lifelong fixture in the Mahoning Valley. For these reasons, he stands out more than any other figure of his day.

At his funeral in 1927, the number of mourners who showed up was so great the church was unable to accommodate the masses. They waited outside in the cold before joining the funeral procession to his final resting place. Inside the church, Uncle Joe Butler was eulogized by his contemporaries as "Youngstown's First Citizen." The esteemed title was earned in an era when ruthless business tactics were honed and perfected, when many industrialists uncaringly acquired stupendous wealth. Few emerged without some negative label. Butler, however, largely escaped these monikers of disrepute because he instead earned the respect of his fellow citizens. In return, they dubbed him their "First Citizen."

ONE

A Family Tree Full of Ironmasters

WHEN JOSEPH GREEN BUTLER, JR., was born into quite modest circumstances in 1840, he could not have predicted the astonishing transformation of America's economic, political, and cultural landscape that he would witness during his long life. He matured and built a successful career in what historians would later call the Gilded Age, roughly the period from the end of the Civil War to the end of the century.[1] He edged into retirement and pursued several personal building projects in the Progressive Era, and he lived long enough to witness most of the Roaring Twenties.

When he was 80 years old, Butler completed his three-volume *History of Youngstown and the Mahoning Valley*. At the end of volume one, he inserted a chapter titled "Personal Reminiscences" in which he recounted various bits of local history that did not fit smoothly into the main text. His personal point of view, however, was more than simply an invocation of author's privilege, for Butler himself had been an eyewitness to many of the significant events that marked the development of the Mahoning Valley. Butler's career in iron and steel reads like a history of those industries. He wrote, "I saw the invention and adoption of the Bessemer and the open-hearth steel processes; the opening of the Lake Superior Ore Region; the introduction of coke as a fuel; the invention of the by-product coke process; the introduction of gas, both natural and artificial, in steel plants; the development of markets from almost nothing to their present stage, together with the gradual growth of transportation facilities that has gone with these things. In fact, it has been my privilege to watch the growth of industry in this valley from what might almost be regarded as its true beginning."[2]

Many of Butler's contemporaries in the iron and steel business, Andrew Carnegie, Henry Clay Frick, Charles Schwab, and others, would earn larger fortunes, but it was Butler's interest in and commitment to the iron and steel industry that made him an endearing national figure among its leaders and earned him the affectionate title "Uncle Joe." Few men of his time did more, worked harder, or gave more of themselves personally to improve the social condition of their community than Joseph G. Butler, Jr. He relentlessly promoted Youngstown and the Mahoning Valley and carried his community's banner throughout the industry. Likewise, he promoted his country on the world stage.

Butler was proud of his ancestry, which he could trace to the Normans who fought with William the Conqueror in 1066. The authors of *The Butler Family in America* explain, "Their original name was Walter, from Walter, one of their ancestors; and Theobald Walter came to Ireland with Henry the Second in 1172 and had the office of Chief Butler of Ireland conferred on him, the duty attached to which was to attend at the coronation of the Kings of England and present them with the first cup of wine. From the office of 'Butlership of Ireland' they took the name Butler."[3]

The first ancestor in Butler's direct line to immigrate to America was his great-grandfather, Thomas Butler, who arrived in Pennsylvania in 1759. Born on January 2, 1740, near Dublin, Thomas married Ann Dalrymple in 1765. They had 13 children. Thomas Butler was an iron foundryman and collier. He and his six sons became well-known furnacemen. During the Revolutionary War he was with George Washington at Valley Forge.[4]

The tenth child of Thomas and Ann Butler, Joseph Butler, was born January 7, 1779, in Huntingdon County, Pennsylvania. [We shall refer to him as Joseph Butler (first) to distinguish him from other Joseph Butlers in the generations to follow.] He moved to Bellefonte, Pennsylvania, with his father and brother, James, and they used their furnace skills to help produce the famous, high-quality Juniata blooms.

In 1807, Joseph Butler (first) married Esther Green, his employer's daughter. Together they had eight children. After the birth of her eighth child in June 1821, Esther Green died a month short of her 29th birthday. Her mother, Hannah Green, raised the children. In the same year that he lost his wife, Joseph Butler (first), at the age of 41, was elected sheriff of Centre County and served for three years. He later married Rachel Gould Parker with whom he had five more children.[5] It was from the first union with Esther Green that Joseph Green Butler was born on May 13, 1814, marking the third generation of Butlers born into the iron industry.[6]

The Butler Family in America carries the following description of Joseph Green Butler: "In general appearance he was very much of a Quaker, and always went clean shaved, no beard; he was fond of dressing in grey. Was not a religious man in the eyes of the world (being a Universalist) but was a great Bible reader, living up to its teachings closely. Levity was not a part of his character. He was the soul of honor in all its dealings and gained a name early in life that remained with him always, that of an 'honest man.'"[7]

One. A Family Tree Full of Ironmasters

To one Temperance Orwig, these characteristics, along with his education and skill, made him a very suitable young man. Temperance, one of 11 children, was born in Salem, Ohio, in 1815 to Quaker parents Jacob and Rebecca Mains Orwig. They believed in the immorality of slavery and the injustice of the unequal treatment of women in society.[8]

One of Temperance's grandsons later described her as "a bright, keen woman, full of energy and grit, small in stature, always of slender build."[9] Her Quaker background proved a good match for her husband's intellect and religious beliefs.

The newly married couple made their home in Centre County where Green Butler was employed. The time spent with his father in the mineral rich and densely forested Juniata Valley region of central Pennsylvania made him a respected authority in the construction and operation of charcoal blast furnaces. Joseph G. Butler, Jr., would later write of his father, "Many years of experience in the building and operation of blast furnaces had made him an expert in that calling, and he was frequently called on by early ironmasters of this region for advice."[10] By the time he was 24, Green Butler had successfully managed several furnaces.

Joseph Green Butler, Sr. (The Mahoning Valley Historical Society, Youngstown, Ohio).

In western Pennsylvania, the growing demands of Pittsburgh iron manufacturers began to hasten the decline of the Juniata Valley. By 1830, western Pennsylvania had 34 iron furnaces servicing Pittsburgh consumers. The steam power revolution at this time caused a tremendous demand for iron. This brought greater competition and lower prices which benefited customers. But this was bad news for producers of the Juniata Valley that were already challenged by the decline in raw materials.[11] Because of these reasons, in 1838 Green Butler joined the exodus from the Juniata Valley.

The Juniata Valley had supported three generations of Butlers for more than 40 years. It was the place of Green Butler's birth and that of his father. Temperance had given birth to two sons, Ithamar and Miles. Despite sentimental attachment to the region, the economic reality far outweighed emotional ties. The depletion of crucial raw materials hastened Green Butler's exodus. The iron industry was spreading west of the Appalachian Mountains where new ore fields had been discovered. New iron-producing regions were growing in places like Pittsburgh as well as further west. It was to Pennsylvania's Shenango Valley that Green Butler decided to relocate in search of economic security.

News of newly discovered ore tracts attracted Green Butler to Mercer County. Of keen interest there existed no iron-producing furnace in the county to supply the local needs. The ready supply of bog ore and timber for charcoal further convinced him that Mercer County was the spot. Confident in his abilities, though short of capital, he took a chance and at age 23, Green Butler set out for Mercer County with Temperance and their two children.[12]

Mercer County was sparsely populated when the Butler caravan arrived

Temperance Orwig Butler (The Mahoning Valley Historical Society, Youngstown, Ohio).

in 1838, but signs of growth were evident. In 1830, the county's population was 19,729, 28 people per square mile. By 1840, the county's population had reached 32,873. The area was known more for agriculture and wool growing.[13]

William McKnight, in his *History of Northwestern Pennsylvania*, describes the village of Mercer, the county seat, in 1840: "The dwellings are neat and substantial, and display a pleasing variety of architectural embellishments.... Daily lines of stages pass through on the Pittsburgh and Erie turnpike." The town also had an academy, five churches, a foundry, and some stores and taverns.

The location of a blast furnace was critical to its success. It is important to understand how they were built, where they were erected, why they were constructed as they were, and how they functioned. In addition, the danger created by the heat of the inferno, as well as the delicacy of its science, needs to be understood. A better explanation than historian George W. Hughes's offering is hard to find: "The blast furnace at the beginning of the nineteenth century was simple in construction, consisting of a mass of stone work, either round or square on the outside and barrel shaped on the inside, and lined with sand stone, ranging from twenty-four to forty feet in height and about twenty-four square at the bottom. The furnace was usually built against the side of a hill to avoid the necessity of hoisting the coke, ore, and limestone to the top of the furnace; ... The furnace was always built on a stream large enough to furnish water for an over-shot water wheel that furnished power to force the air into the furnace against one-half to one-pound pressure per square inch."[14]

To minimize transportation costs, blast furnaces were located near abundant sources of iron ore and timber for fuel. Green Butler purchased an ideal spot of land in Sandy Creek Township that had the necessary water source, timber, and good ore. But he was also intrigued by news of a proposed canal to be built through this portion of the county. (Construction of the Beaver and Erie Canal, also known as the Erie Extension Canal, began in 1827. The north-south course linked the Ohio River to Lake Erie. When it was completed in 1844, Green Butler was divested from the area.)[15]

Pennsylvania enjoyed a robust economy through the mid–1830s, but overproduction and imports plagued the iron industry at large. But 1837 saw the onset of a financial panic. Banks failed and other businesses went bankrupt. The iron market became saturated, and manufacturers struggled to find customers. The depression would last for several years. While Butler was organizing and constructing his new furnace in 1838 and 1839, the economy could not have been much worse.[16]

Another issue that hurt Green Butler's chances was a stagnant population. Mercer County's growth had increased dramatically in the 1830s, but during the 1840s, the population stayed virtually the same. The lack of a growing consumer base dampened projected sales of iron products.[17]

After Green Butler purchased his property, he realized that his financial situation was not good. He grew weary and hesitated to move forward with construction. Consequently, on January 24, 1838, he placed an advertisement in the local newspaper, the *Mercer Luminary*: "The subscriber, having purchased a property in Mercer County for the purpose of erecting a blast furnace, is desirous of obtaining a partner. The property is good—good ore, plenty of it—timber in abundance—all within four or five miles of Crooked Creek, to which place it is supposed the Shenango Canal will be completed the ensuing season." Finding the will and determination to move forward, he made it clear that he was eager to begin construction. "It is desired that any persons wishing to enter into a business of this kind would apply soon," he announced, "as the subscriber intends making such arrangements as that he may be able to attend to the erection of a furnace, himself, if he does not procure a partner soon."[18]

Soon after, Butler was approached by an able iron man in his own right, William McKinley. This father of the future president, like Green Butler, was also descended from iron men. McKinley had been engaged in the iron trade and would remain so throughout his life. McKinley was a known investor in iron interests like Butler's furnace. He shared interests in Columbiana County and Trumbull County, Ohio, for nearly two decades. In 1834, he owned a lot in Niles, Ohio. In terms of property, McKinley surely had the assets to back the project. Biographer Charles Olcott described him as "an industrious worker, and a good business man, who, though never prosperous in a large way, was always able to provide for the necessities of his family."[19]

Nineteenth-century furnace construction followed a pattern where the hillside was cleared of trees and vegetation. Then, large stones were placed at the base and gradually set one on top of the other against the hillside until they reached the height of the hilltop some 30 feet or so high. In a paper he delivered in 1917, Joseph G. Butler, Jr., described the construction of these early blast furnaces: "The stack was usually located against a bluff, the double purpose being to make construction cheaper by using the hill to reinforce one side and enable a patient mule to perform the functions of a skip hoist by dragging the ore to the top of the hill. A short bridge connected the stockhouse with the top and the material charged was wheeled from this point and dumped in at the open top."[20]

Construction of Green Butler's furnace went on throughout the winter of 1838, but it was not until the spring of the following year that the furnace was ready for blast. Since Butler likely supplied more capital than McKinley, he reserved the right to choose the name of the furnace.

Furnaces were usually named after their location, like the Centre Furnace, or were named after popular presidents, statesmen, or, most commonly, in honor of women.[21] For Butler, the naming of the furnace was an easy decision. The most important person in his life was his wife, and in her honor the furnace was christened Temperance Furnace in the spring of 1839.

J.G. White, in his *History of Mercer County*, wrote, "When the furnace was in blast it made a roaring noise which could be heard a long distance, while from its mouth was emitted a continuous stream of sparks, which could be seen for miles at night."[22] Green Butler devoted his full attention to Temperance Furnace. It was a demanding position. Since a furnace was in blast night and day, good ironmasters were on hand at all hours. Historian Joseph Walker explained, "The manager of an iron furnace in the first half of the nineteenth century had a complex and exacting job; he needed an almost impossible combination of talents and skills to find the answer to all the problems that faced him day by day. He was of necessity a technician, a production expert, a personnel director, a transportation control agent, a salesman, an expediter, an economist, a market analyst, a currency expert, a credit manager, a bill collector, a purchasing agent, an investment counselor and a bookkeeper." Walker added "a charcoal furnace in production needed large quantities of food and fuel for man, beast and furnace hearth; and these requirements necessitated the ownership of large areas of land for farm crops, gardens, orchards, and forests."[23]

The Butlers resided in a nearby farmhouse. In this structure, on December 21, 1840, Temperance gave birth to the couples' third son, Joseph Green Butler, Jr. The child, throughout his life, proudly and endlessly proclaimed, "I was practically born in the business, my entrance on the stage of life having been made within two hundred feet of the casting house of a blast furnace."[24]

Besides the financial risks of operating a furnace, there was always the catastrophic risk of a furnace burning down, which is just what happened to the Temperance Furnace in 1840. Most likely a faulty lining of the inner wall was the cause. The intense heat generated within the furnace could reduce the stack to rubble if the firebrick along the inner walls was poorly lined. Fortunately, no one was injured in this incident at Temperance Furnace.[25]

Green Butler managed to rebuild Temperance Furnace but was sobered by the experience. Thus, he decided to move his family to Niles, Ohio, after accepting a position at James Ward & Company, a new rolling mill operation. McKinley had recently moved to Niles and likely helped Green Butler secure a position.[26]

James Ward and his brother, William, had moved to Niles from New

Lisbon to build a rolling mill. The village was located on the Pennsylvania and Ohio Canal (P & O), which ran from New Castle, Pennsylvania, to Akron, Ohio, where it connected to a canal to Cleveland. The P & O Canal, which opened in 1840, provided access to the markets of Cleveland and Pittsburgh. A small iron furnace operation provided Ward with pig iron for his rolling mill.[27]

Green Butler, Sr., was hired to manage the company store, a position that provided more security and less risks than operating a furnace. Butler would find out just how fortuitous it was moving to Niles. In 1845, Temperance Furnace forced Butler and McKinley into bankruptcy. They were forced to sell the furnace that same year.[28]

For the Butlers, however, relinquishing the daily control of Temperance Furnace provided a new beginning. When the family arrived in Niles in 1842, the family found a typical village. One historian writes, "In the 1840's Niles resembled scores of other country hamlets in Ohio. It boasted little more than a tree-shaded, unpaved street, lined by clapboard houses, a country store, a small church, and a bridge across the creek." Still another adds, "In this quiet spot the people had few social advantages. There were no railroads and few wagon-roads. The stages to and from Pittsburg were the only means of communication with the world."[29] With the completion of a canal through the village, however, those doors were opened to provide some semblance of economic and social opportunity. It was in Niles where a young Joseph G. Butler, Jr., spent his early days of childhood and where his memories of boyhood were formed, soon providing him with the opportunity to get into the business of iron making and setting the stage for his life's work.

Two

Going to Work for James Ward

NILES WAS A BUSY LITTLE VILLAGE when the Butlers arrived. In 1806, James Heaton had constructed a gristmill and a sawmill there on Mosquito Creek just north of the Mahoning River. In 1812, he built the Maria Furnace. Around this developed the small settlement of Heaton's Furnace. Heaton retired in 1830, but in 1834, he platted the village and named it Nilestown in honor of Hezekiah Niles, a Baltimore publisher of the nationally circulated protectionist *Niles Weekly Register*. In 1843, the post office shortened the village name to Niles.[1] In the early 1840s James Ward arrived and soon became the village's new industrial leader.

Ward was born in Staffordshire, England, in 1813 and immigrated with his father to Pittsburgh at the age of four. Pittsburgh in 1817 was in its early days of iron production, and being an iron man himself, Ward's father found the location to be an ideal spot for a forge to produce wrought iron nails. Young James spent his youth from the age of 13 at his father's forge. His interests in the business expanded, and he eventually settled on the engineering aspect of the process. For the next nine years he traveled about learning the trade.

In 1841, brothers James and William Ward and Thomas Russell established an iron business in Lisbon, Ohio. A flood ruined their operation, so the trio looked to relocate to Niles. By 1841, the Mahoning Valley was already recognized as a growing iron-producing region, and there were blast furnaces in the valley that could furnish pig iron to rolling mill operations. In addition to the plentiful coal, Ward knew that the Pennsylvania and Ohio Canal could ship his bar iron, sheet iron, and cut nails to Pittsburgh and Cleveland.[2]

The completion of the James Ward & Company rolling mill in 1842 gave Niles an economic boost. According to Joseph Marion Butler, the few skilled iron workers at the Ward mill frequently had to swap duties: "James Ward was manager—practical all round man, and the engineer, his brother, William Ward, was blacksmith and heater. Wm. [sic] Russell was puddler and roller and J.G. Butler was manager of the store and took his turn at the muck rolls when Russell was puddling; the others changed about also."[3] Ward's was the first puddling operation in the Mahoning Valley. Puddling was described as an indirect process of creating and purifying pig iron. "[T]his operation, occupying 2 to 3 minutes, the purification of the pig iron and the process of puddling advanced by stages, known as **melting, clearing, boiling, balling** and **drawing**. To achieve quick melting the door and other openings were closed, the furnace was fired vigorously, and the pigs turned once or twice by the puddler or his helper."[4] Thus, a skilled puddler was vital to the success of the operation. But just as vital were the pull ups, younger boys who raised and lowered the furnace doors.

Moving to Niles marked a new beginning for the Butlers. Despite its size, the village offered a broader scope of social and business activities than the community surrounding Temperance Furnace thanks to the Pennsylvania and Ohio Canal. There were more neighbors and more friends for Joe Jr. and his brothers and a less hectic job for their father. Niles had a tremendous impact on young Joe who said later, "my memory is filled with recollections of its quaint customs and its people."[5]

For Butler Sr., the Ward Company store kept steadier hours compared to managing his Pennsylvania furnace. Temperance befriended the McKinley and Allison families. The three Butler boys, Ithamar, Miles, and Joe Jr., were followed by James Irwin (1843), Edward Steven (1846), Emma (1850), William (1860), James Ward (1852), Emma Eliza (1855), and Alice (1857).[6]

Butler Jr. remembered family life as happy. "The home was then more sacred and the family life more intimate," he wrote in his autobiography. "Our family during the days at Niles grew up together and our evenings were usually spent in the family circle.... Parents and children gathered around the evening candles to read, talk, and enjoy one another's society. The friends of one were the friends and associates of all." He added, "We were all taught that work took precedence of play as soon as we were able to do useful things."[7]

The boys spent their spare time in the spring and summer months swimming and wrestling. But the most popular activity among boys and men alike was pitching horseshoes.[8] During the winter months amusement centered around the river and creek. Butler remembered, "There was a time when the Mahoning [River] froze over each winter and furnished, not only excellent skating, but also a good driveway for sleighs and sleds."[9]

A childhood friendship formed with William McKinley, Jr., the son of his father's one-time business partner. As Butler's career progressed in the iron and steel industry, McKinley's took a turn toward the law, politics, and government service. In due course, the Niles native would become the 25th president of the United States.

Aside from the usual games and sports, Butler sought out other opportunities for fun. The arrival of a stagecoach or a canal boat offered the curious citizens not only a glimpse of the colorful passengers traveling through Niles but also the unknown world beyond the village. Butler once helped a comedian put on a show in a canal warehouse, and he always found a way to visit the circus when it made its local encampment. For the rest of his life, whenever a circus pitched its tent near town, Butler would be a regular visitor. Years later, he wrote to a friend, "I never miss a good circus or menagerie. There is a well-founded belief that the elephant in The Barnum and Bailey Circus recognizes me on their annual visit." Butler remembered getting a glimpse of the great circus promoter himself, P.T. Barnum, strolling the deck of a packet boat on the canal early one morning. The whole town tried to get a look at one of the most popular entertainers of the day, the Swedish Nightingale, Jenny Lind, whom Barnum was promoting.[10]

Butler at ten years of age. A familiar face around Niles, Ohio (The Butler Institute of American Art Archives, Youngstown, Ohio).

For most children, winter months were spent in school at the Old White Schoolhouse, a simple structure dressed in white clapboards. The most commanding feature was the teacher's pine desk, which sat on a platform and demanded attention when the occupant sat before his pupils. Public schooling in the mid–19th century was poorly financed and supplies, as well as teachers' salaries, were minimal to say the least. The situation in Niles was typical. "The principal studies were spelling, reading,

A Group of Niles Boyhood Friends. Front row, left to right are J.M. Brush, William Ward Jr., Butler, and John Dithridge. Standing, from left to right are James Ward Jr., George L. Reis, Irvin Butler, and William B. Berger. From Joseph G. Butler, Jr., *Recollections of Men and Events* (New York: G.P. Putnam's Sons, 1925).

writing and arithmetic, and classes in each of these were held daily," recalled Butler.[11] Most students had to make do with secondhand material. It was common for children in one family to share the same set of books. Butler also remembered using slate to write and the difficulty in acquiring it. "The children of wealthy parents were able to buy slate pencils from the store at a penny apiece, but a great many pupils had to make their own pencils by hunting small pieces of soft slate and whittling these down into something like the form of a pencil." Ink was another luxury that was homemade from pokeberry juice.[12]

A favorite teacher at the Niles schoolhouse was a man named Alva Sanford. He arrived in Niles shortly after the Mexican War and was known about the village as "Santa Anna," apparently due to his resemblance to the Mexican general. Butler explained, "his methods of discipline and punishment were unique, running largely to ridicule. The boys and girls were on opposite sides of the schoolhouse, and one mode of punishment was to send a boy to the girls' side of the house and place him between two girls. This once happened to young McKinley." Another form of school punishment was to force a pupil to stand in front of the entire class. It was common to use corporal punishment. When all else failed, a birch switch was employed.[13]

Butler spent much of his time reading, a habit he maintained throughout his life. He later wrote, "I believe that the most desirable habit that can be formed in youth is that of being entertained by reading, or other practices that improve or expand the mind."[14]

A close friend, Eliza Ward, remembered that Butler and McKinley were the best students among boys of their own age. "Every Friday night," she wrote, "we had a spelling bee at school. We chose sides and stood up, and Joe Butler always stood at the head of the class. There was always a present on the last day to the one having the most credits, and the presents were always divided between Joe Butler and Helen McKinley."[15]

Arriving home one day in 1853, young Butler learned that the family would be leaving Niles. His father decided to take a position in nearby New Wilmington, Pennsylvania, managing the Tremont Furnace. It was a return to a familiar position and duties for Butler Sr. He was hired to replace William McKinley, Sr., who likely was engaged in moving his family to Poland, Ohio.[16] Young Joe Butler was leaving the only place he knew to be home.

The small village of New Wilmington offered even less for young Butler, though his father expected more. While older brothers Ithamar, now 17, clerked in the office and Miles, 15, worked in the plant, Butler Sr. sought work for Joe. "Father tried to get me a job in the only store in the village. I was turned down on account of my size. The Storekeeper Clark said I would have to stand on a stool to reach the scales." He ended up working by his father's side, watching and learning about the operation of a furnace.[17]

During the process of making pig iron, impurities in the form of slag would float to the top of the hot iron and were left over after the furnace was tapped. This slag was then collected and teamed to a location in the woods where it was dumped. Butler's father thought his 13-year-old son could physically handle this task. On one such trip to the woods, recalled Butler, "the cart, horse and driver all went over the dump together, and I had a narrow escape from injury or death, as the slag was hot. After this experience I gave up that job and managed to keep busy otherwise." Fortunately for Butler, the family's stay in New Wilmington lasted less than a year. James Ward brought Butler Sr. back to Niles to re-take charge of the company store. "We were not sorry to leave," Butler remembered.[18]

Joe Butler, Jr., was enthusiastic about the return to Niles. "We moved our household goods by wagon, and I was assigned the task of driving, or rather leading the family cow on the journey of about thirty-five miles," he said of the two-day journey. "It was a great trip," he recalled.[19]

Nothing had changed in the village during the Butler family's near yearlong absence. The village in 1854 was experiencing a gradual industrial resurgence because of the Ward Company.[20] Butler quickly fell back into the same social sets that had given him so much mental stimulation and personal satisfaction in the past.

After Butler Sr.'s return to Niles to manage the Ward company store, he remained intimately engaged in the iron industry. In the mid-1850s, he explored the iron ore fields in the Lake Superior region of Michigan and became involved in the construction of a blooming forge there.[21]

While young Butler's formal education ended at the age of 13, his informal education was just beginning. "Father was not well off and was unable to give us all an education. I had to choose between going to school and going to work. I chose the latter," he explained. Butler and his brothers went to work in the Ward company store under their father's supervision. For Butler, it was a moment that marked the transformation from youth to adult, a genuine turning point in his life. He recalled later that going to work in the company store "ended what may be called my boyhood, for from that time on I was actively engaged in [the iron] business, with the thoughts and aspirations of a man, rather than those of a boy."[22] Upon entering his teen years, he was no longer interested in the carefree adventures of youth.

Most of the Ward Rolling Mill store's customers were company employees and their families. There was a concentration of Welsh immigrants employed at the Mineral Ridge coal mines just south of Niles that frequented the store. To better serve these Welsh customers, young Butler decided to learn their language. Butler took nightly lessons from one of the locals, Mrs. Benjamin Rosser. Though far from fluent, he was soon able to exchange sentences with the local population. However, Butler recalled, "The result of this was that I was overworked, as nearly all of the [Welsh] customers came to me to be waited on."[23]

In all, he spent about three years as the store clerk where he acquired a great deal of knowledge about business practice and methods. For instance, most company-owned stores of the day and subsequent ones were designed to indebt their employees to the company. Since cash was rare and seldom used, goods could be bought from the store on credit, but the prevailing value of labor often was not enough to cover the cost of the goods purchased.[24]

Purchasing on credit further tied the fate of employees to the company. "The men were paid principally in store goods," said Butler. "When a man went to work in the mill he was given credit at the store, and many of them bought so much that they were always in debt." Added to this, some companies, including Ward's, paid their employees with company-issued scrip that could be exchanged only at stores owned by the company. Only on Christmas and the Fourth of July would the Ward employees be paid in currency. "There was little money in circulation," remembered Butler, "and frequently the entire payroll of the mill would take no more than fifty dollars in cash."[25] Paying workers with scrip rather than cash quashed their ability to participate in a free market and further indebted them to the company. A young and naïve Butler could not see the model in place then. It's likely that a mature, business savvy Butler would never admit to its true designs and certainly not identify with the historian Hardy Green's take about company towns and their support structures: "Business exists to make a profit, not to coddle employees."[26]

When Butler was 16, a simple event occurred that changed the course of his life. His father was working inside the store when a distraught James Ward, Sr., appeared and informed the elder Butler, "Our Shipping Clerk is on a drunk and I want one of the boys to come and help me out. There is a boat due soon which we must load for Cleveland." Butler remembered his father's response: "Mr. Ward, there are my three boys. Take your choice." Without hesitating Ward chose the youngest, Joe Jr. Butler was so intent on impressing Ward that he worked through supper and by 10 p.m. had the boat loaded and had in hand a bill of lading signed by its captain. At that late hour Butler made his way from the canal dock to Ward's residence where he announced the completion of the job to his boss. Ward instructed his young employee to return the next day for a permanent job in the shipping department. The unfortunate clerk was discharged, as Butler recalled, "and father was notified to get someone else to take my place in the store."[27]

Being a clerk meant having a variety of responsibilities. Butler's days were long and his assignments far reaching. Wagons or boats delivered pig iron from Youngstown or Mercer County to Niles. Loading and unloading was strenuous but important work. "When we started in to load a boat," said Butler, "it was a continuous performance ... until the task was ended. I worked many a time from dark to daylight." Another task was seeing to the company horse and buggy, but this chore had its perks. When it was not in company use, Butler was permitted to take the horse and buggy around town. "I was probably the only young man in Niles who could occasionally visit his lady friends in real style or take them out for a drive."[28]

Not many of the young men of the village were given these opportunities. Others were subjected to the hard labor and conditions of the rolling mill and the dangers inherent therein. Butler surmised there were about a dozen boys who worked as "pull ups" in the mill. Before child labor laws were enacted in the next century, many youngsters were forced to work long and strenuous hours and were subjected to extremely dangerous situations to help support their families. Yet one local historian, John Struthers Stewart, recalled his youthful fascination with iron making, remarking, "Most boys looked forward to a life in the furnaces or the mills." The whole process was a fascinating and mesmerizing experience. "The operations of casting in the old sand beds," Stewart remembered, "was a sight of which we never tired, and when a visitor from foreign parts came to town it was our pride to take him to see this wondrous sight." Not all, however, were possessed of such romantic notions. For many boys in Niles, school was not an option. Sympathetic to the lads, Butler approached Ward about opening a night school at the mill. With Ward's approval he took the helm using the same *McGuffey Readers* from his own school days. Butler was proud of his efforts. At the very least, he thought, "I was doing something educational"[29] for himself and his charges.

Butler began to pursue the limited cultural interests and society refinements available in the little village at the time. "I was fond of dancing and was regarded as a good dancer," he recalled. "Likewise I liked reading and the society of refined young women better than the rougher sports."[30]

However, having an inclination toward the more genteel offerings did not preclude the ability to defend oneself. One such incident involving Butler took on a life of its own. When he was 18, he became entangled in a scrap with one of the blacksmiths in the village. As the story was told, Butler "licked the biggest blacksmith in Niles." Years later, during the McKinley presidency, a business associate named Caleb Wick supposedly wrote to the 25th president seeking a political appointment for Butler. Due to Butler's exploits with his fists as an 18-year-old, Wick felt Butler to be an excellent choice for Secretary of War. After much consideration, President McKinley supposedly answered Wick's request. "I have gone carefully over your account of that sanguinary encounter with the Niles blacksmith," he wrote, "and in my judgment Mr. Butler is entirely too belligerent for the job."[31]

In 1856, John Lewis, a Welsh coal miner in charge of the mines at Mineral Ridge, entered the Ward Company office carrying a large chunk of what everyone present thought was slate. The slate, Lewis said, resembled the black band iron ore he once mined in Wales, and he asked James Ward for a chance to test his suspicion. A few days later, according to Butler, "Mr. Lewis returned with a large chunk of the stuff calcined into genuine black band ore of good value. This, I believe, was the discovery of black band ore in the United States." Prior to Lewis's discovery, black band

Two. Going to Work for James Ward

Engraving of Falcon Iron Works of James Ward and Co. From the 1856 Map of Trumbull County, Ohio, published by Gillette, Matthews & Co., Philadelphia, PA (The Mahoning Valley Historical Society, Youngstown, OH).

ore was imported and used to make Scotch pig iron. The local ore, previously misidentified as worthless slate, led to the production of American Scotch, a high-quality pig iron that provided a boost in sales for the local coal mining and iron industries. It took some years to win over the skeptical foundry operators, but Butler argued, "Our black band product was fully equal to the best brands imported."[32]

By 1857, he began to take an interest in politics. Many discussions among the men occurred on the porch of Eph Woodworth's Tavern, "a sort of village club house where congenial spirits met and discussed local and national affairs." Certainly, there was talk about the coming of the railroad and the effect it would have on the old Pennsylvania and Ohio Canal. Even James Ward joined in on these discussions, and Butler used these occasions to note his position on various issues and his affiliation with the Republican Party. Butler's lifetime association with the Republican Party, however, was influenced by his father. Butler Sr. became a Republican after the Whig party met its demise. He subscribed to Horace Greeley's *New York Tribune* and supported John C. Fremont in the 1856 presidential campaign. Through the *Tribune*, the Butler family followed the Lincoln-Douglas debates, and after Lincoln won the Republican presidential nomination in1860, Butler's father visited the candidate in Springfield, Illinois, and claimed he was cordially received.[33] Butler credited

Ward more than his father for his career choice. "My admiration and affection for Mr. James Ward Sr. helped to awaken in me the desire to become an ironmaster myself."[34]

Although Butler was heavily influenced by both his father and Ward, their religious fervor could not convince the young man to join a church. Though he believed in God and considered himself a Christian, Butler was never pulled toward a specific denomination. He often expressed that his parents' tolerant beliefs of others steered him away from any one church or denomination.

Under the influence of James Ward, Butler learned the operation and managerial aspects of business. His interest in numbers, bookkeeping, and production calculations would be nurtured in the immediate years ahead with the Ward Company. The capitalist ideology that he would come to embrace as a young investor on the rise in the industry was first introduced and shaped by his association and experience with James Ward.

Prompted by his heightened sense of curiosity, Butler ventured about the grounds making numerous observations concerning the re-melting of scrap iron that lay strewn around the mill. "After the pig iron had been refined in the furnace—a process somewhat like that of puddling, it was rolled into muck bar," Butler said. "This was then made up into bundles, reheated and rolled." As he studied the process, he theorized that there had to be a more efficient way. "I discovered that it was the custom to make the piles of muck bar and scrap by sort of guess work," Butler explained. "I compiled a table which made a great saving; that is to say, when the bar or tire was rolled out, the lengths would be just about right and there would be very little waste, where prior to that there had been very great waste and loss." Butler presented his observations to Ward. Iron men like Ward were generally leery of new ideas that came their way. Promises of improved efficiency, a better product, and greater profits were generally looked upon with a skeptical eye. The only way to get ahead was through hard work. But Butler's calculations proved successful. "I think this was really the turning point; my employer saw that I could be of some use outside of the ordinary duties of a shipping clerk."[35] Ward soon promoted him to company bookkeeper.

Not only did Butler prove to be an opportunist, but he also proved to be a young man who wanted to make sure that he possessed the necessary tools to complete a job successfully. When the Ward Company took on two new partners, the new management offered Butler the position of office manager where he would oversee all the financial operations of James Ward & Company. After careful consideration he would accept on one condition. "I said I would not take the job unless I could go to Pittsburgh and take a course in Duff's Commercial College."[36] Butler was clearly setting himself up to succeed and minimize the chance of failure not only for himself but, for the company. "Accordingly," concluded one historian, "Butler's appointment into the company proved beneficial to its overall operations."[37]

Established in 1851 by Peter Duff, a Scottish immigrant, Duff's Mercantile College was the first business college in the United States specializing in accounting and the overall training of "young men to meet the needs of the business world." The partners agreed to Butler's request and he completed the six-week course in half the time.[38] Joseph G. Butler, Jr., was prepared to meet the new challenges.

Three

Ironman

BUTLER SR. TURNED TO PUBLIC SERVICE when he was elected Trumbull County sheriff in 1860 and again in 1862, a job that prompted him to move the family from Niles to Warren, Ohio, the county seat.[1] He later served as clerk for both Weathersfield and Warren townships. When his father won the election, Butler Jr. chose to remain in Niles to work for James Ward. "This pleased Mr. Ward," Butler wrote in his autobiography, "and resulted in his taking me, with the consent of his good wife, Aunt Eliza Ward, into the family. They had one son, James Ward Jr., about my age, and we were together a great deal, which seemed to please both the father and mother."[2] Though the Butler family's iron tradition was well established, Joseph G. Butler Jr.'s passion for the industry was aroused not by his father but rather by James Ward.

Butler's new surrogate parents were not limited to James Ward and his wife. Ward's brother William Ward and his wife also looked after Butler. Their daughter recalled that one evening when Butler headed for the office, her mother ordered the young man to "go to bed now. Our boys are going to bed and you go to bed too." William attempted to restrain his wife's maternal instincts toward Butler but to no avail. Butler cherished his relationship with the Ward families, especially James Ward, who indeed became a beloved father-figure.[3]

The election of Abraham Lincoln as president in 1860 began a chain of events that led the country to civil war. When the Civil War began in April 1861, three of Butler's brothers, Miles, Irvin, and Edward Butler, enlisted and saw considerable action. All three were wounded while fighting for the Union cause. Butler always maintained that the lives of his brothers were shortened because of their military service.[4]

Butler himself did not enlist. He maintained that it was Ward who convinced him that he "could aid the Union cause more effectually by helping to increase the production of iron, then badly needed."[5] One recent historian supports the likelihood "that much of Youngstown's pig iron was sent to the Fort Pitt Foundry in Pittsburgh"[6] where armaments were manufactured.

Three. Ironman

In the summer of 1863, while Ulysses S. Grant laid siege to Vicksburg and Robert E. Lee took the fight to Gettysburg, Confederate General John Hunt Morgan crossed the Ohio River with a large force of cavalry to raid towns in Indiana and Ohio. For many Americans, the war was fought in far off places and towns whose names were strange and unrecognizable. Blocked from re-crossing the Ohio River into West Virginia, Morgan headed north in Ohio. Despite being pursued by Federal regulars and local militias attempting to thwart the rebels advance, Morgan reached northeast Ohio. Much of the Mahoning Valley grew alarmed. Was he targeting the iron forges of the Mahoning Valley for destruction? For all the villagers of Niles knew, Morgan's attack upon their community was imminent, and they took the threat seriously. If the war was coming to Niles, the villagers decided to resist the Confederate raiders.[7]

Ohio's governor in 1863 was Youngstown industrialist David Tod. Taking advantage of the local connection, Butler sent a telegram seeking the governor's approval to burn the bridge leading into Niles to foil Morgan's advance. Supposedly, Tod replied that he would take the suggestion "under advisement." The villagers waited dutifully for the governor's response, but it never arrived, and the bridge was spared. Looking back fondly years later, Butler remarked of the suggestion, "I think it is still 'under advisement.'"[8]

Rather than sit idly by, Butler and a group of volunteers formed a unit and headed south to confront the raiders.[9] The ill-advised band, including 22-year-old Butler, reached the village of Canfield by evening and took rooms at a hotel where they discovered a fine supper awaited them. Only later did they learn the meal was intended for a Youngstown unit that had ordered the dinner. Butler was anxious and pressed the captain to advance after the evening meal, but he was outranked and ignored.

The captain's delay spared Butler and the boys from a potentially dangerous confrontation. Morgan surrendered on July 26 near Salineville on the southern border of Columbiana County. "The capture," Butler recalled years later, "had been made just before we arrived." Upon their return to Niles, they were hailed as heroes. "Our bosoms heaved with pride," Butler remembered.[10]

Fortunately, the Mahoning Valley remained distant from any actual fighting. As Butler recorded, "the anxiety, the cares and the sorrows of war were felt here, but the sound of battle was absent."[11] After the excitement of Morgan's raid subsided, a sense of normalcy, if there was such a thing during war, returned to the village. The men returned to their places within the community, and Butler returned to the Ward office.

During the height of the Civil War, opportunity sought out Butler once again and lured him into a world beyond the comforts of home. The

Chicago firm of Hale & Ayer was one of many Great Lakes manufacturers that purchased pig iron from Mahoning Valley suppliers. Prior to 1860, Chicago iron firms had found it cheaper to import pig iron from Ohio and Pennsylvania rather than produce their own. Between 1860 and 1868, there were no iron producers in Illinois, so iron manufacturers in the state were forced to seek pig iron producers elsewhere.[12]

Hale & Ayer had been longtime customers of the James Ward Company and knew well of Joe Butler. The firm's owners, Samuel Hale and John Ayer, on one business trip to the Niles operation in 1863, indicated that they had been impressed with Butler's managerial abilities. They offered him a position as a purchasing agent, which would require him to travel about the country securing pig iron at the best possible rates for the Chicago firm. According to Butler they made him "a very liberal offer."[13]

Chicago was a major transportation hub experiencing its own business and industrial growth and a far cry from the Mahoning Valley. It offered more than its share of opportunities to those who sought them. After much thought Butler concluded that this was an opportunity worth pursuing.[14] But, Butler would not accept until after discussing the matter with James Ward. The mentor had guided and nurtured his young protégé. He had made a substantial investment, but more than that, the affection between the two was genuine, and Ward wanted to protect his young friend.[15] After more consideration, however, Ward realized that if Butler took the position, the departure would create an opportunity for another young man to embark on a career with the company. As Butler concluded, "it occurred to Uncle James Ward that perhaps his son could take my place." James Ward, Jr., was Ward's only son, and he and Butler were like brothers. Butler accepted the offer from Hale & Ayer and with Ward's consent left the Ward Company.[16]

Butler began his new job as purchasing agent for Hale & Ayer in November 1863. "I went to the metropolis of the West and found that my new employers evidently had something in view for me of which they had not given me all the information they could have given," he wrote. "There seemed to be nothing in particular at their Chicago offices for me to do, and I stayed around for some little time with a rather hazy idea of what my duties were to be." Finally, the Chicago firm sent their new purchasing agent on the road, and Butler's first assignment was to call on pig iron producers in Cleveland and the Mahoning Valley. Sending Butler back to Ohio was wise since he was intimately familiar with its iron manufacturers. They were his previous competitors when he was with the Ward Company, and he was aware of their products and business tendencies. Hale & Ayer depended heavily on pig iron from Ohio and Pennsylvania and relied on Butler to secure good prices.[17]

But the Chicago firm had bigger plans to purchase an operation in the Mahoning Valley, either the Ward company or the mills of Brown-Bonnell in Youngstown. Hale & Ayer soon began negotiating with Brown, Bonnell and Company, which had been organized in 1854 by Joseph, Richard, and Thomas Brown, and William Bonnell and eventually had become the largest employer in Youngstown. The Chicago firm bought an interest in the Brown-Bonnell Mill and appointed Butler to be their representative in Youngstown. Butler later reflected, "I really think they never had any idea of utilizing me in Chicago. My principal business was that of purchasing agent."[18] In that role his primary function was to act as a sort of stockbroker, but instead of buying and selling stock in companies, he was to buy and sell iron. A successful purchasing agent had to know what was driving the demands for iron and had to pay close attention to the trends, especially considering the effects of the war. It was another opportunity for Butler to learn the business.

In 1864, Samuel Hale and John Ayer looked to further expand their presence in Youngstown and organized a manufacturing operation called the Lake Superior Nut & Washer Company. In addition to Samuel Hale and John Ayer, the new company listed as its owners, Gustavus Simonds, George Simonds, and Joseph G. Butler, Jr. The company's name indicated its finished product, which also included bolts, railroad track bolts, and railroad spikes. It was one of the first fabricating plants in Youngstown.[19] The new venture gave the owners the means to take raw materials, and without relinquishing control, transform them into a finished iron product ready for market.

The Lake Superior Nut & Washer Company operated successfully in Youngstown but in 1867 was offered inducements to move the business to Indianapolis. Gustavus Simonds and Butler's brother, Irvin, who had recently come into the business, followed the company west to manage its affairs for a short time.[20] It had been Butler's first opportunity as a business owner. He had impressed the men from Chicago in a short time with his hard work, his no nonsense approach to business, and most of all, the positive financial effects that resulted from his decisions.

Through his travels, he saw and experienced much of the country. The trips to Chicago yielded opportunities to witness technological advancements taking place in the industry. In May 1865, while attending a meeting of the American Iron and Steel Association, Butler was able to observe the first steel rail rolled in the United States at the North Chicago Rolling Mill in nearby Wyandotte, Michigan. Increasingly, he was exposed to the cultural offerings of big city life as well. It was in Chicago that he took an early interest in art, and at the age of 25, he borrowed $100 to have his portrait painted by the up-and-coming portrait artist William Cogswell.[21] It was an interest that would eventually turn into Butler's passion.

By the summer of 1864, Butler had already been away from the James Ward Company for almost a year. Although he had been with the Hale & Ayer firm since the previous November, he was never distant mentally or emotionally from the Wards. No one could have foreseen the events that would bring such shock and sadness to his life at a time when so many positive changes were unfolding.

On the night of July 27, 1864, a man known to be a frequent visitor to a recently widowed woman who lodged in one of Ward's cottages, shot and killed the senior James Ward. The citizens of Niles were shocked at the murder of their leading citizen. Butler was devastated by the loss of his mentor and father-figure. Many years later, still haunted by Ward's tragic death, Butler wrote, "under circumstances so painful that not even the lapse of more than fifty years has softened" that unexpected and untimely loss. Throughout his life Butler paid homage to Ward and credited him for everything good that came his way. "There is no doubt in my mind," Butler wrote, that Ward "changed the whole course of my life and that I owe to him the opportunity to succeed, as well as much of whatever is worth while in my later life."[22] Ward's death "would have a far-reaching and damaging effect on the industrial structure of Niles, as well as most of the Mahoning Valley," concluded one local historian.[23] At the funeral for James Ward, Sr., Butler served as a pallbearer.

While in Chicago, the Hale and Ayer sales agent borrowed $100 to have his portrait painted by William Cogswell in 1865. *Portrait of Joseph G. Butler Jr. (25 years of age), 1865*, by William Cogswell. Oil on board (The Butler Institute of American Art, Youngstown, Ohio. Gift of Mr. J.G. Butler III, 1951).

Though some mills saw an increase in demand for war materiel, according to historian William T. Hogan, the Civil War's effects on the iron industry were not entirely positive. He wrote, "The industry, located principally in the northern states—Pennsylvania, Ohio, New York, and New Jersey, which produced 75% of the pig iron—depended upon the southern states for a relatively sizable share of its market, and this was lost during the war years. Expansion of the nation's railroads was curtailed and rail demand declined sharply. The market was not replaced as might be expected by war-time activity since the conflict was carried out on a modest scale in comparison with twentieth-century wars. In fact, ordnance requirements were so limited that it was not until 1863 that pig iron recovered to the 1860 level."[24]

Mahoning Valley iron producers were not as dependent on rail production before the war and produced more iron for local consumption before hostilities began. This would change after the war. Still the government's war demand for Mahoning Valley iron, though limited, was enough to sustain the local industry. By December 1864, prices for both bar iron and workers' wages rose to all-time highs in the Valley. In 1863, bar iron sold for $95 per ton, and before the war ended, it sold for as high as $168 per ton. At the end of the war Butler observed that the price of iron "remained up." Though the war brought death and destruction to the country, it brought economic gains to the Mahoning Valley where iron and coal owners in particular grew wealthy.[25] Youngstown had 4,000 inhabitants at the end of the war and was poised for expansion After four years of war, the time was at hand to build for the future.

"Youngstown felt the spirit of the times," wrote Butler, "and with the removal of the dark war cloud began to bestir itself—to get out of the rut." The new village council of 1866 outlined an $80,000 improvement program to better the streets and install sidewalks along Federal Street. The same year also marked another significant improvement in the business career of Joseph Butler. In the fall of 1865, while still representing Hale & Ayer, Butler received word from a local business associate, "Uncle Billie" Pollock, that David Tod wanted to meet with him.[26]

David Tod, born in 1805 in Youngstown, was a man known for his many successes in life ranging from business to politics. A biographical profile published in 1893 said of David Tod, "As a business man he was far-seeing, an accurate calculator, and of great confidence, always sanguine of success. His friends shared his confidence; they trusted him and sought out his advice." As the Valley's leading industrialist who built his wealth upon his coal mining enterprises, Tod served one term as Ohio's governor before returning to Youngstown to retake control of his business empire. Tod was successful in practically everything in which he became involved, and there was no reason to believe that the Girard Iron Company would be anything less than a great success. If the new venture succeeded, his other companies would also profit since the furnace was designed to use Tod's Brier Hill coal.[27]

Butler met with Tod at his Brier Hill Iron and Coal Company office. For some time, Tod had been contemplating a new business venture that included William Richards and William Ward, James' brother. The three were looking for someone to oversee this new company.[28] Ward, of course, had known Butler for most of his life and enthusiastically recommended him for the new position. Tod, the famous War Governor of Ohio, also was no stranger to the young upstart.

On this latest visit to Tod's office the former governor got right to the point. Butler recalled, "He told me he was thinking of building a blast furnace at Girard, and wanted me to take charge of the office end of it." But the offer made to Butler was more than that. Tod offered him an equal partnership if he was willing to invest an equal share of the needed capital. Each partner was to contribute $25,000, which just so happened to be Butler's total savings. It was a handsome sum, "all the money I had," he wrote. Clearly, Butler had become a wealthy young man through careful management of his earnings. His business decisions thus far had served him well.

There was no reason to over-evaluate the proposition, and Butler eagerly agreed to join the distinguished partnership. On February 5, 1866, the new partners signed the formal agreement creating the Girard Iron Company. William Richards was named manager and, "the said Butler, it is agreed, shall be the General Agent of the Company and as such Agent shall have charge of the books, monies and affairs of the company, the purchase of stock, sale of iron and assisting the said Richards in the discharge of his duties, the said Butler agreeing hereby to devote his attention faithfully and diligently to the business of the firm."[29] James Ward's young hand-picked store clerk was now part owner of an exciting new business proposition.

During the summer of 1865, Harriet Voorhees Ingersoll, the daughter of a United States Navy Lieutenant, paid a visit to an aunt who resided in Youngstown. Harriet was also the cousin of Connecticut politician Charles Ingersoll, who would be elected governor in 1873. Butler was immediately struck by her beauty and charm as were most of the other young men who met her.

Harriet Ingersoll was born in 1844, in Warren, Ohio, the first of four children to Jonathan and Catherine Seely Ingersoll. Her father served in the United States Navy and sailed aboard the famed U.S.S. *Constitution*. In 1836, Lieutenant Ingersoll left the Navy to study law, and two years later he married Catherine, who lived in Warren, Ohio. Attorney Ingersoll cultivated a successful law practice in Trumbull County. When the couple's last child was born in 1859, Harriet was already 15 years old. Shortly after,

Catherine died, leaving her aspiring attorney husband a single father of four. Realizing he needed help, Ingersoll sent Harriet to his wife's cousin, Henry W. Seely, who was a lawyer in Honesdale, Pennsylvania.[30]

Located in the northeastern part of the state in the foothills of the Pocono Mountains, the small town of Honesdale provided Harriet with a safe childhood upbringing. The Seely family had deep roots in the area, and Harriet, like her future husband, could claim a Revolutionary War heritage. Harriet's great-great grandfather, Sylvanus Seely, served as a colonel in the Morris County, New Jersey, regiment during the Revolutionary War. After the war, Colonel Seely moved to Wayne County, Pennsylvania, where he ran a successful sawmill business. The Seely family stayed and prospered.[31]

The Henry Seely household provided Harriet the structure, comfort, values, and educational opportunities that any young girl would have longed for. Three years later Harriet returned to Ohio to visit her relatives in Youngstown. She was now an 18-year-old woman and an attractive catch for any of the town's worthy bachelors. Butler quickly set out to court Harriet and succeeded. They were married in Honesdale, Pennsylvania, on January 10, 1866. Butler's brother, Irvin, served as best man. The newlyweds honeymooned in New York City where they enjoyed the local attractions and several plays. After an adventurous journey by rail and carriage, the couple returned to Youngstown to live.[32] The newlyweds stayed with Butler's friend, Reuben McMillan, and his wife for 17 months until they were able to purchase their own house.

The couple's devotion to each other over the years became evident to all their friends. Many admired Harriet's sterling character, but to her husband, it was her constant patience and sweetness that touched

Portrait of Harriett Voorhees Ingersol Butler, n.d., by Ivan Gregorovitch Olinsky. Oil on canvas (The Butler Institute of American Art, Youngstown, Ohio. © c. Ivan Gregorovitch Olinsky or Estate).

him deeply over the years. Yielding to and supporting her husband's tiring agenda throughout their marriage, was a sign of her devotion. Staying behind, tending to the children and the demands of keeping the house in order, especially during the financial setbacks, reflected her role as a woman of this era.

After leaving the hospitable McMillan residence in 1867, the Butlers moved to a new home at the corner of Rayen Avenue and Phelps Street just north of the downtown square. Their first child, Blanche, was born in 1867, daughter Grace was born in 1870, and son Henry Audubon was born in 1872.[33]

The years following the Civil War marked the beginning of a prosperous and progressive era for Butler as well as for the Mahoning Valley iron industry. For the first time in nearly five years the residents of the Mahoning Valley, like the rest of the country, looked forward to a life without war, fear, and bloodshed. Aided in part by his current association with David Tod, Butler was fast becoming a person of recognizable significance in the valley iron scene, and the Mahoning Valley was becoming one of the centers of pig iron production in the United States. Production increased significantly during the years immediately following the war as new manufacturers entered the local market.[34]

Beyond the west end of Youngstown's village limits was a swath of farms whose owners had names such as Manning, Wirt, Tod, Davis, Rayen, Struthers, and Stambaugh. These farms were bordered on the west by the Mahoning River, on the north by the village of Girard, on the south by Youngstown, and on the east by the rising hillside covered with briers from which the section known as Brier Hill got its name. A narrow path meandering through the farms connected Brier Hill with Youngstown.[35] In the early 19th century, large veins of coal were discovered on these farms. Great quantities of coal were mined during the ensuing years and sold to steam ship owners on the Great Lakes via the Pennsylvania and Ohio Canal. Coal mining began the Mahoning Valley's transition from an agriculture-based economy to an industrialized one. The coal proved to be ideal for iron production and attracted new blast furnace construction on the banks of the Mahoning River from Warren and Niles in the north to Struthers and Lowellville in the south. Critical to his development of a lifelong career in iron and steel was the necessary training and experience that Butler received in the immediate years ahead with the Girard Iron Company.

By 1867 Butler's life was far different than it had been five years earlier. The 27-year-old had acquired considerable business experience and was part owner of a new business. He had a wife and a baby daughter and by summertime had purchased a house in which he and Harriet would raise a family. By the time they moved into their home, the village council's infrastructure improvements had not yet begun. The streets were still dirt and became extremely muddy when it rained. Nevertheless, the move was an indication of Butler's commitment to his new hometown. He was also committed to his new business and excited at the opportunities that lay before him.

In addition to the iron industry, the railroad industry expanded dramatically after the Civil War. Between 1866 and 1873, 35,000 miles of new track were laid as the railroad industry became one of the nation's largest employers, second only to farming. The Valley's newfound use of railroads was the final blow to the Pennsylvania & Ohio Canal in 1872. The canal bed itself was left to dry up and became littered with discarded canal boats. The final insult to the P&O Canal occurred when a section of the bed was filled in and overlaid with a new railroad.

Four

The Onward March

A February 28, 1866, editorial in the *Mahoning Courier* suggested the growth of the Mahoning Valley iron industry was about to take off. "The growing importance of Youngstown under the impetus given by the extensive coal fields of the Mahoning Valley, has become famous at home and abroad." The expanding railroad system that was beginning to envelope the Mahoning Valley would further strengthen the economy and transform Youngstown into an industrial behemoth. The editorial continued, "Although we number at present but five or six thousand inhabitants, we are giants, of small stature, but possessed of enormous strength in resources, which will soon be developed ten-fold."[1] Local companies began to dot the landscape seemingly overnight; one was the Girard Iron Company.

The owners made plans to construct a blast furnace, the likes of which the Mahoning Valley had not seen before. William Richards had recently returned from Wales. Inspired by a furnace he had studied on a tour of his native homeland, he envisioned building such a structure back in Ohio. Richards, who managed David Tod's Wood furnaces, persuaded the former governor to undertake the project. They would locate the furnace in Girard along the Mahoning River. Tod and Richards privately owned the land and sold the site to the new firm for a price of $100 per acre. The operation would lease coal rights from one of Tod's banks.[2]

Not being wholly familiar with modern blast furnace technology and operation, Butler took steps to prepare himself. "I knew nothing about the practical end of the business, but was forced to learn it," he recalled. Studying Sir Isaac Lowthian Bell's *Chemical Phenomena of Iron Smelting* proved invaluable.[3]

Butler thought the Girard furnace would be the eighth wonder of the world.[4] It was the first in the Valley constructed entirely of brick. An old engine salvaged from a Mississippi River steamboat powered the mill. High spirits were quickly dashed.

Richards's memory had failed him. The bosh, the wide middle section of the furnace located above the hearth and below the stack, was constructed almost entirely upside down. The furnace was a complete failure and had to be completely rebuilt. The blunder was a tremendous financial strain. "We were young and enthusiastic," recalled Butler, "and drove along without refinancing, expecting and hoping that eventually the enterprise would be successful."[5]

In time, it proved to be "a very good furnace" yielding a quality product that utilized a combination of Tod's Brier Hill coal and Lake Superior iron ore. The company initially employed 30 men and produced on average 20,000 tons of iron annually. It made a modest profit. The furnace's early success, wrote Butler, justified the faith that Tod placed in him.[6] The owners overcame the initial gaffe that would have broken the spirit of men of lesser means.

Butler was full of determination and energy. He was efficient, practical, and calculating, characteristics first sharpened under the Wards. He knew one way to make a profit was to take chances. He took another when he was invited to join the Tod-Stambaugh Company, a coalmining firm along with John Tod, and Evan Morris. The company leased the Peter Kline farm near the Church Hill section of Liberty Township in 1868. They even built a railroad from Liberty to Lowellville to deliver coal to the Struthers furnace.[7]

The Kline farm provided excellent coal to Valley furnaces for years. Butler's decision to invest in the Tod-Stambaugh Company proved a fruitful one. The company supplied coal to local and distant consumers as rail lines connected the mines to the markets of the Great Lakes and Ohio River. The partners needed to shore up the firm in preparation for further expansion, but Butler lacked the extra capital to invest and relinquished his partnership. He refused to take out a loan not wanting to overextend himself. Later the company did extremely well, and Butler missed out on greater profits.

Youngstown was incorporated as a village in 1850. In June 1867, village officials ordered a census, which revealed a population of more than 5,000. Upon application, the village was declared to be a city of the second class, a designation that required a new governing structure. Butler decided to enter politics, and in April 1868 he was elected to serve on Youngstown's first city council joining Chauncey Andrews, Richard Brown, Homer Hamilton, and William Barclay. Andrews, Brown, and Hamilton had previously served on the village council.[8] During these prosperous times the city council continued infrastructure upgrades, improved police protection, and created a volunteer fire department.

In *The Search for Order*, historian Robert Wiebe notes that many local leaders who otherwise would have participated in civic causes became preoccupied with their own business investments especially during economic uncertainty. Wiebe wrote, "Men struggling to learn new skills or to preserve old ones in a rapidly changing economy could not afford to think about city-wide issues. Without stability at home or on the job, the civic spirit had no place to take root."[9] The cause of civic improvement would have to be put on hold for Butler and others as business leaders tried not to panic as the growing economic outlook grew dim. Although Butler was emerging as a new player in the Youngstown community, he was forced to refocus his efforts on the uncertain economic situation affecting his own business interests.

Butler's business philosophy was set early in his career working for James Ward. There he was schooled on the importance of protective tariffs. He learned of the negative impact the depression of 1837 had had on the construction of the P & O Canal and of the revitalization of the early iron industry brought about by the Tariff of 1842. When the iron tariff was lowered, the growth of the Mahoning Valley's iron industry slowed and worsened as the Panic of 1857 took hold. Although Butler witnessed the industry survive the panic thanks in part to the demands of the Civil War, the lesson of tariff protection was not lost on him. To entice domestic consumers, he and many others like him believed it was necessary for American iron producers to have protection against foreign imports to keep domestic pig iron rates more attractive. Order and protection were the themes carried forth by the country's business leaders.

The one matter that the federal government moved forward with during the 1870s was organization, a result of the Civil War. As Wiebe showed, all levels of government, particularly at the national level, sought order to make sense out of the carnage heaped upon the country during the war years of the 1860s. Local governments like Youngstown, took steps to provide better organization of services by improving their infrastructure and their safety forces. Even labor, led by the growing number of railroad workers, took steps to organize for better pay and working conditions.

New ventures fueled an increased need for business loans, but the few existing financial institutions lacked the necessary assets to fully satisfy the growing need for credit. Recognizing the need for more solvent lending institutions, David Tod saw another opportunity. From July until November 1868, Tod gathered friends and various business associates from the Valley and organized the Youngstown Savings and Loan Association. It was the first savings bank in Youngstown and opened that December with a capital of $600,000, offering six percent interest on the dollar. Its Board of Directors listed the elite of Youngstown's business world including Tod, John Stambaugh, Chauncey Andrews, Richard Brown, and Freeman O.

Four. The Onward March

Arms. Among the other directors, with lesser means but handpicked by Tod, was Joseph Butler.[10]

Youngstown's industrial growth brought a surge in population. More housing was needed to accommodate the increasing number of workers and their families, many of them immigrants from Europe. These projects needed financing. Business leaders were practical, no-nonsense men aware of the social order and their place at the head of society, and they were also aware of opportunities for profit. Simply put, sitting on a board of directors was a personal investment for each director and was another means by which to gain wealth.

When Tod died in November 1868, the Mahoning Valley lost its leading statesman and industrial leader. He led many movements in the Valley beside coal, iron, and transportation interests. He supported the construction of the P&O Canal and later led the effort to build the first railroad in the Valley. His leadership left the Valley on solid footing for industrial expansion. For Butler, Tod's death was another personal loss. In some ways, in four short years, Tod had become a mentor for Butler. Looking back on the relationship, Butler said, "I lost at that time my then best friend."[11]

Butler was saddled with another loss when his brother Irvin took ill and died in Cleveland on December 27, 1868. "My brother was delicate," Butler once said, "a gentle, lovable character." They once shared a brief business partnership in 1866. After the war, Irvin settled in Tennessee where he purchased a charcoal furnace. Butler agreed to join the business venture, but after a visit south to inspect the operation, they realized they didn't have enough money to improve the faulty structure. They sold the furnace to investors with deeper pockets. Butler blamed war wounds for Irvin's premature death.[12]

By the late 1860s, the Brier Hill coal that fed the Valley's furnaces was becoming scarce. The days of raw coal or anthracite fuel were coming to an end not only in the Mahoning Valley but throughout the country as large veins were being mined to extinction. As the business manager of a blast furnace, Butler had to search for other fuel sources.

The transition from anthracite to coke fuel had been underway in the iron industry for some time, especially in the Pittsburgh district. Coke was the product of burnt coal much like charcoal was the product of burnt wood. Railroad cars loaded with raw coal ran up alongside brick and earthen ovens that resembled beehives, thereby acquiring the name of beehive coke ovens. The rail cars emptied the coal into the top of the ovens that were then sealed. Over the next few days, the impurities were slowly burned off resulting in the leftover coke. It was discovered that this coke served as a useful fuel for blast furnaces.

The use of coke as a fuel in the United States could be traced back to the 18th century. Its popularity took hold out of necessity as raw coal veins were being depleted. The emerging center of the coke industry was the Connellsville area of western Pennsylvania, 57 miles southeast of Pittsburgh on the Youghiogheny River.[13]

One of the early leaders of the Connellsville coke industry was Henry Clay Frick. Born in 1849, Frick was involved in several family-run businesses. While employed in his grandfather's distillery in the Connellsville region, Frick recognized the coming role of coke and soon invested his entire savings, as well as what he could borrow, to acquire all the coal mines and ovens that he could.[14] Within a decade he was a millionaire, the undisputed king of the coke industry.

In 1868, though, Frick was just starting out when he met Joseph Butler from the Girard Iron Company, whose search for a new fuel source led him to Connellsville. After examining Frick's coke, Butler felt that it could be used in the Girard furnace along with the current Brier Hill coal for as long as the latter supply would last. He quickly began negotiations with Frick. An agreement was reached on the steps of Butler's Youngstown-bound train.[15]

Thus, the Girard Iron Company became the first furnace in the Mahoning Valley to make pig iron from coke. The combination of Connellsville coke and Brier Hill coal produced "what we thought ... was a very satisfactory and economical fuel," Butler concluded. Over the next 20 years this combination would become the dominant fuel used in Valley furnaces. Butler also claimed that it was the first coke agreement for young Frick as well. "I would be ashamed to tell you the price," paid young Frick, he reflected years later, "and I think he would also."[16]

Although Butler focused on his responsibilities as furnace manager, the absence of Tod left the company rudderless. William Ward had the experience to lead the new company during the adjustment after Tod's death, but he was pre-occupied with the James Ward enterprises in Niles where his nephew, James Jr., had become the majority owner after his father's murder. He continued to pursue other ventures and started William Ward & Company, which constructed and operated the Ward Furnace from 1870 until 1875.

Richards also expanded his interests and likewise in 1870 built a blast furnace in Warren. Butler always thought highly of Ward and Richards, but their interests were clearly elsewhere. And with Tod's passing it was inevitable that outsiders would look to take the former governor's place at the Girard Iron Company.

The A.M. Byers Company, owned by Alexander MacBurney Byers, was interested in purchasing the Girard Iron Company to supply pig iron

Four. The Onward March

The Girard Iron Company managed to overcome its initial construction problems. From Joseph G. Butler, Jr., *Recollections of Men and Events* (New York: G.P. Putnam's Sons, 1925).

to his Pittsburgh rolling mills. Butler regarded Byers as a practical man. Like Butler, Byers had entered the iron business at an early age, managing a stone stack furnace at the age of 16 in 1843. He had the distinction of managing the first Pittsburgh blast furnace to use Lake Superior iron ore. Byers eventually had business interests in Cleveland and Pittsburgh and would soon own interests in the Mahoning Valley.

When Tod died, his interest in the Girard Iron Company transferred to his sons. In time, both Ward and Richards relinquished their interests. This left Butler as the last original partner. Tod's sons were natural leaders, inheriting much of their father's business traits in addition to his coal and iron operations. In 1870, when Ward and Richards were pursuing their other business ventures, Byers struck a deal with the Tods. As Butler had noted, the company had been yielding a small profit since its ominous beginning. The fiasco of the original furnace construction so severely limited the company's long-term reinvestment ability that it limped along aided by capital on notes endorsed by the late Tod. Difficult times were marked by the charge of 10 percent interest on the notes. Hence, the Tods needed little convincing to sell out to Byers. Butler grew increasingly frustrated by the loss of the Tods as partners and by the declining economic conditions. Nevertheless, he stayed on at the Girard Iron Company.[17]

As a sales agent for the Girard Iron Company, Butler sold much of his company's pig iron to rolling mills in Pittsburgh on account of the cheap railroad rates. Keeping a high tariff in place helped to make domestic pig iron more attractive to Pittsburgh rolling mills than pig iron produced overseas. Mahoning Valley iron sales, much of it to Pittsburgh's finishing mills, increased tenfold between 1856 and 1872. According to iron industry historian Kenneth Warren, the Valley was by far the largest supplier of pig iron to Pittsburgh even outdistancing Allegheny and Juniata Valley producers.[18]

To sustain profits, owners increasingly began to lobby their political representatives. According to Wiebe, industry and community leaders had no qualms about using political influence to protect their business interests. The Wool and Woolens Act of 1867 was one attempt to secure protection by seeking higher tariffs on imports. Leaders of the Mahoning Valley iron industry were no different, and Butler became intimately involved in these efforts. Years later Butler proudly proclaimed, "I have appeared before all the Congressional Ways and Means Committees from 1872 down to the present day, whenever a new Protective Tariff was to be formed."[19]

In 1870, several local iron manufacturers formed a lobbying group that attempted to discourage Congress's plans to lower the tariff. Thomas Struthers was named president, John Stambaugh, vice-president, and Butler, secretary. Stambaugh and Struthers were old family acquaintances whose ancestral homesteads abutted each other where the famous Brier Hill coal was eventually discovered. Stambaugh and David Tod became partners when the Brier Hill Iron and Coal Company was re-organized, and Stambaugh became president of the company after Tod's death. In 1869 Struthers had started operation of the Anna blast furnace along the Mahoning River near Lowellville, which was fed by Stambaugh's coal from the nearby Liberty and Vienna Township mines.[20]

The group lobbied the Valley's congressman and future president, James Garfield, emphasizing the opinion of the Mahoning Valley iron men on the latest tariff effort. Garfield served on the powerful Ways and Means Committee. The Mahoning men argued with typical business rhetoric, "Resolved, that any forced reduction in the price of iron by reduction in the tariff, will necessarily compel those engaged in the business to reduce the expenses of manufacturing, and this reduction can only be effected by reducing the wages of laborers in our furnaces and mines, thus inaugurating such direct conflict with labor as we have ever striven to avoid."[21]

Garfield, a self-proclaimed Free Trader, worried iron men over recent comments. His biographer wrote, "he had publicly said that if an industry did not need protection he saw no reason for giving it any. Of such a man, they [the Mahoning Valley iron men] could not be sure. He might think they did not need it." The Youngstown owners provided what they thought to be ample facts to support their cause. Some letters threatened Garfield's reelection bid, but Garfield, the former Civil War officer, would not be intimidated. "The fact is," Garfield said, "some Youngstown and Niles people, in trying to beat me out of the nomination, started a story, purely for political effect, that I was opposed to the tariff interests and by their persistent falsehoods made the impression upon the minds of many in the valley that I was hostile to the manufacturing interests.... The fact is, many of these men want a representative that they can own and carry around in their pantaloons pocket." Garfield was clearly in a difficult position. "It may perhaps be my misfortune," he wrote, "that I occupy that position which is never popular with any party, a middle ground. If I may say it without being absurd, I should claim to be theoretically a Free Trader, but practically a Protectionist." The Mahoning group urged Garfield to oppose any reduction of the tariff on pig iron.[22]

The tariff bill passed in the House but initially failed in the Senate; however, parts of the tariff bill, including a reduction on the pig iron duty, were attached to a tax bill that passed in June with Garfield supporting the majority. Garfield's support of the tariff reduction showed his defiance toward local interests, and his lack of support so infuriated the iron men of the Mahoning Valley that they looked unsuccessfully for a pro-tariff candidate to run in the fall election. Although the Valley iron men afterward remained hostile to Garfield, Butler and Garfield became friends and remained so until Garfield's death on September 19, 1881, six months after being inaugurated as the nation's 20th president.

The tariff battle that fueled the tension between labor and owners would define the decade. The reduction, although modest compared to the high rates of the 1860s, was considered a compromise within the Republican majority on the committee. The cut was due to mounting pressure from the growing representation of the Western farmers who felt high rates on manufactured textiles and machinery were harmful to their interests.[23]

As much as local leaders lamented the congressional action, British iron producers rejoiced. The tariff reduction, reported *The London Mining Journal*, was "most satisfactory to the British ironmaster." *The Miners' Journal*, an American publication, on the other hand, pledged to "put in nomination good substantial Republicans who have some business capacity, and who will carry out the desires of the people and not use nearly all their time in working for themselves."[24]

Butler's support for protective tariffs, specifically those that kept a high duty on imported pig iron, would remain consistent throughout his career. His subsequent appearances before the House Ways and Means Committee echoed this philosophy as his lifelong identity with the Republican Party and its conservative business principles became further entrenched.

By the early 1870s the city of Youngstown, though not yet the county seat, was showing off several improvements. One of the first efforts to bring a public display of art in addition to the architectural designs in buildings came in the movement to honor Youngstown's Civil War dead, an idea that Governor Tod had first proposed in 1864. The memories of the recent war were not lost on patriotic citizens, especially with the country's centennial approaching.

Cost for the memorial was estimated at $10,000 to $15,000, and it was hoped that most of the funding would be raised through private donations. It was during the fundraising campaign, after the cornerstone was set, that Youngstown was named the county seat and it was decided to build the new county courthouse at the monument site, so a new location in the middle of Central Square was chosen. After several years, work on the monument was completed, and the dedication was held on July 4, 1870.[25]

The Grand Opera House was built in 1872, and gas service was extended to homes and businesses north of Federal Street. Three local newspapers—the *Mahoning Vindicator*, the *Mahoning Register*, and the *Youngstown Courier*—supplied citizens with the news. Also available were the *Cleveland Leader* (in daily, weekly, or tri-weekly editions) and the *Cleveland Herald*.[26] Improvements were made in transportation as some of the city's major thoroughfares were finally paved, and a horse-powered trolley and rail system was transporting citizens down Federal Street from Brier Hill to Crab Creek.

The post–Civil War railroad expansion had kept the iron mills running at full capacity. Between 1868 and 1873, 33,000 miles of track were laid, but this overbuilding and risky speculation eventually led to ruin for many. During the war, the Philadelphia investment firm of Jay Cooke & Company had been the government's largest financier. It also became the financial sponsor of the second trans-continental railroad. However, Cooke's company had severely overstepped its financial capabilities and declared bankruptcy on September 18, 1873. When other investment houses and banks soon followed, the demand for new rails fell off, sharply affecting the iron industry immediately. Youngstown and its iron industry were hit hard.[27] Most of the Mahoning Valley's 21 blast furnaces were impacted. Hundreds of other businesses throughout the country failed, throwing thousands of laborers out of work, as a major economic depression developed throughout the country.

The New York Stock Exchange closed for 10 days. The Panic of 1873 became a global affair as the economies of several European countries such as Britain, Germany, and Austria-Hungary fell into depression. In the next two years, 18,000 U.S. businesses failed.

Butler described the panic: "Ghostlike smokestacks, idle men, relief societies that doled out bare necessities of life, want and hunger displaced the prosperity of but a year before." Pig iron orders dried up. The Valley's operators shuttered their furnaces. "The Panic dragged wearily along for approximately six years."[28]

The depression caused extraordinary concern for local industrialists as well as for President Ulysses S. Grant. The Civil War hero, now the nation's 18th president, took a laissez-faire approach to the troubled economy, but his measures produced little improvement. Cash, in large circulation during the war, became almost non-existent, and the Mahoning Valley mills that managed to stay open paid their employees in company-issued scrip. This occurred extensively across the country.

Congress attempted to intervene by seeking to increase the nation's paper money supply by $100 million. Grant vetoed the plan, however, arguing that it would cause inflation and weaken the domestic economy. Garfield, was elated with the President's veto when he wrote, "For twenty years no President has had an opportunity to do the country so much service by a veto message as Grant has, and he has met the issue manfully." But for the remainder of the decade of the 1870s, the search for order continued with attempts to reform government and curtail tax evasion. None of these tactics had an immediate impact toward economic recovery. Industry was left to slug it out on its own. Garfield, already alienated from his disconcerted iron constituents because of his failure to back the protectionist tariff, still represented their feelings in general when in a December 1874 letter he wrote, "It is not part of the functions of the national government to find employment for people—and if we were to appropriate a hundred millions for this purpose, we should be taxing forty millions of people to keep a few thousand employed." Things limped along until 1879 when "the mills began to hum again with oldtime industrial activity."[29]

Butler spent the 1870s employed at the Girard Iron Company. When A.M. Byers took over, he retained Butler as general agent for the furnace, which supplied iron to Byers's Pittsburgh mills. Coal mining in the Valley peaked in the mid–1870s as mills increasingly turned to coke as a fuel. In 1875, for example, a furnace in Milwaukee recorded using as fuel one part Brier Hill coal mixed with three parts Connellsville coke.[30]

Collectively, however, area mines continued to produce more than one million tons of coal annually through the early 1880s. But with the laying of new rail lines from Youngstown to Pittsburgh, most local furnaces made the transition to Connellsville coke first tried by Butler at the Girard Iron Company in the late 1860s. The dependence on Connellsville coke increased during the 1870s as new technology and greater ore deposits allowed for larger blast furnace construction.

The A.M. Byers Company, Girard, Ohio (author's collection).

Larger blast furnaces nearly doubled iron production, but the dwindling Mahoning Valley coal supply could not keep apace. The year 1875 also marked the beginning of the end of the Valley's black-band ore supply, which had diminished significantly and was being replaced by Lake Superior ores that had been first shipped to Valley furnace operators on the P&O Canal before the Civil War.[31] Railroad expansion continued, and low transportation rates gave industries the ability to continue operations despite the growing distances between iron producers and raw supplies.

Congress also began to scrutinize its decision-making process utilizing more legislative hearings and introducing subcommittees for closer examination of issues. The House Committee on Ways and Means continued to take on such matters as tariffs. One of the protectionist stalwarts of the committee from 1869 to1889 was William "Pig Iron" Kelley, a Republican representative from Pennsylvania. Kelley was a strong advocate of protective tariffs, especially those that protected the iron industry in Pennsylvania. One of Kelley's colleagues once said of him that he was "the acknowledged champion of protection and it was conceded by all that he was competent to frame the tariff legislation, the leading question at that time."[32]

In 1876, during the economic turmoil, several brave investors including Butler formed the Mahoning Iron Company. The partners purchased a blast furnace in Lowellville. Butler, who still managed the Girard Iron Company, had little time to devote to the new company which soon fell victim to the economic conditions affecting the industry and filed for bankruptcy. Butler was determined not to be associated with the proceedings and petitioned the court to exclude his name from the bankruptcy declaration in exchange for paying his one-sixth share of any debt owed to creditors.[33]

By 1877, iron that had sold for $35.00 a ton in 1873 plummeted to $10.00 a ton. Wages for furnace laborers during the same period fell from $1.75 per 12-hour day to $1.00. Coal sold in 1873 for $3.20 per ton but in 1877 sold at just $1.00 per ton. Coal miners who were paid $1.00 per ton of mined coal saw their pay cut to $.50 per ton in 1877.[34]

The *Youngstown Vindicator* came out strongly for the working class "so far as they keep law and order on their side."[35] In July 1877, railroad workers across the country, supported by coal miners, struck over wage cuts bringing industry to a standstill. A rumored railroad strike in Youngstown never materialized. However, the ripple effect of the distant strikes did hit Youngstown since Pittsburgh rolling mills stopped ordering iron from the Valley's furnaces.

Baltimore; Chicago; Martinsburg, West Virginia; and Pittsburgh were the scenes of deadly violence in which police, local militias, and federal troops were deployed to disperse striking workers, who had been joined by displaced citizens and other sympathizers. The *Vindicator* blamed management and wrote, "We doubt if any class of laborers are more intelligent than railroad engineers, and none more conservative or patriotic, and it is a foul slander upon them to say that they justify or endorse the incendiarism or destruction of property that has followed the misstep taken by railroads in the reduction of wages already too low."[36]

Pittsburgh was hard hit as thousands of freight cars were taken over or destroyed by strikers. Several of the freight cars in Pittsburgh contained firebrick for the lining of the Girard Iron Company blast furnace. Unfazed by the reports of violence, a determined Butler set out for Pittsburgh to locate and secure his company's firebrick. A chance encounter with the president of the Pennsylvania Railroad Company, Tom Scott, proved beneficial. During the Civil War Scott had helped to organize rail and telegraph services to assist the Union war effort. Butler convinced Scott, in the midst of the chaos around him, to locate the brick and set it on its way to Girard as soon as the company re-established control over the road. "I was told afterwards that when the strike was over these carloads of brick were the first shipment made to the Valley," recalled Butler.[37]

On August 24, 1877, the *Toledo Review* summed up the Valley's situation: "There is a scarcity of money; an approximation to starvation among the laborers, and the happy, smiling faces are the exception not the rule. The sway of Radicalism has had its withering effect upon the hitherto prosperous people and beautiful city of Youngstown. Like other cities it has felt the scorching breath of panic breathed over it; but unlike most cities, it has felt the flame too hot and for too long a time."[38]

"In a nation geared to promotion and expansion," wrote Wiebe, "stagnant years had traditionally carried a special frustration. They were, quite literally, soul-searching times, for throughout the nineteenth century a great many looked upon economic downturns as a moral judgment, precise punishment for the country's sins."[39] Eventually, employees returned to work. Throughout the depression of the 1870s, Butler had remained the manager of the Girard Iron Company. He was the only original partner connected with the company, and he missed his former associates. Though he had no way of knowing it, 1878 would bring Butler an opportunity that would change his life and his fortunes.

Five

Taking Hold at Brier Hill

DURING THE NATIONWIDE RAILROAD STRIKE, John Stambaugh did his best to keep the Brier Hill furnaces ablaze as orders from Pittsburgh's finishing mills plummeted. But Stambaugh was intimately involved with several other business concerns that required frequent travel.[1] His absences during this period of transition in the local iron industry necessitated a more stable presence on site.

Sales had fallen off due to the depression and the violent labor strikes, and sales agents from Youngstown's blast furnaces could barely give pig iron away. Although Butler resisted dropping prices so low that they would yield no profit, he grew increasingly concerned by the situation. Part of his frustration was due to the poor state of the economy, though another cause was the deteriorating relationship with the owner of the Girard Iron Company, Alexander Byers. Although he respected him immensely for his business accomplishments, Byers was an outsider and Butler never developed a close relationship with him.

Ten years with the Girard Iron Company provided Butler valuable experience. The associations with the Tods and Stambaughs at the Girard Iron Company provided Butler with invaluable business lessons. The risk of investing one's personal assets, the ups and downs of the business cycle, the trials of being an owner, the managerial structure of a company, the day-to-day headaches, and the effects of a major economic depression were things that Butler experienced firsthand.[2]

Butler's resume was strong, consisting of a steady 10-year record with the Girard Iron Company. But the time was right for Butler to test the waters for new opportunity.

On a train trip home from Philadelphia, Butler encountered John Stambaugh. Though the meeting appeared happenstance, Stambaugh had an agenda. Unknown to Butler was the fact that on January 8, 1878, the stockholders of the Brier Hill Iron and Coal Company had appointed a committee to pursue his services. They were also interested in Thomas Pollock, an experienced furnace manager whose father William was a stockholder in the company.[3] Butler would later reminisce about the train encounter with Stambaugh. "He told me they were thinking of re-organizing the concern and asked me how I would like to come to Brier Hill. I told him I believed I would like it."[4]

The stockholders offered Butler the position of general manager. In exchange for agreeing "to devote all his time, care, skill, and diligence in the business and management, and especially in engaging and contracting for all materials and supplies, all the labor and employees, superintending their services, taking care of the property of the Company of all kinds, and properly marketing and disposing of all products and securing the results of sales,"[5] Butler would be paid $2,000 annually in quarterly installments. This was more than he was making at the Girard Iron Company.

If for any reason the company closed for three months or longer, Butler's pay would be cut accordingly. This clause reflected the stockholders' concern for weak or unstable market conditions, as it was common as well as practical for operators to shut down their furnaces if orders fell. The language also indicated concern over labor strikes. If a strike occurred, Butler was to hire new workers and keep production going. He had an option to purchase a minor share of company stock. Pollock was made a founder in charge of operating the furnaces, subject to Butler's discretion. Butler was to meet with the Board of Directors once a week.[6] With that, the new Brier Hill Iron & Coal Company management and operational structure were in place.

Butler signed on without giving Byers advanced notice. His departure from Byers's Girard Iron Company would be complicated. He had not even given Byers a chance to negotiate a counteroffer. Byers was too proud to be treated in such a way, and he decided to hold onto his brash upstart manager if not physically, then at least, financially. Butler was undeterred, and he wrote Byers a final letter severing his services and forsaking his financial investment with the company. It was not until some years later under the advice of his attorney that Byers compensated Butler for his original investment.[7]

Butler's name was now recognized not only within the Valley's iron industry, but also within the Mahoning Valley itself. His new position with the Brier Hill Iron Company meant that Butler was now associated with one of the most respected establishments in the Valley. When he left the Girard Iron Company, he departed confident in his abilities to persevere, and he left as an ironmaster, thus satisfying a lifelong quest.[8]

Butler soon realized that he had the full confidence of his new bosses.[9] For Butler, the Brier Hill organization became his second family, and Governor David Tod, even in death, loomed as the patriarchal figure. Lest anyone forget, Butler had been handpicked by the governor to be a partner in

Five. Taking Hold at Brier Hill

the Girard Iron venture, and he never sensed that his value was in any way inferior to Tod's or John Stambaugh's descendants. Butler's ability at his craft legitimized his position, perhaps even more than the direct descendants of the founders because he, more than they, had proven his worth. Nevertheless, Butler's colleagues on the board were more than just business partners. They were a close-knit group of friends and family. Among them was John Stambaugh's son, Henry, whom Butler considered his closest friend.

Once Butler gained his bearings, he began taking steps to improve Brier Hill's situation. At the time he was hired, the company had two furnaces on the property, the Grace and the Sallie furnaces, named for Tod's two daughters, and the Tod furnace that stood a quarter of a mile away. All had been out of blast for some time.[10] About the yard, the effects of the nation's railroad strike were still evident. Tons of pig iron lightly coated with rust were stacked in the yards. Butler did his best to sell off as much of it as he could during the period of low demand, even if that meant getting less than ideal prices. His next move was to secure large supplies of ore as he and Pollock worked toward relighting all three furnaces.

By mid-summer, the Grace Furnace was up and running, but the summer proved a slow season for pig iron. Midway through 1878, iron production in the Valley continued to dwindle. The furnace at the Brier Hill Iron Company stayed in blast, one of only eight Valley furnaces in operation. The furnaces at the Girard Iron Company, Brown-Bonnell & Company, Struthers Iron Company, Andrews Bros., Himrod Furnace Company, Andrews & Hitchcock, and the Eagle Furnace Company were the only others still in blast. These eight furnaces yielded a meager 400 tons of pig iron a week. Thirteen other blast furnaces in the Mahoning Valley sat dormant. High grass and weeds almost hid the nearly 22,000 tons of pig iron that lay strewn across the stockyards of the Valley.[11]

The top blast furnace operators learned how imprudent it was to rely solely on the Pittsburgh market. This had been driven home whenever an economic depression or strike shut down iron production, which was usually shipped by rail to Pittsburgh. The *Youngstown Vindicator* noted, "Up to the Panic of 1873, the major part of pig iron sold in this valley found its way to Pittsburgh where it was used for mill purposes. Since 1873, our manufacturers have discovered that there was more money in making a better quality of iron, and today but little is shipped to Pittsburgh, the great bulk of it being sold at other points for foundry and Bessemer purposes."[12] The Brier Hill Iron and Coal Company with Butler as manager learned to look beyond the Pittsburgh market to places like Wheeling, West Virginia.[13]

The Board of Directors began an aggressive course to purchase companies too financially weak to survive the depression. One vulnerable enterprise was the Girard Rolling Mill. It was renamed the Corns Iron Company after one of the investors, Joseph Corns. Butler was made a member of the Board of Directors.[14]

Although the era was marked by government reform, it would be well into the next century before safety in the workplace was given its proper focus. Owners and operators of business had free rein to test new ideas without much thought to consequences. To owners, casualties were often counted as an unfortunate, though accepted, part of heavy industry.

Working at the base of a blast furnace remained one of the most hazardous jobs. The same pitfalls that threatened ironworkers at the stone stack furnaces of the 1840s plagued workers at the blast furnaces of the 1870s. But Butler and Pollock continued the company's upgrades.

Pollock's presence during this phase was vital. His father William was considered an expert in blast furnace construction, and he later became successful with his own company that specialized in the practice. Iron producers had begun utilizing the gas given off by blast furnaces to heat the blast around 1859. By putting a bell top on the blast furnaces, the gases given off could be captured and redirected down to the stoves and boilers. Butler recalled the process when it was first tried in Youngstown. "It was thought highly dangerous by workmen, and there was at first some difficulty in getting them to work around the stack."[15] Butler recalled the bell top design at the Girard Iron Company furnace back in 1868. The furnace men there were very apprehensive and feared that trapped gases would explode. Yet the idea proved very efficient despite the inherent dangers associated with its application.

In late 1878, a tragedy occurred at Butler and Pollock's furnace. As Butler explained the circumstances to a *Youngstown Vindicator* reporter, "We had just completed the rebuilding of a hot-blast oven, making it substantially as good as new, and were ready to connect the same with the main pipe leading to the furnace. The oven had been drying out for ten days previous by fire being kept up with the fuel, and it was thought best to complete the drying process by turning on a small amount of gas from the down flues of the furnace proper, but by some means, just how we are unable to arrive at an exact conclusion until one or both of the injured men recover, too large a quantity of gas penetrated the oven. This was lighted, it is supposed by Anderson, one of the parties injured. Our founder [Pollock] says he gave no order to that effect. The lighting of so large an amount of gas in so small and confined a space caused the explosion." Two laborers were seriously injured by the flying brick and iron, and the foundry man died from his injuries the next day. The *Vindicator* praised Butler for his candor in describing the events.[16]

Five. Taking Hold at Brier Hill

The Valley had experienced several labor strikes in the past decade. The most serious occurred in 1869 when more than 1500 laborers walked off for more than four months. During the panic year of 1873, replacements were brought in by Youngstown owners to end a work stoppage.[17] In the spring of 1878, a strike began at the Youngstown Rolling Mill Company. Management promptly discharged them. In April, 24 puddlers, members of the Amalgamated Association of Iron and Steel Workers, walked off the job to protest the implementation of a sliding scale, a formula that tied the puddlers' wages to the price of iron rather than hours worked. By using a sliding scale, manufacturers could reduce the puddlers' wages any time the price of iron dropped. Some companies quickly accepted the puddlers' demands because they could not afford to shut down, and by the summer of 1879 half a dozen mills had given in to the demands.[18]

Organized labor, however, was still in its infancy despite the large-scale violence of the railroad strikes and the early victories of the Amalgamated Association of Iron and Steel Workers. Disunity still existed within the early union movements because skilled laborers, like puddlers, would not want to assimilate with the unskilled workers who included blast furnace fillers and day laborers. Recent European immigrants and African Americans typically filled these jobs. As historian John Bodnar noted, "The craft-dominated Amalgamated Association of Iron and Steel Workers could never really bring itself to extend a cooperative hand to the mass of unskilled strangers."[19] Strikes initiated by skilled workers were not joined by the unskilled and, thus, were easy for management to overcome. The notion of strength in numbers among the workers was slow to develop, and this would prove fortunate for Butler.

Several months after Butler took charge, Brier Hill finally started to take a positive turn. But it was not until September 1879, before prices for iron started to rise. Butler and Pollock had blown in another of the company's furnaces in late August, one that had been down since 1872.[20] It came just in time, for the economy began to recover rapidly. "Iron prices doubled and tripled," Butler remembered, "the demand was heavy, work was plentiful and the distribution of charity happily came to an end."[21]

The economic upswing carried with it increased wages for puddlers, heaters, and rollers as dictated by the sliding scale.[22] But the wages of local furnacemen were not attached to the sliding scale. Theirs remained fixed. Although blast furnace workers unionized in the late 1870s, it remained difficult to obtain advances without support from skilled workers. Creating a work stoppage was not always the answer because owners simply replaced them.

However, in January 1880, organized furnace workers demanded a 25-cent increase to their average daily wages of $1.25. Owners were given

24 hours to acquiesce or face a walk-out. But the Brier Hill furnace men also wanted the right to determine job assignments. "Upon consultation," the *Vindicator* reported, "the owners concluded to refuse the request and proceeded to dampen their furnaces." It was just the sort of crisis Stambaugh foresaw when Butler's contract was drawn up, and the new manager was given full control to deal with it. Butler ordered Pollock to dampen one of the two operating furnaces until replacements were found. Managers at Brown, Bonnell and Company and the Andrews Brothers Company did likewise.[23] This method of strikebreaking was typical of owners.

A week later the *Vindicator* reported "The furnacemens' strike so far is detrimental to themselves alone, their places having been filled by other laborers, who are not members of any union." Butler had faced his first serious labor dispute and had kept the furnaces producing with only a brief interruption. Had he failed, he risked forfeiture of three months' pay. "It was a bitter and memorable strike," Butler concluded.[24]

Much of his managerial philosophy was learned from David Tod. It was Tod, who in response to a series of strikes by area coal miners in 1860, introduced legislation in the state house in Columbus that would have made it a felony to strike. However, coal miners around the state rallied to defeat that measure.[25]

In the 1870s and 1880s, adherents of Social Darwinism as espoused by Herbert Spencer, the English philosopher and sociologist, applied the concepts of survival of the fittest and natural selection to politics and sociology. When applied to the business world, this philosophy suggested that strong companies and their leaders would survive and advance while weaker companies would fail or be swallowed up by larger ones, a concept embraced by such contemporaries as Andrew Carnegie and Henry Clay Frick. Social Darwinism also seemed to favor the strong hand of management over the working hands of labor. Surely, Butler applied this tactic to keep his furnaces producing. But labor's troubles eventually were forgotten in the excitement that accompanied the Valley's industrial recovery.

By 1880, the transition from an economy based on coal to one based on iron accelerated. The number of men working at blast furnaces and rolling mills totaled 4,048, far outdistancing the 3,157 coal miners in the Mahoning Valley. A simple name change would soon reflect the transformation of the Brier Hill Company.[26]

Under Butler's recommendations, improvements continued to take place at the Brier Hill operation. Furnaces were refurbished and investments in new technology helped to transform the company into a modern industrial plant. Stoves and furnaces were added as the company took advantage of strong economic conditions and their proximity to local firms that began specializing in iron-related services. William Tod &

Company, for instance, built a 120-ton hot blast oven for the Brier Hill Iron and Coal Company.[27] The additions were indications of profit and confidence. The company, through Stambaugh and the Tods, was widely connected with many of the leading industrial and financial enterprises in the Valley including banking, rail, coal, limestone, and primary and secondary iron concerns. Its holdings were numerous and diverse, and the trend continued. Attention soon turned to the newly developed ore fields in the Lake Superior region.

Access to raw materials remained vital. During the last 15 years, iron manufacturers shifted from coal to Connellsville coke. Limestone quarrying was underway in western Pennsylvania, but a ready supply of iron ore was still elusive. Although the discovery of native ores gave birth to the local iron industry in 1803, it was clear by the 1840s that new sources were needed to sustain iron production. The black-band ore discovered at Mineral Ridge had produced the high quality American-Scotch pig iron at the James Ward and Company in Niles. But that local vein was not large enough to meet the needs of all the Mahoning Valley's furnaces. In the old days depleted ore fields meant the end to local iron-producing enterprises, but improved transportation modes meant iron producers no longer had to rely on local resources.

Ore mining in the Lake Superior region before 1877 was primarily confined to Marquette County in Michigan's Upper Peninsula. It began in earnest in 1856 when 7,000 tons of ore were shipped from Marquette at a value of $28,000. But the discovery of ore in the Menominee Range in 1873 along the border of Michigan and Wisconsin led to one of the most productive ore-mining operations in history.[28]

Eventually the ore discovered on enormous tracts around the upper Great Lakes was mixed with local ores to produce iron and ultimately, steel. The first shiploads to the Mahoning Valley arrived by way of the canal in the 1850s. After the railroad boom, furnace owners enjoyed cheap transportation rates, which aided iron production as tons of ore began rolling into Valley mills. The introduction of massive quantities of ore gave rise to larger blast furnaces, which gave birth to iron production on a large scale. Iron producers fortunate enough to be near canals and then railroads enjoyed lower shipping costs, an advantage enjoyed by the Mahoning Valley district. Locally, the use of Lake Superior ore first took place at the Sharon Iron Company in Mercer County, Pennsylvania in the 1850s when Butler was in his teens.[29]

Iron producers of the Mahoning and Shenango Valleys took advantage of the new discoveries and their massive yields. Within a decade all 15 of the Mahoning Valley's furnaces and all 23 of the Shenango Valley furnaces relied on Lake Superior ore. The days of self-sufficiency were over.[30]

By 1880, as much as 84 percent of the ore used in the Valley's six main furnaces came from Lake Superior mines and was transported on such rail lines as the Cleveland and Mahoning Railroad started by David Tod in the 1850s.[31] Railroad expansion continued to play a vital role in the area's industrial development. When the great railroad-building era was complete, four major lines passed through Youngstown—the Pennsylvania, the Baltimore and Ohio, the Erie, and the New York Central. "In addition," noted Harlan Hatcher in his history of the Western Reserve, "the flow of Great Lakes ore and the rise of big companies encouraged the construction of the Pittsburgh & Lake Erie, The Lake Shore & Eastern, and the local Youngstown & Austintown roads—busy industrial belt lines serving the plants, rolling ore down to the valley and coal up to the lake in stupendous quantities."[32]

These developments were welcomed, but the Mahoning Valley still lacked a steel producer. The prediction, urging, and outright clamoring for a steel manufacturer in Youngstown had grown steadily since the late 1860s, but it was not until 1881 that the first attempt to organize a steel concern was made. At this time there were only 13 Bessemer plants in the country.[33] Butler felt a Bessemer steel plant would be most efficient, and thus, most profitable. The feeling was shared among several blast furnace operators, and these interests, including the Brier Hill Iron and Coal Company, came together collectively to pursue this goal.

Butler, Stambaugh, and George and Henry Tod represented the Brier Hill faction. T.W. Kennedy, manager of the Struthers Furnace, Butler remembered, "believed that he alone possessed the secret of making good Bessemer pig iron" and brought this brash attitude to the mix. Butler did not share Kennedy's high opinion of himself and felt only one man possessed the right qualifications—Captain Bill Jones of Pittsburgh. At the time, Jones worked for Andrew Carnegie, and he was, said Butler, "one of the most important practical men in the Carnegie plants ... an inventor and a manager of great ability."[34] Butler pursued Jones aggressively meeting with him several times in Pittsburgh. Interested in the proposition, Jones also traveled to Youngstown as negotiations heated up, leading Butler to report that the Captain would join the new Youngstown Bessemer Steel Company.

Although negotiations between Butler and Jones had gone well, discussions among the interested blast furnace operators did not. They were able to pool $450,000 in subscriptions from among their group, but a disagreement over property valuations arose between the Struthers' representatives and the other parties. The dispute was enough to sink the whole project. For the moment, plans for a Bessemer steel plant in Youngstown were dead. "The project was abandoned," as Butler put it, and would not be seriously revisited for another decade.[35]

Five. Taking Hold at Brier Hill

Butler was the driving force and showed once again the business philosophy of the Brier Hill men. They were aggressive, but by no means, hasty in their efforts. Before another serious attempt to construct the Mahoning Valley's first steel plant emerged, Captain Bill Jones died tragically from injuries sustained from an explosion at a Carnegie plant in Pittsburgh leaving Butler without the best candidate to make Bessemer steel in Youngstown.

By 1882, Butler helped to make Brier Hill the envy of the Mahoning Valley. The Grace Furnace had earned the title of champion iron producer by putting forth 100 tons of pig iron per day. The Tod Furnace yielded 75 tons per day compared to the 65 tons at the furnace at the Girard Iron Company. Grace reigned over both the Mahoning and nearby Shenango Valley.[36]

In the spring of 1882, a group of local investors decided to start a mining operation in Marquette County, Michigan, to feed their Youngstown area furnaces. With a capital stock of $1,000,000, the Youngstown Iron and Mining Company was organized. John Stambaugh was made president and Butler was named vice president.

The company's vein was projected to yield 50,000 tons of ore the first year. Not only was the ore expected to supply the iron furnaces surrounding Youngstown, but it looked to be ideal for the Bessemer process of making steel.[37] By injecting air into cast iron in a liquid state to remove carbon, the Bessemer process created a stronger metal known as steel, a product that had been manufactured in the United States since 1864, but one not yet made in the Mahoning Valley. The Menominee Range near the Wisconsin border, and the involvement of Mahoning Valley iron men in this region would soon change all that.

In 1882, the Brier Hill board decided to reorganize the operation and used the occasion to alter its name. With their coal mining interests fading, the board shortened the company name to the Brier Hill Iron Company. Butler continued as General Manager.[38] Butler also proved to be the company's man on the spot. He regularly took business trips to Cleveland and New York and continued to trek to Wisconsin and Michigan to check on ore operations.

No longer could Butler be considered a rising iron master. By the opportunities made available to him through his association with the Brier Hill men, he had become much more. Butler had become a true Brier Hill man. He was now viewed as a successful businessman. With his accumulation of wealth and status, he was able to make additional financial investments. In short, he had become a capitalist and would maintain that status for the remainder of his days. The new status encouraged Butler to become more active in his other interests at this time, namely politics.

Added to all these activities, he continued his efforts of public improvements serving on Youngstown City Council.

In 1883, the Brier Hill Iron Company was listed as one of five companies in the United States manufacturing spiegeleisen, a unique type of pig iron made by introducing manganese ore to other common iron ores. This product was thought to be well suited for rail production. After Butler secured a large supply of concentrated manganese ore, a contract was signed with the Joliet Steel Company to provide 2,000 tons of spiegeleisen. Butler maintained that Brier Hill Iron was the first company to produce this type of pig iron. But they soon found out that their furnaces were ill-equipped for the job and jeopardized the lucrative contract with Joliet Steel.

Butler would not abandon the plan to produce spiegeleisen. He contacted his friend Julian Kennedy, an up-and-coming blast furnace engineer and Yale graduate from Poland, Ohio, who worked for Andrew Carnegie in Pittsburgh. Kennedy recommended the services of a fellow Yale graduate named Edward L. Ford.[39]

The 27-year-old Ford got his start in the industry at New York's Albany and Rensselaer Iron and Steel Company. His most recent experience had been with the Cambria Iron and Springfield Iron companies. Once aboard at Brier Hill, Ford helped to draft plans for the construction of a special blast furnace to produce spiegeleisen.[40] His efforts helped to salvage the contract with Joliet Steel though, in the long run, the Brier Hill Iron Company finally abandoned the production of spiegeleisen. Ford stayed on, however, and Butler grew fond of the young man, eventually introducing him to his daughter, Blanche. The young couple would marry in 1887.

In the nearby rolling hills of Pennsylvania, quantities of limestone existed that could sustain iron manufacture on a large scale. When added to molten iron, limestone helped to separate the impurities from the liquefied metal. Recognizing its potential, the Brier Hill Iron and Coal Company looked to secure a long-term financial foothold there. The company, under Butler's management, operated the Brier Hill Limestone Company in Hillsville. However, in 1881 the company sold the Hillsville mine to the Carbon Limestone Company. Brier Hill Iron and Coal then purchased another quarry in Hickory Creek Valley, and in 1885 Butler organized the Tod, Butler & Company. Henry Tod served as chairman, Butler was named secretary, and William B. Schiller was made treasurer and general manager. Tod, Butler & Company would soon become the Bessemer Limestone Company of Pennsylvania.

On June 2, 1887, the Bessemer Limestone Company of West Virginia was incorporated. The principal investors in the new company were three nail manufacturing companies in Wheeling, West Virginia, and one individual—Joseph G. Butler, Jr. The company was capitalized at $60,000 based on 600 shares at $100.00 per share. Butler bought 299 shares. An incorporators' meeting was held on June 23, 1887, and bylaws were adopted. A Board of Directors was chosen, and Butler was elected president.

Another Bessemer Limestone Company was incorporated in 1888, for $60,000 with Butler elected president. Five days later, Butler offered to sell Bessemer Limestone of West Virginia to Bessemer Limestone of Pennsylvania. On September 29, 1888, a special meeting of the West Virginia stockholders was held who agreed to the offer and sold Bessemer Limestone of West Virginia to Bessemer Limestone of Pennsylvania for $6,000.[41] These quarries would continue to supply the Mahoning Valley mills for decades.

Six

Iron's Demise and the Promise of Steel

ON MARCH 5, 1888, JOHN STAMBAUGH, president of Brier Hill Iron Company, died. As a sign of respect, most of the businesses in Youngstown closed from 1 p.m. to 4 p.m. on the day before the funeral. In his eulogy, he was feted for his charitable heart. "No representative of any work that was for the amelioration of suffering, or for the benefit of the poor, ever appealed to him in vain, and his gifts were not meager, but measured by the need." Butler was one of the eight pallbearers.[1]

For Butler, John Stambaugh represented the third businessman whose career, values, and life's work were worthy of respect and admiration. As had James Ward and David Tod, Stambaugh recognized Butler's energy and talent and entrusted him with ever-expanding responsibilities. The roles Stambaugh had fostered for Butler aided his manager's growing stature in the local iron scene. Butler observed not only Stambaugh's distinction in the iron industry, his business know-how, and his impulsive kindness toward his partners and his community, but also Stambaugh's thirst for books, travel, culture, and desire for public improvement. Stambaugh was once president of the Youngstown Opera House Company, and it was his donation of land that helped create the city's first hospital. Butler wrote, "He was benevolent in impulse and deed, possessed of keen business foresight and judgment, and the welfare of his employees, business partners and the community was always of vital interest to him."[2] Noticeably absent are comments regarding Stambaugh's treatment of strikers.

Butler was absorbed with his role as General Manager of the Brier Hill Iron Company and his many responsibilities as president of the Bessemer Limestone Company, which, by the early 1890s, operated three quarries, employed 150 men, and produced 250,000 tons of stone annually.[3]

Finding Stambaugh's replacement as the head of the Brier Hill Iron Company was an easy task for the Board of Directors, and they looked no further than George Tod. The third son of the late governor, Tod had been with the company since 1861 and certainly had the family connection and company seniority.

Thought by Butler to be rather gruff, Tod was an intimidating figure in the office and around the furnaces. "Most of us at Brier Hill were more or less afraid of him," recalled Butler. Nevertheless, Tod's reign as president would last for the next 20 years during which some of the most progressive and far-reaching changes that the company and the industry had ever seen took place.[4] Early into Tod's presidency the new generation of leaders of the Mahoning Valley's iron producers would be tested. For Butler, these hurdles were opportunities.

In 1888, 14 iron manufacturers in the Mahoning Valley had formed an organization known as the Mahoning Valley Iron Manufacturers' Association whose primary goal was to combat increasing freight rates set by railroad agents. The MVIMA, which listed as a member the Brier Hill Iron and Coal Company, also collected data and statistics on the production of pig iron. The group eventually grew to include the iron concerns of the nearby Shenango Valley. To attract buyers, Youngstown's iron producers ended up competing against each other by lowering their prices to sell pig iron to Pittsburgh area rolling mills. The competition drove down the price of Youngstown pig iron until the mill owners realized they were hurting themselves as well as each other financially. The situation became so advantageous for Pittsburgh rolling mills, noted historian Kenneth Warren, that the Mahoning Valley's pig iron at times sold cheaper than that made in Pittsburgh.[5]

The MVIMA, later known as the Bessemer Pig Iron Association, eventually came together to combat the Pittsburgh influence by securing orders in mass and then distributing them among the association members. After the death of its president, Henry O. Bonnell, in 1893, a successor was found in Joseph Butler. Butler's stature grew among the local iron producers as he frequently returned from Pittsburgh with orders of 50,000 to 100,000 tons of pig iron, which would be distributed among the member firms. The Bessemer Pig Iron Association helped to ease some of the natural mistrust inherent in the highly competitive iron scene while providing a degree of stability for the local industries.

The pig iron manufacturers and rolling mill owners still longed for a steel mill in Youngstown, but building a steel plant would require a very substantial financial investment. If it were to be done, the project would have to be a joint venture. Without cooperation and trust nothing would happen. Even the Mahoning Valley's rolling mills demanded steel, but the process to acquire it bordered on absurdity. Iron produced in Youngstown had to be shipped to Pittsburgh to be transformed into steel. It then came back to the Valley's rolling mills as steel bars for further rolling and processing. Youngstown mills not only paid for the changeover to steel but also for shipping both to and from Pittsburgh.[6] It stood to reason, therefore, that a steel plant in the Mahoning Valley would create a new market for the local iron mills. And finally, a group of local iron producers emerged ready to change this situation, and Butler's role would prove invaluable to its success.

Youngstown's city fathers made great strides in providing services to the community during the latter part of the 1880s by expanding electrical service, paving roads and sidewalks, and improving infrastructure. And there were more people to serve. Through natural population growth, a continued influx of immigrants, and a series of annexations, Youngstown's census increased from 15,000 in 1880 to more than 33,000 by 1890. For example, in 1889, the area known as Brier Hill, which was home of the Brier Hill Iron Company, was annexed into the city.[7]

The late 19th-century industrial scene was a transformative time in the Mahoning Valley. For Butler it was a time of professional, financial, and social growth. It was also a time of transition for the Butler clan as he and Harriet raised their three children to early adulthood during the late 1880s and early 1890s. Eldest daughter Blanche had married the rising iron chemist E.L. Ford in 1887. The other children, 19-year-old Grace and 16-year-old Henry, studied abroad in Berlin during 1889 and 1890. Harriet Butler accompanied the children. Butler made sure that every educational advantage was available to his children.[8] Butler himself had yet to travel abroad, evidently entirely too busy with business matters.

The economic troubles of the 1870s seemed so distant, especially since things had gone so well in 1889. American iron producers had increased output by 1.3 million tons from the previous year and for the first time had surpassed Britain's total production of iron and Bessemer steel. That good feeling carried over into the 1890s and masked any signs of economic trouble. But the signs were there. Like the depression of the late 1870s it was the failure of America's railroads in the early 1890s that sent Wall Street investors into a panic. Iron and now new steel centers felt the effect of the collapsing rail industry as diminishing orders slowed production. Mahoning Valley iron producers were keenly aware of this situation. A failing rail industry could mean only one thing—a failing iron industry. C. Seymour Dulton of William Tod & Co., an engine-building firm that serviced many of the local mills, charged that other factors were also at play. In April 1892, he claimed that railroad companies were holding back their orders for rail early in the year in order to place larger orders at the end of the year to claim greater dividends.[9]

Regardless of the motives, the iron and steel industries depended heavily on expanding railroads to keep their furnaces lit.[10] The first years of the 1890s would prove this. In 1892, for example, the nation's rail production was 1.6 million tons while steel production was 4.9 tons. These numbers fell over the next five years. Not until 1897 would rail production equal this amount again. Likewise, from 1893 to 1895, steel production remained stagnant averaging 4.8 million tons. It was a crucial period for the Mahoning Valley's iron industry and for its first steel producer.[11]

King iron was on the verge of being dethroned, not so much because of the current railroad concern, but because of the growing demand for steel in general. The future of the Mahoning Valley was in steel, and this fact had been understood by Butler and the other parties involved in the first attempt to make steel in Youngstown in 1881.

From his earliest days Butler had been a man of numbers and efficiency, and he continued to rely on facts. The signs of iron's demise were clear as the popularity of steel continued to climb along with the new skyscrapers it was helping to construct. Steel was much stronger than iron, and its production was proving more efficient. Muck bar, for example, cost iron producers about $24.50 to make, whereas a billet of steel could be cast for $22.00. This cost comparison helped many iron producers to see the direction of things to come. "It seems to me," observed one local iron man, "that the iron manufacturers will be driven into making steel."[12] The questions for the Mahoning Valley were: who would venture successfully in the direction of steel manufacturing and, more importantly, when?

The fiery competition among the local iron producers of the day, in their desire to outdo the other, ultimately led to progress for Youngstown. Competition was good for the local economy. The investments, the replanting of outside businesses into Youngstown, and the building of new enterprises garnered much attention from envious communities such as nearby Warren.

Steel production could have started in the Mahoning Valley as early as the late 1850s had James Ward recognized the process William Kelly had tried to sell him. Four long decades later, the Valley appeared ready. Joseph Weeks of Pittsburgh, editor of the iron and steel trade journal, *American Manufacturer*, told a *Vindicator* reporter "I see your people here are going into the business, and the only thing that surprises me is that they waited so long. With all the natural advantages possessed by Youngstown, its excellent railroad facilities for shipping to every point you should have had a large steel works here making billets long ago." But Weeks saw an advantage in Youngstown's procrastination. "A large steel plant can be erected at present much cheaper than two or three years ago. Further than this the improvements have almost revolutionized the business, and the new plant will have the advantage of securing many improvements that those that were built several years ago do not possess."[13]

When Butler entered the industry in the late 1850s, "pig iron," he recalled, "was just pig iron ... if it worked, it was good iron; if it didn't work, it was bad iron."[14] But by the 1880s, the iron masters recognized the need to adopt scientific methods of metallurgy. In an article for *The Iron Age* Butler wrote, "I remember, incidentally, when we first started in the analyzing business in real dead earnest at Brier Hill. This was in the eighties. For certain purposes foundries would not use anything but imported Scotch pig iron. We solved this problem by sending out and getting samples of all the well-known brands of Scotch pig iron and had them thoroughly analyzed. We then pursued the matter further by an analysis and proper combination of ores, and it was not very long until we were making the American Scotch, which was the equal of the imported." These analyses were done by Brier Hill Iron and Coal's chemist, C.A. Meissner. With the new product, the company made inroads into newer markets, and Meissner's value skyrocketed.[15]

Brier Hill had been the first iron operation in the Mahoning Valley to erect a laboratory and employ a chemist. Butler wanted to hire another. "I wanted ... a young man for a chemist, who ... would be able to run a furnace later on; and if he had some business ability, that would not be amiss." In January 1890, Butler hired a chemist named Rollin Steese to work at the Brier Hill Iron and Coal Company's laboratory. The 22-year-old Steese was studying chemical engineering in Cleveland at the Case School of Applied Sciences when he left in his junior year to accept Butler's job offer.[16] Steese joined C.A. Meissner in the Brier Hill lab. After watching Rollin Steese in the lab for six months, Butler made the young chemist a superintendent at one of the furnaces.[17]

Later in life Butler often reflected about those up-and-coming stalwarts of the Valley's iron and steel industries who got their start at the Brier Hill training school, as he often called it. Meissner, the first chemist employed by any of the Mahoning Valley blast furnaces, as well as Rollin Steese, Julian Kennedy, Thomas McDonald, E.L. Ford, and others would emerge from under Butler's watchful eye and mature into steel men of influence. Almost 60 years later, Rollin Steese would fondly recall, "We were a very happy community up there making pig iron."[18]

In the fall of 1890, members of the British Iron and Steel Institute, including Sir James Kitson and Jenkin Jones, came to the United States to tour the leading iron and steel centers. Butler was a member of the entertainment committee and traveled with the delegation. After visiting Youngstown, the British visitors offered to purchase the Brier Hill Iron Company. They were turned down.[19] The Brits left Youngstown on October 12 and spent a few days in Chicago before heading south to Birmingham and several other cities in Alabama, Tennessee, Kentucky, and Virginia.[20]

Six. Iron's Demise and the Promise of Steel

The 1890s were marked by new technology as a growing reliance on science began to replace the antiquated rule of thumb methods of iron production and by new business practices that favored consolidation and merger. Within this industrial evolution only a handful of the Mahoning Valley's iron leaders, Butler among them, possessed the necessary qualities to safeguard their interests while working to preserve the local iron industry for at least another decade and lay the groundwork for the inevitable shift to steel.

Butler's preparation for these changes was a lifetime in the making. His childhood was remarkable compared to others of his day. There were not many like Butler who could boast of having been born literally into the iron industry. Neither Carnegie, Frick, Tod, nor even Butler's mentor, James Ward, could make such a claim. Although Butler's employment at such a young age was expected for most children of the era, certainly his opportunity at management training was rare. His goal for as long as he could remember was to become an iron master following in the footsteps of his father, grandfather, and James Ward. Before he reached his mid–30s, he had achieved that. And as he entered his early 50s, he became much more than an iron maker and successful pig iron salesman. He was a leader in local industry and was beginning to be noticed on the national scene. Since childhood his natural instinct had been to educate himself and pursue useful information. Now as an adult he focused this thirst for knowledge more specifically on the iron business. His search for data strengthened his understanding of the current market scene, and his accumulation of historical facts related to the iron industry became more than a hobby.

The early opportunities presented to him by James Ward were by no means physically strenuous; however, he recognized the value of these lessons and made the most of them. At each succeeding level of advancement his hard work and determination made others take notice of him. His insistence on taking a crash business course at Duff's Commercial College before assuming management of the James Ward and Company was a testament to his determination and need for preparation.

Butler wanted to know not only the current iron scene, but also its entire history. He examined developments from the early Iron Age to the first furnaces in colonial America as well as their impact on the industrial development of the Mahoning Valley. He studied the technological advances in iron production through the ages as well as the emerging role iron had on society and developed an insatiable appetite for all things related to the historical evolution of the iron industry.

Likewise, his curiosity in the historical development of the Mahoning Valley, a story closely linked to his own, would become a lifelong interest.

He was proud of the Butler iron tradition established in post–Revolutionary War America and the role his grandfather and father had played during the young nation's westward expansion. And he was proud of his own contributions to and rise in stature within the local iron industry. He became a close friend of the most famous iron historian of the day, James Swank, and for nearly three decades the two would share correspondence relating to historical facts and current data of the iron and steel industry. His growing knowledge enabled him to speak as an authority on the subject, and this ability was noticed by his contemporaries. Relentless energy, thorough preparation, and determination were traits that came to characterize J.G. Butler, Jr.

On December 21, 1890, Joseph Butler celebrated his 50th birthday. He was secure financially, socially, and politically. He had sent his wife to Germany while his son and youngest daughter were in school there, had served four terms on Youngstown's City Council, was becoming influential in national politics, and enjoyed countless friendships with prominent men of influence.

His children also were heading down successful paths. Stressing the value of education, Butler and Harriet, his affectionate and supportive wife, had raised three well-rounded offspring—Blanche, Henry, and Grace. Although Butler did not conform to any specific church, the children were exposed to religion. Blanche once won a Bible at the First Presbyterian Sunday school after answering 107 catechism questions.[21] The couple's marriage was a model of devotion to each other and their family as they shared close relations with each child despite the enormous amount of time Butler spent on the rails in search of markets for the Mahoning Valley's pig iron. He developed an especially devoted relationship with his daughter, Blanche. She had taken an interest in writing poetry, and Butler encouraged and supported her creative efforts.

In 1891, not long after Harriet and the children returned from Germany, the Butlers moved to a new address. After living in the former Presbyterian parsonage on the corner of Rayen Avenue and Phelps for 23 years, Butler purchased a home at 525 Wick Avenue from George D. Wick, who had built the house in the 1880s.

After returning from Europe and graduating from the Rayen School, Henry had gone to Harvard where, in 1897, he became the first Mahoning County–born resident to graduate from that Ivy League university. Grace married Detroit businessman Arthur McGraw in 1891. The couple settled in Detroit where Arthur was a director of the Wolverine Manufacturing Company.[22]

By this time, Wick Avenue was known as one of the premier residential areas for Youngstown's wealthier citizens. As one local historian

Six. Iron's Demise and the Promise of Steel

The Butler estate on Wick Ave., Youngstown (The Butler Institute of American Art Archives, Youngstown, Ohio).

noted, "Wick Avenue was so attractive that there were Youngstown postcards showing the tree-lined street and elegant homes."[23] The move symbolized Butler's permanent place in the elite Youngstown social class after a 30-year climb. He methodically started to fill the new house with original paintings that he had been collecting for the last decade or more. Going back to his days in Chicago, he had developed an interest in art that soon turned into a passionate pursuit. His modest collection at this time, about two dozen works, would eventually lead to one of the most prized private collections in the area. His continued success at the Brier Hill Iron Company not only lifted his status among Youngstown's upper class, which was made up primarily of iron men, but also helped to expand his role within their business circles.

Throughout 1891 and into 1892 the Mahoning Valley Iron Manufacturers' Association met with agents of the various railroads of northeast Ohio and southwest Pennsylvania to negotiate a rate reduction in order to stay competitive. In his March 1885 letter to the *Iron Age*, Butler had acknowledged that railroad rates had been reduced on raw materials including coke, iron ore, and limestone. He added, "the railroad

A group of friends and business leaders at Brier Hill. Left to right, Simon Perkins, George Tod, Henry Tod, Henry Stambaugh, Butler, Rollin Steese and Robert Hazletine. From Joseph G. Butler, Jr., *Recollections of Men and Events* (New York: G.P. Putnam's Sons, 1925).

people have done a very handsome thing in the way of assisting the owners of furnace plants in this valley, not only in the reduction of rates, but in adjusting other and discriminating rates to and from near-by competing points."[24]

Hoping to effect a similar response, the Mahoning Valley Iron Manufacturers' Association in early 1891 sought to lower shipping rates 10 cents per 100 pounds on finished iron from the Mahoning Valley to Chicago. Nearly 11 months passed before the petition was rejected by the railroad agents. In the meantime, struggling to compete, the Valley's iron mills shut down.[25]

Persistence would pay off in the spring of 1892 as Butler and the Valley's iron representatives finally convinced the railroad operators that both industries, railroad and iron, were dependent on one another and that a modest cut in shipping rates on iron would go a long way for their immediate business security. Idle mills benefited no one. The local men reminded the rail agents of the business they had lost during the first half of 1891 when the Mahoning Valley iron mills had shut down. Pointing to the declining iron industry and competition from southern mills, the local iron manufacturers successfully persuaded the railroad agents to see the cut as something mutually beneficial.[26]

In 1891 and 1892, the campaign to create a Youngstown steel plant took a major step forward when George D. Wick, one of the Valley's

Six. Iron's Demise and the Promise of Steel

leading industrialists, stepped up. The Wick family was one of the first to settle in Youngstown, and they had established their financial footing in the coal industry. Their interests eventually moved into finance, but they invested largely and successfully in the iron industry. George Wick proclaimed in April 1892, "the obstacle in raising the necessary stock here is owing to the jealousy among the manufacturers, each seeming to have the idea that someone else wants to get ahead of him. At one time I had $450,000 subscribed toward a steel plant, when it fell through, owing to one of the parties withdrawing. This was a year ago, and had the project been carried into execution, we would now have a fine steel plant in operation and be at the head of the procession. The demand for steel is rising at a rapid rate and the sooner we build a plant here the better."[27]

Joining Wick in this organizing group were Myron Wick, H.O. Bonnell, James Neilson, and Butler's son-in-law, Edward Livingston Ford of the Brier Hill Iron Company. Ford became superintendent of the Youngstown Steel Company and established himself as one of the finest up-and-coming men in the industry. This group of men represented several of the Mahoning Valley's leading iron concerns including the Union Iron and Steel Company, Brown-Bonnell, Mahoning Valley Iron, Andrews Brothers, and the Brier Hill Iron Company.[28]

With the railroads finally cooperating with the iron interests, the Mahoning Valley organizers hoped to push ahead with construction of a steel plant; however, in front of them lay another stumbling block. The Amalgamated Association of Iron and Steel Workers, made up primarily of skilled puddlers, had been in the middle of bitter negotiations with owners over a new pay scale. Owners feared that any prolonged disagreement between the two sides would bring unnecessary tension to the industry.

A strike and any violence would affect all the blast furnaces and mills in the Mahoning Valley. Butler and the Brier Hill Board of Directors feared the potential outcome from the puddlers' impasse. A drop in pig iron orders would force the company to shut down their blast furnaces, which would have a disastrous effect on the company's bottom line just as they had invested heavily in the new steel plant that was not yet built.

H.O. Bonnell forewarned the local puddlers just how precarious a predicament the iron industry was in. So fragile was the situation and so forthcoming was mass steel production, that any drastic move on their part could tip the scale against them and the iron industry as a whole. "Steel is rapidly and surely supplanting puddled iron in almost every place in which iron has been a necessity," he explained echoing Butler's and George Wick's previous assessment. "One ton of steel billets or slabs can be laid down in the mills of this valley today at a lower price than it is possible to produce a ton of puddled iron," he informed the skilled laborers. It was inevitable, he predicted, that "steel will take the place of muck bar, and the puddlers' occupation will be gone." A strike, therefore, would only hasten this development. "It would seem," Bonnell reasoned, "that the workmen should be careful not to take any stand that will result in stoppage of all these puddling furnaces."[29]

In May 1892, during the labor negotiations, the Mahoning Valley steel plant organizers embarked on a fact-finding trip to Birmingham, Alabama. "The object of the Southern trip," one member told the press, "is to inspect and examine the leading steel plants of the South with a view of ascertaining the most approved methods and the lowest cost of producing a merchantable quality of steel." To the group's chagrin, they returned from Birmingham after a week to report that "there are no steel plants there except an experimental one that was erected."[30] Undeterred they pressed ahead.

A stalemate between the two sides in Pittsburgh led to one of the deadliest strikes in American history. In the summer of 1892, there occurred an event whose repercussions would be felt by the iron and steel industries for decades. As Thomas Misa observes in *A Nation of Steel: The Making of Modern America 1865–1925*, "For labor historians, and for many workers, no single event has generated as much passion as the 1892 lockout at Carnegie Steel's Homestead plant."[31]

Andrew Carnegie and Henry Clay Frick, chairman of Carnegie Steel, saw the Amalgamated Association of Iron and Steel Workers as an impediment to their plans to mechanize and modernize their holdings. Carnegie placed Frick in charge and left for his castle in Scotland. Frick refused to recognize the union, and by late June negotiations had deteriorated. Historian Les Standiford writes, "By this time workers in Homestead understood there was no hope of reprieve. With Master Carnegie gone to ground in his Scottish retreat, spies planted in their midst, scabs already summoned from distant points, and three hundred mercenary Pinkertons and Coal Field Police on the way to Homestead, there would be no peaceful settlement. As the headline in the [*Pittsburgh*] *Post* blared: IT LOOKS LIKE WAR."[32]

Frick ordered the Homestead mill to be shut down on June 29, hours earlier than the planned walkout by the workers, which made the stoppage a lockout rather than a strike. Frick's decision to employ armed Pinkerton men to control the Homestead mill led to a violent gun battle on July 6, 1892, and many workers and several Pinkertons were killed. The ensuing riot in the town, which was just up the Monongahela River from Pittsburgh, was quelled only by the arrival of 8,000 members of the Pennsylvania National Guard.

Six. Iron's Demise and the Promise of Steel

"It was common knowledge that the monumental profits earned by Carnegie Steel in the 1890s grew directly from the defeat of unionism at Homestead," wrote Paul Krause in his book on the Homestead Strike. "Without the encumbrance of the union, Carnegie was able to slash wages, impose twelve-hour workdays, eliminate five hundred jobs, and suitably assuage his republican conscience with the endowment of a library."[33]

Most townspeople supported the workers. The mayor of Homestead was a skilled worker in Carnegie's mill and was a member of the Amalgamated Association of Iron and Steel Workers, which meant that, as Standiford points out, "there was little distinction between the town's government—or its very population, for that matter—and the organizing body of the strike itself."[34] The Homestead lockout and its aftermath provided lessons to both labor and management, and these lessons were certainly studied by the men trying to start Youngstown's first steel mill.

Seven

First Steel in Youngstown

THE SUMMER OF 1892 PROVED to be one of the most momentous periods in the Mahoning Valley's industrial development. Three events—a new steel plant, striking ironworkers, and the onset of iron's demise—competed for ink in the local press daily. The only positive article of the three was the prospect of a new steel plant called the Ohio Steel Company, and even that story was touched with high drama and charges of unfair play by the time it unfolded.

After the formation of the Ohio Steel Company was announced early that summer, the first decision that needed to be made was where to locate the great plant. Land needed secured for the enterprise, and the organizers began the search for the best possible deal. What ensued was intense competition between Youngstown and several Mahoning Valley cities to land the plant. Private land-owning citizens of Youngstown also looked to cash in on the venture.

The steel men had set their sights on Hawkins Farm, a stretch of land north of the city and west of the Mahoning River near the Girard border. "This land was rather swampy," recorded local historian George Higley, "and the river overflowed at times requiring very deep foundations of large blocks of quarried stone. When excavations were made they frequently filled with water before the massive stones could be lowered." Getting to the farm was difficult, Higley explained, "Access to the site was over Credit Mobilier Bridge to Goose Island, then through the McMaster brick yard where the road ended in the plant."[1] The farmland encompassed 100 acres but was nowhere near large enough. The organizers hoped to purchase additional acreage adjoining the farm; owned by several different families. This made negotiations difficult.

In July 1892, Butler hosted a meeting of local investors and interested citizens to help raise $15,000 to help purchase the site. His connection with the steel movement was initially on behalf of the Brier Hill Iron Company, heavy investors in the new project. When news of the fund-raising movement became public, the neighboring communities of Girard,

Struthers, and Niles initiated a bidding war to lure the project away from Youngstown. A variety of enticements such as free land and tax abatements were offered. The project became more attractive as the strike by the Amalgamated Association of Iron and Steel Workers shut down local iron operations. One unnamed mill owner told a *Vindicator* reporter, "The life of an iron manufacturer is not a bed of roses just now.... The shutdown of seven weeks had the effect of demoralizing things generally, and it will be a month yet before everything gets to working smoothly."[2]

Throughout the summer the bidding war was front-page news, and the headlines told the story. July 28: "Merchants Begin the Donations"; August 11: "It Is Certain, Youngstown Sure to Lose a Vast Industry on Account of Selfishness"; August 30: "The Steel Plant Question Reaches a Crisis"; September 3: "Girard Calls and Goes Youngstown $10,000 Better."[3] The organizers kept silent as Girard and Youngstown practically begged for the project. In August, Girard, by offering their land for free, emerged as the leading site.

Recognizing this critical development, Butler and his Youngstown associates increased the fundraising goal from $15,000 to $25,000 to assist the Ohio Steel Company in purchasing Hawkins Farm. The wrangling that occurred between the two communities was fierce. Property owners held out for more money, while the steel men expected to get the land for free. What was not stated, although subtly implied, was that the majority of the interested Youngstowners, including the Brier Hill Iron Company, owned real estate near the proposed site, and they looked to gain financially if the new project was built in their neighborhood. Their greed, suggested the press, was sure to force the project from its rightful location from Youngstown to Girard.

Butler addressed the allegations in an open letter to the *Vindicator* when he wrote, "The Ohio Steel Company is not asking for any donations or begging for anything. It is purely a matter of business, and will be decided on business principles, or, in other words, if the 86 and three-quarter acres of land is donated free to the Ohio Steel Company, making it equal to the Girard offer, the steel plant will be located on the Hawkins farm site, otherwise it will be located in Girard."[4]

Butler's comments were disingenuous. Girard never really stood a chance of getting the plant, but the bidding war was real. Pitting Girard against Youngstown, and the ensuing tactics, sweetened the deal for the Ohio Steel Company. So, although the stockholders may have intended to locate the plant in Youngstown all along, they succeeded in securing the inducements they desired by luring interested parties into a competition until conditions were to their liking.

On September 14, 1892, Butler and Henry Wick announced the

selection of the Hawkins Farm for the location of the Ohio Steel Company. "It Is Ours, The Steel Plant to Be in Youngstown," proclaimed the *Vindicator*. The $25,000 raised by Butler from the local businessmen to assist the land acquisition paid off. His persuasive skills were vital to the deal. In addition, Youngstown's mayor and city council agreed to adjust the city limits so the new plant would be outside of Youngstown's boundaries and could thus avoid taxes.

A spokesman for the Girardites said their group "had given up all hopes of securing the site, for a week ago they discovered that they were being used as a 'cat's paw' to pull chestnuts out of the fire for the Youngstown men. For this reason, they did not renew their offers."[5]

Plans for the huge plant would make it the third largest steel producer in the country behind the Edgar Thompson Works in Pittsburgh and the South Chicago steel plant in Illinois. It would produce up to 1,200 tons of steel per day manufacturing billets, rail slabs, tinplate bars, and sheet steel bars beginning July 1, 1893. The citizens and business interests of Youngstown rejoiced. Finally, the age of steel was at hand in the Mahoning Valley.

Not only was Butler named to the Board, he was also the new vice-president and, along with Henry Wick (president), named a manager.[6] Butler had the most recent experience in running an operation at the ground level and could assess the company's immediate needs better than anyone else. Julian Kennedy, an up-and-coming local engineer, was hired to develop the design plans for the new plant. Before coming to Youngstown, he had to finish his work on the mechanical engineering plans for the new Ferris Wheel at the World's Columbian Exposition in Chicago.[7]

The Amalgamated Association of Iron and Steel Workers' demands for higher wages in the summer of 1892 caused widespread strikes in several states. Locally, a lengthy seven-week strike forced furnaces to shut down. Fortunately, violence was avoided. Once the strikes ended, furnaces were relit, workers returned, and the mills came back to life. Brier Hill's Grace furnace set its best mark by casting 270 tons of iron in one day in December 1892.

While Valley furnaces continued to produce only pig iron, steel production in Pittsburgh was in full swing. The *American Manufacturer* reported that "Radical changes" were underway at Pittsburgh's iron mills; "they [were] being converted into steel producers." The conversion of the plants not only led to modernization with the most up-to-date equipment, but also required less labor than iron and thus was more efficient.[8]

The transformation in Pittsburgh was a prelude to the future of the Mahoning Valley's iron scene. Although Youngstown had officially embarked in the direction of steel, the new plant, the only local steel project planned so far, was under construction whereas Pittsburgh's conversion appeared wholesale. The Ohio Steel Company was a long way from pouring its first heat of steel.

On October 14, 1892, Butler, Henry Wick, chief engineer Kennedy, and assistant engineer Singleton King walked Hawkins Farm plotting the locations for buildings and railroads to serve the new steel plant.[9] However, as Butler and his colleagues trudged the old pasture that autumn day sowing seeds for the future, they were unaware of future developments. Survival would once again depend on strength, adaptability, and flexibility.

Turbulence in the national economy, uncertain markets, and labor unrest, had weakened several Mahoning Valley mills, and their vulnerability caught the attention of investors from New York. In addition to an attempt to acquire the Brier Hill Iron Company, these New York capitalists were interested in securing every rolling mill and furnace in the Mahoning Valley. The out-ot-staters represented larger companies that were consolidating smaller companies to integrate the various stages of production. Historian Naomi Lamoreaux explained, "Because blast furnaces could not be run intermittently or at less than capacity, economical operation of a steel works required the maintenance of a smooth, continuous flow of output from the blast furnaces to the Bessemer converters to the rolling mills.... The result was a radically new approach to business. In contrast to the small manufacturers, who adjusted their production to conform to fluctuations in market demand, large firms sought to operate their plants at full capacity, regardless of the state of business."[10] They believed that more could be produced for less and sold for less though still at a profit, and at a price that would undercut the smaller independent producing firms. In addition, shutdowns and start-ups were cost prohibitive. The New York syndicate recognized the array of iron resources within the Mahoning Valley and aggressively sought to buy out firms they believed to be struggling financially. And within the Valley, there were vulnerable iron operations eager for a buyout and interested in making a deal.

Local owners, including the directors of the not yet constructed Ohio Steel Company, were asked to name a price. On December 9, 1892, the *Vindicator* reported, "If the sale as contemplated goes through the total amount paid for all the properties will reach $7,000,000.... If carried out as intended all the mills and blast furnaces between Lowellville and Warren including Hubbard, will pass into the hands of one concern."[11]

Such a sale would have ended local ownership and put the future into the hands of outsiders. However, one month later, the gigantic deal was called off. When asked for an explanation, George Wick told a reporter it was "a stringency in the money market that caused a shutdown of investments, and that was probably the principal reason for it not going through according to the scheme laid out."[12]

In November 1892, Governor William McKinley was in town to speak at the annual Garfield Club banquet. He also attended a private dinner at the home of Henry Wick. Butler was there to greet his old friend. Talk turned to the Soldiers' Monument that stood on Central Square. After its dedication in 1870, a payment disagreement arose with James Caldwell, who had delivered the granite shaft from the railroad station to the square. Caldwell was never paid, so he went to court to seek restitution. In lieu of payment, however, he was granted legal title to the monument. Twenty-two years later, he remained the legal owner of the monument. A disappointed McKinley urged the locals to solve the problem. A committee was formed to negotiate a settlement. Caldwell accepted $40 to settle his long outstanding bill and deeded the monument to Butler, Bonnell, and King who in turn deeded it to Youngstown Township.[13]

The Ohio Steel Company suffered a setback on January 16, 1893, when the organization's vice-president, Henry O. Bonnell, died. The industrialist had taken ill in late 1892. The Board of Directors of the Ohio Steel Company unanimously chose Butler to take his place. Though he modestly attributed his selection to the large stock that the Brier Hill Iron Company owned in the Ohio Steel Company, Butler had done as much for the creation of the new company as anyone. He rallied investors for the fundraising drive to assist the land purchase and communicated to the press the often-complex process of site selection for the new steel plant.

After hiring Julian Kennedy, Butler wasted little time and aggressively pushed to hire another young talent, Thomas McDonald, to become the new company's plant manager. McDonald worked for Henry Clay Frick at the Carnegie Steel Company. Butler felt so strongly about McDonald that he offered him an annual salary of $5,000 during their first meeting in Pittsburgh. Butler, like his mentors before him, was proving a natural at recognizing young talent. McDonald's impact on the Valley's steel development over the next three decades would prove enormous. The offer made to McDonald was met with some resistance from the Board of Directors, but at Butler's insistence it stood. McDonald accepted and came aboard in February 1893.[14] With Kennedy and now McDonald in place, the plans for operation proceeded.

McDonald was the man who possessed the best understanding of the Bessemer process, and much deference was given to him. McDonald also had a strong, forceful personality which helped him persuade the directors to alter their original plans by enlarging capacity from one or two 8-ton Bessemer converters to two 10-ton units. These changes came with a huge price putting McDonald's and Butler's reputations on the line. Fortunately for both, McDonald's experience proved invaluable. Throughout the 1890s, Butler's admiration and respect for his superintendent grew, as did the support of the Board of Directors after the company's slow but constant growth. Butler would later write, "When he [McDonald] was engaged, Mr. Henry C. Frick was in Europe. After Mr. Frick returned he told me that if he had been at home we should never have secured Mr. McDonald for the management of our plant."[15]

McDonald's reputation in the Mahoning Valley would rise to legendary status. In an era of consolidations and mergers, successive owners of the company recognized in McDonald the same qualities that Butler had in 1893. When the United States Steel Company came into existence at the turn of the century, it invested heavily in the Mahoning Valley's iron and steel industry. The giant steel producer began erecting a mill across the Mahoning River from Girard in February 1916 and created a company-built town that grew around the operation. This village was later named McDonald in honor of the mill's general superintendent. In his autobiography Butler wrote, "I feel that if I ever did a favor to the Mahoning Valley it was when I induced Mr. McDonald to come to Youngstown."[16]

In the spring of 1893, readers of the *Vindicator* learned about New York's rising star, the new Manhattan Insurance Company skyscraper. At 17 stories, it would be the tallest office building in the world all because of the strength provided by its new steel skeleton.[17] It was another sign that steel was on the rise both figuratively and literally. The previous two decades were marked by record-setting railroad expansion as thousands of miles of track crossed the country. Railroad magnates preferred steel over iron because of its strength and durability. And as the great railroad-building era ended, the new steel-framed buildings rising in America's major cities foretold the next great market for steel.

Steel was on the verge of transforming the American landscape by freeing architects and builders from the limits imposed by iron and challenging them to design buildings of unimaginable heights.[18] The signs were obvious that iron was becoming less desirable to longtime customers. Steel was the future and Butler's beloved iron industry continued down the irreversible path to its ultimate demise.

The event that affected the economy for the rest of the decade was the Panic of 1893. Primary causes included a run on the gold supply, the bankruptcy of the Philadelphia and Reading Railroad, and the failure of the National Cordage Company, a rope company that had tried to corner the world market for hemp. Historian Charles Hoffman reported that 125 railroad companies went into receivership. Companies stopped paying dividends and laid off workers. Public confidence in the government, financial institutions, and private business went into free fall.[19]

In *Self-Help in the 1890's Depression*, H. Roger Grant writes, "The economic scope of the depression of the 1890s was staggering; American business enterprise lay in shambles." Soon after the Panic, the nature of the disaster began to emerge. By September 1893, 172 state banks, 177 private ones, and 47 savings and loan associations had closed; by October, 158 national banks had folded; and by year's end company failures totaled a whopping 15,242. Prominent casualties included Oliver Iron and Steel; the Atchison, Topeka, and Santa Fe Railroad; and the Union Pacific Railroad. During the summer, 12 of the largest ore steamers on the Great Lakes never left their home ports, while many mine operators were wiped out by the hard times. "Factories are shut everywhere," became an oft-repeated description of the economic decline. Grant also noted that 40 percent of the men working in the iron industry lost their jobs.[20]

The Panic came just as the organizers of Youngstown's first steel plant were attempting to arrange financing. Original projections in 1892 had put the cost of the new mill at $600,000, but that was soon increased to $750,000 and then to $1,000,000. Due to McDonald's various upgrades the costs rose still higher. The timing could not have been worse.

After the Panic became a full-fledged depression, the owners grew wary, and construction was delayed. Assistance soon came, but it was not from within the Mahoning Valley. Instead, it took a group of investors from outside the Mahoning Valley to help the Ohio Steel Company meet its mounting costs. In 1894, the *Vindicator* reported, "the capital again was increased to $1,500,000, by far the largest incorporation Youngstown had ever known."[21]

Butler described in stark detail the desperate state of the national and local economies in 1893. In his *History of Youngstown and the Mahoning Valley* Butler wrote, "There was a disagreement between iron manufacturers and their employes [sic] over the wage scale that expired on June 30, 1893, and the mills closed down on that date to remain closed until a settlement had been reached ... but before the summer was over a national crisis had supplanted the mere quarrel over an adjustment of the ironworkers' wage scale.... For almost two years Youngstown not only stood still but went backward." Youngstown's working men were reduced to beggars in the streets. The situation throughout the industry was without precedent. Historian Victor Clark wrote, "Between the fall of 1892 and of 1893 the number of men employed in the six largest rolling mills at Youngstown fell from 6,700 to less than 500. Never in the history of the American iron trade ... were there so few furnaces in operation as in October."[22]

Smoke filled skies, for decades a symbol of Youngstown's prosperity, gave way to clear skies, a depressing sight to anyone associated with the iron industry. Butler remembered, "Few of those who depended upon a daily wage for subsistence had sufficient funds to stand even a short siege of idleness, and the most thrifty, and even those of comfortable means, felt the pinch of poverty."[23]

The iron and steel manufacturers that emerged from the 1880s and struggled through the instability of the 1890s not only had to embrace science, as the Brier Hill Iron Company had, but also had to adapt to the rapidly evolving new business philosophies. Historian Naomi Lamoreaux in *The Great Merger Movement in American Business, 1895–1904* observed, "In the competitive struggles that followed the Panic of 1893, manufacturers first resorted to the trade associations and gentlemen's agreements that had seemed to work in the past. When these failed, they experimented with more highly structured organizations, such as selling agencies and pools. Finally, when these, too, proved unable to stem the decline in prices, they turned to consolidation for relief."[24]

Two examples of competitors coming together for their common financial gain were the Bessemer Pig Iron Association (formerly known as the Mahoning Valley Iron Manufacturers' Association) and the proposed Ohio Steel Company. Before these monumental efforts, the relationship among Valley iron men was more fraternal or social in nature. But in competition where sheer survival and existence were at stake, the influence of associations was indeed limited.

Not surprisingly, Butler served as president of the Bessemer Pig Iron Association. In the old days, an experienced pig iron salesman like Butler would go out and haggle over the sale price by the ton. But this approach was outdated. Simply naming a lower sales price to his old friend Charles Schwab, for example, was no longer a practical business tactic when dealing with rivals. Competition, Butler began to understand, "covers a great many more things than simply naming the lowest selling prices." In addition to price competition, Butler cited "rivalry at all points—in developing new markets, in improving the quality of the goods and adapting them better to the uses for which they are intended, and in reducing the cost of production and distribution."[25]

Though Butler saw that the future was in steel, he was still deeply engaged in iron production and seeking markets for local producers of pig iron. Steel was produced through the Bessemer process by burning out the required amount of carbon contained in iron. Therefore, the continued use of iron was necessary for steel production since any steel maker had to produce iron first before altering the chemical makeup to create steel. Emerging steel producers had a choice: make their own iron or purchase it from suppliers. Locating consumers for the Valley's pig iron was essential for the local iron industry's survival. As head of the Bessemer Pig Iron Association, Butler did this as well as anyone.

Harper's New Monthly Magazine carried in its March 1894 issue a detailed essay on how steel was made, including a dramatic account of the role of the Bessemer converter: "At the beginning of the blowing, only sparks and a little brown smoke are seen; ... as the silicon becomes exhausted, the oxygen turns its attention to the carbon; the fact is immediately announced by the appearance of a true flame, which grows rapidly, until it fills completely the mouth of the converter, and dazzles the spectator by its brilliancy. The temperature rises quickly; the flame becomes fuller, clearer; the metal, stirred by the heavy blast, boils, and particles from it are expelled from the vessel; the roar of the flame becomes deafening; the projections of metal become more frequent; and to one unaccustomed to the spectacle it would seem that a continuance of the proceedings must wreck the entire establishment."[26]

The steel was then poured into ingot molds. After the molds cooled, they were stripped away revealing the steel ingot, which would be reheated in one of the company's four soaking pits and then transferred to the blooming mill for further processing into billets or plate. The Board of Directors, having approved McDonald's request for increased capacity, expected the plant to produce 1,000 to 1,400 tons of steel per day.[27]

Despite the stagnant economy, Youngstown's new steel plant was finally completed. On February 4, 1895, a milestone was reached, and Butler and a hopeful group of new steel men in the Mahoning Valley expected to have cause for celebration.

The prevailing spirit of cooperation that day, fostered by a common desire to make good on a new investment, warmed the hearts of many of the new owners who once had looked at each other as fierce competitors. The thermometer read four degrees below zero, not particularly unusual for a February day in the Mahoning Valley. The much anticipated start-up of the Ohio Steel Company could not have come at a better time for the Valley. The expectation of 600 to 700 new jobs at the steel plant was encouraging news to idle iron workers.[28]

At around 10:00 a.m. several hundred interested citizens, curious onlookers, and business leaders amassed on the grounds of the old Hawkins Farm where Butler's handpicked engineering and design team of Kennedy and McDonald was about to unveil the workings of the new enterprise. "At the time it was started," recorded Butler, "the plant of the Ohio Steel Company consisted of four cupolas, two 10-ton converters, four 4-hole soaking pit furnaces, one 34-inch blooming mill, and one 3-high 23-inch mill on which could be rolled four inch billets, small billets one and one-half inch and larger, and sheet and tin plate bars."[29] The advances of the Pittsburgh steel industry showed McDonald and others that newer plants with modern equipment could undersell competitors who did not modernize.

Seven. First Steel in Youngstown

There were no blast furnaces. Instead, blast furnaces from nearby plants would supply iron for the converters. In this respect, the steel plant served as a new outlet for local blast furnace operators. This was part of the original plan and induced many of the Valley's furnace operators to support the steel plant project. It would be five years before the Ohio Steel Company operated its own blast furnaces.

For now, iron from nearby blast furnaces shipped in by rail cars. Upon arrival, the molten iron was injected into the massive converters where it was charged with a blast of cold air at 25 pounds per square-inch to eliminate the carbon from the chemical makeup. Next, ferro manganese was added to bring about the necessary carbon level that produces the chemical composition of steel.

In any event, it was a brilliant sight to see on that February morning when molten metal streamed into the south converter quickly filling the large iron-plated vessel. Butler recorded that several hundred people watched as "the long, brilliant flames roared from its mouth, while showers of sparks fell on the surrounding snow."[30] The frigid temperatures throughout the night nearly froze solid the poorly insulated water pipes of the great plant, which could have prevented the day's festivities. But McDonald and his new crew worked through the early morning hours to fix the problem and to keep the start-up on schedule.

Another incident with disastrous consequences, however, was barely averted thanks to the keen eye of a skilled blower and those trained men working on the converter platform. A drop in hydraulic pressure caused by a faulty supply line left the converter momentarily crippled with molten steel inside the vessel. "If the blower had not had presence of mind to stop on discovering this," wrote Butler, "and had attempted to turn the converter back, he would have dumped its liquid contents on the wet, frozen ground, caused an explosion, killed most of the crowd, and wrecked the plant." Fortunately, the catastrophe was averted. Later that afternoon, the company's first steel ingots were rolled in the plant's blooming mill. Butler put it simply, "The manufacture of steel in Youngstown had begun."[31]

The bold prediction made nearly 30 years before that steel would be made in the Mahoning Valley was finally realized.[32] Butler's contributions toward the milestone were considerable, ranging from organizational efforts to the selection of McDonald as superintendent and Kennedy as chief engineer. Although the first flow of steel was cause for celebration by those who made it happen, the rest of the Valley remained depressed. But at least the flame was lit.

The ensuing period was a defining one in American business. Lamoreaux says the depression that followed the Panic of 1893, spawned more mergers than at any other time in history. When firms had a distinct advantage over their rivals, collusion or price-fixing was no defense. However, she notes, "In such industries, firms frequently joined together in associations ... to defend the industry as a whole against some external threat (e.g., unfavorable tariff legislation) rather than to restrict output or support prices.... Agreements were rarely successful among manufacturers who produced staple goods, that is, in industries in which the strategy of mass production prevailed."[33] Typically, the external threats facing iron producers came from foreign competitors, low tariff proponents, and other industries.

In this period of transition strong financial backing was a necessity. Mills backed by the unlimited capital of Andrew Carnegie or J.P. Morgan could and did swallow up weaker rivals. The businesses that lacked capital surrendered to mergers and takeovers. The takeover and consolidation movement had a far-reaching effect on the Mahoning Valley's industrial scene. In a way, the formation of the Ohio Steel Company was one such example that united local business concerns under one head because it brought the companies that mined raw materials and those that operated blast furnaces, rolling mills, and finishing plants under a single board of control.

In truth, the organizational structure that Butler helped to construct took a great deal of persuasion, and its creation would influence the local steel industry for generations. One of Butler's contemporaries in the industry, Henry E. Passavant, reminisced in a 1922 letter to Butler about their seminal efforts at consolidation, which was a miniature version of what J.P. Morgan would create in 1901. "At that time," wrote Passavant, "we had in embryo the present United [States] Steel Corporation, and I really think you and I were the only ones who appreciated what it really meant."[34] Although their efforts brought the various owners together for the purpose of making steel under one corporation, the various parts, such as the many pig iron manufacturers, remained independent and maintained their separate identities.

The mergers that evolved in the Mahoning Valley during the 1890s, however, were orchestrated by outside interests, though this was by no means the first attempt to do so. Brown, Bonnell & Company, for example, a Mahoning Valley fixture since before the Civil War and synonymous with its iron industry, had been sold to outside interests in 1879.

Given Butler's involvement in so many varied business activities, it was inevitable that his interests would occasionally clash. From the outset the Ohio Steel Company with Butler as vice president leased the blast furnaces of the Brier Hill Iron and Coal Company, where Butler was general manager and sat on the board, and this arrangement proved to be most efficient. But after three years of steady progress the Ohio Steel Company was in a financial position to bid on the furnaces. A proposition was made to purchase the famed furnaces, and although Butler and the Brier Hill board were receptive, in the end a deal could not be reached between the two companies. Rollin Steese, who worked for Brier Hill, recalled the negotiations with Ohio Steel. "We had set a dollar price for our property. It was accepted but we had a rider which demanded stock at $125 a share, not cash. They offered cash but refused stock. The deal was called off. This was clearly a case of two fools meeting."[35]

Butler's other major business interest, the Ohio Steel Company, did not elude the buyout movement before the close of the decade. By 1896, the Ohio Steel Company was in full production putting forth 400,000 gross tons of steel annually, very different from that frozen February day in 1895. This output benefited local pig iron producers including those at Brier Hill. In 1897, Ohio Steel consumed an average of 1,200 tons of pig iron per day.[36]

Without their own furnaces, steel mills were at the mercy of prevailing market conditions or greedy iron producers. But building a blast furnace was an expensive undertaking, and the decision to do so could make or break a company. Butler and the other board members of the Ohio Steel Company cautiously approached the idea in 1898 after the Brier Hill Iron and Coal Company had refused to sell them their two blast furnaces the previous year. William H. Baldwin, secretary for the Ohio Steel Company, wrote in the annual report for the fiscal year ending June 30, 1898, "On May 19, 1898, the Company decided to issue bonds to the amount of $1,000,000 for the purpose of obtaining money for the erection of two blast furnaces." The report added, "During the three years and five months since starting on February 4th, 1895, the mill has made 833,858 tons of steel."[37] In February 1899, it became part of the new National Steel Company. Historian Peter Krass explains, "Behind National Steel was the flamboyant financier William H. Moore, a former judge who was no stranger to the merger game, having formed the Diamond Match Company and the National Biscuit Company, trusts in the matches and baking industries. He had also created the Tin Plate Company in December 1898, an amalgamation of thirty-eight firms, and in April 1899 he would organize thirty companies into the American Sheet Steel Company and nine companies into the American Steel Hoop Company."[38]

Moore offered the Ohio Steel Company stockholders $275 per share, an astonishing figure since the shares had never sold for more than $130. Butler and his fellow board members accepted it.[39]

With the sale to the Moore interests, the Ohio Steel Company became one of eight iron and steel companies in Ohio and Pennsylvania to make up National Steel, which immediately became one of the new giants on the scene ranking third in size behind only the Carnegie and Illinois Steel

Companies. The great transition from iron to steel did not happen in a vacuum. It was a tumultuous time for all concerned. Panic, depression, and finally economic recovery characterized the decade of the 1890s. A new century full of optimism and pride was dawning. Butler's boyhood pal, William McKinley, elected president in 1896, had just successfully led the country to victory in the Spanish-American War and was overseeing the economic recovery, aided, Butler noted, by the president's support of protective tariffs.

As a result of the merger movement, the birth of big business was underway. Butler had demonstrated a deep understanding of the direction that the iron industry was headed. His study of the industry's historical development helped to shape his vision for its future. The industry could no longer be governed by the old methods, and the use of steel was indicative of this. Scientific methods to produce a better product were essential, and Butler embraced this modern concept with enthusiasm. The iron product was evolving and metamorphosing into steel, a better and stronger material. The era of the iron men was closing, and a new generation of steel men was rising. However, the steel industry occasionally would still need help and advice from aging iron masters.

Eight

The Original McKinley Man

JOSEPH BUTLER'S INTEREST IN national politics increased considerably in the 1890s, especially as his childhood friend William McKinley won elections to the Ohio governorship and the presidency. In McKinley, Butler found a politician whose Republican beliefs, especially on tariffs and protectionism, perfectly matched his own.

McKinley, born in 1843 in Niles, Ohio, where the Butler family lived, was descended from an iron heritage as proud and as rich as Butler's. In the early days of the Civil War, McKinley enlisted in the Union Army, where in four years he rose from the rank of private to major. Afterwards McKinley studied and practiced law before embarking on a career in politics. His pursuit of political office eventually took him to Congress in 1877 and to the Ohio governorship in 1891. After McKinley's second term as governor, his backers groomed him for the presidency.[1]

Butler enjoyed politics. As a boy he attended political rallies, and as a young man ran successfully for City Council.[2] By the time he reached his mid-40s, he had become a familiar figure to politicians in Washington, D.C. Because of his leadership in local races and issues, he was named a delegate to several Republican presidential conventions. As a member of management throughout his career, he credited the Republican philosophy for creating America's prosperity. "The policy of protection to American industries," he believed, "has encouraged development of our natural resources and promoted invention and enterprise."[3]

Leading the nation's industrial position of global strength was iron and steel. And those who were leaders in the iron and steel industry—men like Carnegie, Frick, and Butler—exerted their influence on politicians in order to shape legislation that would advance their financial interests.

As a long-time advocate for protectionism, Butler made numerous appearances before congressional subcommittees attesting to the importance of protective tariffs. As a congressman McKinley chaired the House Ways and Means Committee before which Butler testified on several occasions. At these committee hearings Butler repeatedly credited protective tariffs for the industrial development of the United States. Those industries, namely iron and steel, pushed the country's industrial and technological advances. "There is no question that a part of the development was due to the tariff policy," he claimed, that protected "the struggling iron and steel industries against competition from abroad."[4]

Relying heavily on their childhood bonds and their families' long relationship, Butler renewed his friendship with McKinley and supported him as he ascended the political ranks. For many industrialists, reaching out to McKinley was like reaching out to a friend who had championed protectionism. In fact, McKinley was more than supportive philosophically. As a congressman in 1890, McKinley had supported domestic producers by authoring the McKinley Tariff bill, which raised duties on imported goods to the highest levels in American history. Years after McKinley's death, Butler credited the tariff with the construction of the first tin mill of size in the United States.[5]

The Tariff Act of 1890 prompted advocates to create the political slogan, "Bill McKinley and the McKinley Bill." Historian Peter Krass writes, "for men like McKinley, protection was a patriotic duty that allowed infant industries to mature while inspiring internal competition. The tariff, they said, also created jobs and generated revenue for the government. On the other side of the argument, the free traders, which included a minority of Democratic congressmen and the rest of the world, claimed that the tariffs aided and abetted the industrialists and their trusts, while the laboring classes allegedly suffered by having to pay artificially high prices for products."[6]

According to Butler, McKinley's protective tariff philosophy was directly shaped as a young man. "His opportunity to observe closely the struggles of the early iron industry in the Mahoning Valley had convinced him of the necessity of tariff protection for all American industries."[7] Specifically, he believed that McKinley's philosophy was influenced by the trials of his father, William Sr. And when Butler wrote about his friend's experiences, he may as well have been writing about his own. McKinley's political outlook was indeed shaped by the leaders of American industry. McKinley biographer Margaret Leech wrote, "McKinley looked upon the great industrialists as the leaders in the march of national progress, the source of high wages and full employment for all the people, and he thought of their financial backing of his presidential candidacy as a contribution to the patriotic cause of protection."[8] Butler, Cleveland industrialist Mark Hanna, and others eagerly looked to deliver as much support as they could gather to get McKinley elected president.

Hanna, like McKinley, was an Ohio native, born and educated in New Lisbon in Columbiana County. But it was in Cleveland where, with his

Eight. The Original McKinley Man

father-in-law's help, he made a small fortune in the iron and coal industries. By the 1880s Hanna was involved in local and state politics, and after helping McKinley to win the presidency, Hanna was appointed in March 1897 and later elected in 1898 and 1904 to the United States Senate. He also served as chairman of the Republican Party from 1896 to 1904.

Butler and Hanna enjoyed a close friendship during their lifetimes connected by their loyalty to McKinley and their shared experiences in the iron industry. Butler recounted the story of a banquet in Cleveland's Union Club to honor Hanna shortly after McKinley's nomination. Hanna addressed the guests, "Gentlemen, a number of people claim the honor of being the original McKinley man. There are guests in this room who give me the honor. I disclaim it most decidedly. The gentleman by my side is the man who first proposed William McKinley for the Presidency. I introduce him as the original McKinley man and guarantee it—Mr. Joseph G. Butler Jr. of Youngstown." Butler's response rivaled Hanna's own quick wit. "I have never claimed the honor," he stated, "but I have never heard of Mr. Hanna telling an untruth."[9]

Once McKinley secured the Republican Party's nomination at the St. Louis convention in the spring of 1896, Butler was tireless in his efforts to get his childhood friend elected president. He hosted many dinner parties for McKinley supporters at his Wick Avenue residence.[10]

Butler and other business leaders knew that it was critical to get out the vote en masse if McKinley was to overcome the Democratic Party's nominee, William Jennings Bryan. The Nebraskan was the antithesis of Big Business and was well known for his impassioned oratory skills. During the campaign he became the defender of labor and society's downtrodden and spread his fervent message across the country appealing to the working class everywhere.

Historian Wiebe said of McKinley, "His specialty was tariff policy.... Less a leader, he was a far shrewder analyst and a more skilled organizer than the Nebraskan [Bryan]." McKinley could not match the younger Bryan's oratorical skills, so he chose a different strategy. His biographer noted, "McKinley's conception of his candidacy was so passive that he at first gave the impression of intending to make no campaign at all. He had decided to stay home and address only the people who cared to visit him there."[11] Instead of going out among the people, McKinley addressed them from his front porch on North Market Street in Canton. The Front Porch campaign proved to be effective. Throughout the summer and up to election day, tens of thousands traveled to McKinley's residence to hear his orations on the greatness of America and the might of its industrial prowess made possible and bolstered by protective tariffs.

Residents of the Mahoning Valley and Niles, in particular, renewed their affection for their native son. Rallies and other campaign festivities in support of McKinley were frequent. None of these, however, deterred William Jennings Bryan from making a campaign stop in the Mahoning Valley in search of the sizable labor vote.

Bryan visited Youngstown on October 20, 1896, and a crowd comprised largely of workers packed Youngstown's Central Square. Estimates placed the number of Bryan supporters at 75,000, many of whom had been following the candidate around the country. Four thousand iron and steelworkers from Pittsburgh made the trip to Youngstown to lend their support. They informed the *Youngstown Vindicator* that they had made the trip "on their own accord to see Mr. Bryan, but that they were compelled by their employers to go to Canton to see McKinley."[12]

Bryan's foray into what was known as McKinley territory would not go unchallenged. Butler and other industry leaders of the Mahoning Valley quickly rallied supporters to counter Bryan's audacious campaign stop and to show that the district was still impenetrable to would-be rivals.

Plans were quickly made to send huge numbers of McKinley supporters by train from Youngstown to Canton to call on the candidate at his home. The McKinley supporters recruited for this political pilgrimage were the thousands then gainfully employed in local mills and factories. Butler excitedly wrote McKinley of the anticipated show of support coming from the Mahoning Valley. "Our visit to you on Saturday, October 31st, is assuming largest proportions and we expect to make it the visit of the campaign." And he made no secret that the delegation would be made up of "several thousand" Valley workers.[13] How many of those workers were legitimate McKinley supporters cannot be determined but it is safe to say that many were behind him since local labor leaders were involved with the plans. They knew that idle mills benefited no one, whereas those operating at full strength meant work for all.

The demonstration was intended to subtly, if not overtly, persuade labor groups to vote for McKinley, whom the industrial leaders promoted as a man of the people. Owners intended to reinforce the message that McKinley's protective policies would continue to directly benefit the workers of the Mahoning Valley and their families.

Butler helped secure Roger Evans, a local labor leader, to speak on behalf of the workers. Evans's participation at the rally was a loud endorsement of where the Valley's organized labor leaders stood in the election and where they wanted their members to stand as well. Evans's speech, Butler told McKinley, would focus on "what protection has done for the Mahoning Valley and what [McKinley has] already done to help us along."[14] The comments were a direct reference to the McKinley Tariff of 1890.[15]

Butler wrote McKinley that his much-anticipated remarks to the

Eight. The Original McKinley Man

Mahoning Valley crowd should "be the best effort you have made thus far."[16] Indeed, after the traditional parade through the streets of Canton that ended at McKinley's front porch, neither side disappointed the other. Butler estimated the crowd to be about 12,000 and noted that McKinley seemed genuinely touched by the impressive turnout that spilled from his dying front lawn and into the street. "My fellow citizens and friends of the Mahoning Valley," said the candidate, "I am grateful and appreciative of this splendid demonstration from my old friends and constituents ... from my birthplace, the home of my boyhood and early manhood, and the dear old town where I as a boy enlisted in the service of the country."[17]

McKinley's accomplishments would never have happened, claimed Butler, had it not been for some assistance he had once provided his childhood chum. "While boys we frequently went swimming together. On one of these occasions he got beyond his depth, and I undertook to save him. I think we would both have lost our lives had it not been for a mill worker named Jacob Shelar, who rescued us."[18]

Every effort was made to present McKinley as a friend of labor. Collectively, those working in support of McKinley, both workers and owners, throughout Ohio and the country succeeded in getting their candidate elected president of the United States. McKinley captured both the electoral and popular vote. Butler and others involved throughout the Valley certainly aided McKinley, whose margin of victory in Ohio was a mere 50,000 votes. Not surprisingly, his support in the Mahoning Valley was strong. Decades later Butler would write, "Nothing for which I have exerted myself ever gave me more deep and conscientious satisfaction than the choice of McKinley as president in 1896."[19]

Business leaders throughout the country finally would have a man they believed to be one of their own in the executive mansion. For Butler and countless other Republicans, there was every reason to celebrate. The *Youngstown Telegram*, the city's Republican newspaper, wrote of restored confidence and reported that "men having capital to invest are now coming forward with propositions to start new manufacturing plants." And it predicted, "there is every indication that there will be sufficient work at the mills and furnaces to sustain everybody in comfortable circumstances during the coming winter."[20]

Though McKinley favored a course of peace and prosperity, the most notable event of his first term was the Spanish-American War. In the fall of 1897 and early 1898 the United States found itself increasingly drawn into the conflict between Spain and the nationalists who wished to gain Cuban independence. To protect U.S. interests, McKinley, with the assent of the Spanish minister, sent the battleship U.S.S. *Maine* to Havana where it received a cordial reception.

On February 15, 1898, an explosion rocked the ship, and it sank with the loss of 266 American lives. McKinley's hopes for a peaceful liberation of Cuba through diplomacy were dashed. "The warmakers of Congress were in the saddle. 'Remember the *Maine*!' was the national slogan," writes his biographer.[21]

McKinley's response to the sinking finally came in April with a war declaration much to the satisfaction of an enraged public. In little more than four months, Spain surrendered to the United States ceding Puerto Rico, Guam, and the Philippines. The popular notion of the day was that American idealism was being spread further throughout the western hemisphere and beyond. Critics, however, saw the McKinley administration as a reign of American imperialism and, as the *Youngstown Vindicator* put it, a "policy which lusts for empire."[22]

During the McKinley years, Butler, more than any other Mahoning Valley businessman, experienced great access to the president and his inner office, and McKinley maintained a warm friendship with his old friend. Most of the correspondence that existed between the two during the White House years was initiated by Butler as he kept the president informed of goings-on in the Valley or events that surrounded some old mutual acquaintance who had made good. Butler was always quick to lend an encouraging word of support to the president and never hesitated to promote Youngstown and the Mahoning Valley, especially its industrial progress. The president's replies were always warm and cordial and usually came by way of his secretary.

When the president was in Canton, Butler enjoyed an open invitation to see him, and they shared many private moments together. When Butler was in Washington, the doors of the executive mansion were also open to him.[23] The respect and courtesy that McKinley displayed toward Butler by all accounts was genuine and certainly aided in further enlarging the latter's influence within local business circles and promoted an already growing prestige within the industry at large.

By the close of the 1890s, Butler had suffered the loss of both parents. His father died in 1895 and his mother in 1899. Although his parents had moved to Cleveland some years earlier, they did their best to the end to correspond with their busy son in Youngstown. Butler likewise wrote his parents frequently and visited as much as possible when business trips took him north.[24]

Butler admired his parents' devotion to each other, and his love and respect for them was deep, genuine, and sincere. He wrote about them with much praise and affection. Butler sent word of his mother's death to the president and related the fact that she had carefully preserved between the pages of her Bible roses that McKinley had once sent her.[25]

Eight. The Original McKinley Man

At the end of August 1899, Butler wrote to McKinley in Canton, urging the president to call on Youngstown on his return trip to Washington to see firsthand the industrial evolution of his old 18th Congressional District. "Such a busy hive of industry is no where to be seen outside of Pittsburgh," boasted Butler to the president.[26]

The Valley's mills were running at full capacity with enough orders to keep production going for weeks. On January 6, 1900, the *Vindicator* reported, "There is not an iron or steel manufacturer in the city but that is in need of labor, both common and skilled." This need for labor would draw thousands of immigrants to the Mahoning Valley's factories during the coming years. By the following year, the Valley could boast to potential consumers of its 15 blast furnaces, 13 rolling mills, and one steel producer.[27]

In June 1900, McKinley was up for reelection and easily won the Republican Party's nomination. This time Butler attended the convention in Philadelphia as a delegate. For the delegates, the real battle of the convention came not for the president's nomination, which was a foregone conclusion, but rather for the selection of the ticket's vice-presidential candidate. Garret Hobart, McKinley's vice president during the first term, died in October 1899. There had been talk of a McKinley-Roosevelt ticket since Hobart's death. Butler was not shy about offering his opinion on the matter and eagerly jumped into the fray.

Early in the convention Butler found himself seated behind one of the most recognizable figures of the day, a wide grinned and bespectacled man, New York Governor Theodore Roosevelt. The former New York City Police Commissioner and Assistant Secretary of the Navy had recently served in the Spanish-American War and became an instant hero after successfully leading U.S. troops against the enemy at Cuba's San Juan Hill. Like McKinley, Roosevelt and his supporters exploited his military service to further enhance an already established political career. Governor Roosevelt entered the convention harboring a loftier goal of someday becoming president himself, but his name was on the lips of nearly all the delegates as the best candidate for the number two spot.

McKinley determined to stay out of the convention's vice-presidential selection process, giving deference to the decision of the delegates. Roosevelt had made it clear that he was not interested in the position. "In the Vice-Presidency I could do nothing. I am a comparatively young man yet and I like to work. I do not like to be a figurehead. It would not entertain me to preside in the Senate."[28] Butler, along with many others in the party, felt that Roosevelt belonged on the ticket to strengthen McKinley's chances for re-election as he faced his Democratic adversary William Jennings Bryan once again.

Butler did his best to encourage Roosevelt to give serious consideration to the vice president position. "I tried to persuade him that it was his duty to run with McKinley and that he would be a great help to the ticket." During the meeting of the Ohio delegation, Butler recalled that Mark Hanna proposed John D. Long as the vice-presidential candidate. Butler immediately objected, spoke in favor of Roosevelt, and asked for a roll call. "Mr. Hanna was very good natured about it," Butler recalled, "and said: 'Joe, you are always making trouble; I thought you would please me by letting me have my way about this.' The delegation was polled and a very large percentage voted for Mr. Long, but, as I recall it, there were at least a dozen who favored Roosevelt. Other elements were put to work and when the Convention met the next day the nominees were William McKinley for President and Theodore Roosevelt for vice-president."[29]

Once the ticket was in place, efforts to re-elect the president and his new running mate went into full speed. Butler once again lent his unbridled support by rallying the Mahoning Valley in support of McKinley's re-election efforts.

Butler's accessibility to the president's insiders was also an opportunity to aid local Republican office seekers as well. Robert Walker Tayler, a veteran Republican congressman since 1895, held down McKinley's old congressional district. Butler, as a trustee of the Mahoning County Republican Executive Committee, used his influence to bring national party figures to Youngstown to campaign for McKinley and a slew of local candidates like Tayler.

The Democratic Party again chose Bryan as their nominee, and in the fall of 1900 announced that Bryan would again campaign in Youngstown. Butler did not want Bryan's visit to go unchallenged and did his best to secure someone from the McKinley Administration, if not the president or his new running mate, to respond to the Democrat's appearance. In early October, less than one month before the election, Butler was in frantic negotiations with McKinley's secretary, George Cortelyou and Myron T. Herrick, a state Republican stalwart and future Ohio governor, to secure a speaker. By this time, Butler conceded that it was not possible to bring Roosevelt to Youngstown, even though the New York governor was riding the rails through the Midwest, including Ohio, in search of votes. In addition to feeling that a response to Bryan was necessary, Butler also believed or at least conveyed that Tayler was in trouble and, therefore, needed help to win his reelection.[30]

The local Democratic newspaper, the *Vindicator*, did its best to build excitement for Bryan. "It is certain that Youngstown will have one of the greatest, if not the greatest crowd in its history," it proclaimed. "The immense crowd that greeted Bryan here in 1896, will be doubled and the

Eight. The Original McKinley Man

The "original McKinley Man's" house all set for the president's reelection campaign (The Butler Institute of American Art Archives, Youngstown, Ohio).

greatest day in the history of the Western Reserve in the way of political gatherings is assured." Preparations were being made two weeks in front of Bryan's scheduled showing on October 15. A grandstand was built on Central Square to accommodate a large turnout.[31]

"Youngstown never before witnessed such a political gathering," wrote the *Vindicator* on October 15, 1900, "and it is doubtful if it ever will again. For four hours and more the Square was a mass of humanity, waiting for the appearance of the great leader and when he finally did come there was a demonstration that those who witnessed it will not likely forget."[32]

While Bryan preached his Democratic doctrine in Youngstown, Butler had been in Chicago. If he believed the *Vindicator* reports he had every reason to worry about the disposition of the voters in the Mahoning Valley. However, the rival *Youngstown Telegram*, which favored the Republican cause, claimed Bryan had been greeted with little fanfare and reported that the turnout was pitifully small. Butler had worked diligently during this second campaign for McKinley and Tayler. He traveled a good deal, particularly to familiar territories in the Midwest like Chicago, lauding McKinley to friendly associates as well as gauging the mood of the electorate. He was pleased with what he found on these trips and brought "back glowing reports of Republican prospects west of the Mississippi." Just two weeks before the election, Butler predicted that "the election will show great gains for prosperity and protection in nearly all the western states."[33]

On the night of the 1900 presidential election, November 6, Butler hosted a party at his Wick Avenue residence, which was linked to Western Union's telegraph lines. He cabled President McKinley's secretary George Cortelyou requesting an update as results came in, and before the end of the evening, Cortelyou responded with the joyful news of McKinley's re-election. Mahoning County once again delivered for McKinley. "Old Mahoning did nobly well.... Running up a majority." The majority was actually an unimpressive margin. McKinley received 8,953 votes to Bryan's 7,401. Across the Buckeye State, the favorite son's showing was much more impressive, as early estimates of a 70,000 plurality sent all Republicans to bed for the evening quite happy. Butler and company retired for the night in excellent spirits satisfied with their efforts and the knowledge that their good friend would serve as president for another four years. Congressman Robert Walker Tayler also celebrated his re-election to a fourth term.[34]

With victory in hand, an energetic Butler turned his attention back to the business of pig iron. Just two days after the election, he was in Cleveland to attend a meeting of the Bessemer Furnace Association to work on ratcheting up pig iron prices that had fallen to a low of $13.25 a ton from a previous high of $24.00 a ton less than four years earlier. Speculation from all corners was quelled as pig iron prospects began a favorable swing, "Heavy sales of pig iron" were "reported from all the leading distribution centers" just days after McKinley's victory.[35]

The United States in 1900 now led the world in iron and steel production. During the McKinley years, production had been on the rise each year, and the president's protectionism was credited with restoring confidence. Local leaders felt extremely optimistic about the current situation in large part because their mills were flooded with orders.

The last time that Butler saw McKinley was in late summer 1901 at the President's home in Canton. Butler wrote in his autobiography that McKinley had invited him to be a member of his party attending the Pan-American Exposition in Buffalo in September 1901, but due to business obligations Butler declined the president's invitation. After many visits with the president, Butler had formed the opinion that McKinley did not take his personal security seriously and expressed this to his friend. "I want to impress upon you that you are not careful enough of your safety from assault," Butler told the president. "One of these days something will happen which we will all regret." This concern was not taken very seriously

Eight. The Original McKinley Man

by McKinley, who reportedly replied, "Why should any one seek my life—what have I done to justify it?"[36]

On September 6, 1901, while attending the Pan-American Exposition, McKinley was shot by Leon Czolgosz. A mentally unstable individual, Czolgosz had been disgruntled for some time after leaving his job at a Cleveland wire mill. McKinley's biographer wrote, "In revolt against the injustice of the social order, Czolgosz was strongly attracted by the doctrines of anarchism. He came to hate the American system of government, and to believe that all rulers were the enemies of the working people."[37] The stricken president endured his wound for eight days before succumbing on September 14.

Butler was asked to be an honorary pallbearer for his old childhood friend during the funeral services in Canton. "Knowing all the relatives," Butler explained, "I was placed in charge of them." The sadness Butler felt over the loss of President McKinley would linger until the end of his life. In his 1924 account of McKinley's life, Butler blamed the Secret Service. "I have always thought that the secret service men in charge were lax in their duty," he charged. "The assassin with his right hand muffled should have been challenged and investigated before reaching the president. Had this been done," he lamented, "the fatal disaster would not have occurred."[38]

Nine

Big Steel

BY THE TURN OF THE CENTURY the age of steel had arrived. Steel-based products had penetrated nearly every facet of society all but eliminating the demand for finished iron goods. The popularity of steel was seen especially in the construction and rail industries because steel products were found to be stronger and more durable. In November 1900, National Steel Company's Youngstown plant, the former Ohio Steel Company, received an order for 3,000 tons of steel for new rails.[1]

During the shift from iron to steel, many began to see the old practice of ruthless competition as mutually destructive. "The first serious effort to improve conditions," wrote Butler, "was the combination of a number of companies producing different lines of finished steel." However, Butler observed, "they went after one another in precisely the same spirit that the original companies manifested, and the only result was competition fiercer and more relentless than before."[2]

The shift towards specialization did not improve conditions for small manufacturers; instead, the big companies grew larger, and control became even more concentrated. "In 1899," historian Robert Hessen writes, "Carnegie's company had produced 75 percent of all the steel products exported.... In 1900, Carnegie's five major rivals had a total steel output of 3,500,000 tons; Carnegie alone produced just under 3,000,000." The American Steel and Wire Company controlled about 80 percent of the nation's nail and wire production, and the American Tin Plate Company held 95 percent of tin plate production.[3]

McKinley's victory in the 1900 election was cheered by most industrialists, who expected the President to continue his policy of protectionism through high tariffs. "Every Mill Is Working," read a headline in the *Youngstown Telegram* on November 12, 1900. The paper reported, "From the Ohio steel plant down to the smallest industry in the city every plant in the city, with two exceptions, that is in condition to operate, is working."[4] With the mills converted for steel production, increased orders meant little idle time. The new absentee owners were expanding and modernizing

Nine. Big Steel

the Valley's mills and were capitalizing where local owners had failed to do so.

The local critics, who once predicted that the new owners who infiltrated the Mahoning Valley in the 1890s would reap what they could from the local mills and leave the operations and city for dead, were wrong. Record-breaking profits made that notion unthinkable. Large corporations were reinvesting precious dollars back into the plants of the Youngstown district, and the local banking and lending institutions knew this to be true.

In 1900, Asael Adams, treasurer of the Dollar Savings and Trust Company, observed, "During 1898 and 1899 much of the largest manufacturing business of the valley was sold to outsiders and much new capital brought to this city through these transactions. Almost all of this money has been reinvested by the owners." In its huge "Thanksgiving Prosperity" edition of November 23, 1900, the *Youngstown Telegram* noted, "The Republic Iron and Steel Company has taken each mill in both the Brown Bonnell and Valley plants separately and transformed them from the old style mills to the most modern and rebuilt several of them entirely. The tonnage turned out by the men has increased from 10 per cent to 40 per cent, according to the size of the mill. It has increased both the number of men employed at these two plants and their wages."[5]

Butler was pleased with the financial fortunes of his community and all the benefits that a vibrant, healthy economy could bring to local government. For the first time improvements in infrastructure, basic services, and other quality-of-life issues—ones that Butler had struggled to advance as a Youngstown councilman several years before—now appeared to have unlimited potential. In May 1899, a longer and modern Market Street viaduct finally connected Youngstown's Central Square with the high bluff on the south bank of the Mahoning River, and this easier access led to residential and commercial development on the city's south side.[6]

Regardless of the positive financial gains that the Mahoning Valley was enjoying, the incursion of outsiders and their new hold over local developments was a challenge to the Youngstown men. In his *History of Youngstown and the Mahoning Valley*, Butler would later summarize the feelings of the local industrialists: "The close of the last century was a momentous period for the iron and steel industries of the Mahoning Valley.... The day of the individual enterprise which had done so much for this locality seemed to have passed. Investors feared the commanding influence of large combinations of capital, and, while there was an abundance of money and no lack of enterprise on the part of local capitalists, it required supreme courage to engage in that industry on the scale which had become essential to success. The future of the Mahoning Valley seemed at that time rather uncertain, for plants that had done heroic service under other conditions were being constantly dismantled. Control of the local industries had passed to a great extent into the hands of outsiders, whose intentions were not thoroughly understood and whose only motive was supposed to be the operation of these industries in the manner which would achieve the most efficient production."[7] What his writings reflected were his own fears and doubts at this time about the future of his beloved Mahoning Valley iron industry as well as his own financial stake in it.

Despite these fears of outside exploitation and abandonment, quite the opposite result occurred. The opinion of Asael Adams, known for his financial acumen and foresight, carried a good deal of weight. His outlook was promising, suggesting that a business owner's reinvestment was a commitment to the future. "This [reinvestment] can only be expected where capital is confident that a good business future is in store for them," said Adams.[8] The main questions, therefore, for Youngstown industrialists like Butler were clear. Could they continue to exist in this new highly competitive arena, and, if so, was it too late to create another local iron producer with an eye toward steel production to compete against these growing giants?

Because of his comfortable financial status, Butler easily could have walked away from leaders and enjoyed a life of leisure. But it had never been his nature to give up. Arguably, the unfolding drama within the industry had all the markings of a Shakespearian tragedy with a cast of colorful characters all its own. It was just the sort of theater that continued to hold Butler's interest.

James A. Campbell, District Manager for the Republic Iron and Steel Company, was interested in starting his own company. He was approached by George Wick, a vice-president of Republic, who proposed a stock company on a much larger scale. They gathered 55 investors who purchased $600,000 of capital stock. These new stockholders included many of Youngstown's leading citizens including five Wicks, five Tods, three Stambaughs, and Joseph G. Butler, Jr. The new enterprise was named the Youngstown Iron Sheet & Tube Company. The Articles of Incorporation were filed in Columbus on November 23, 1900. The five incorporators were George D. Wick, James A. Campbell, scrap dealer William Wilkoff, merchant George L. Fordyce, and steel man Edward L. Ford. Although Butler was not the leading force behind this new organization, his participation and support were especially significant in securing subscriptions from some of the valley's financially ablest citizens, and in 1904 Butler would join the new company's Board of Directors.[9]

George Wick, who owned most of the new company's stock, became president and treasurer, and James Campbell, a commanding figure in his own right, his piercing eyes staring over a bushy mustache, was named vice-president and manager. A Trumbull County native, Campbell had aspired to be a military officer but ended up clerking for a local coal company instead. He then worked briefly in the hardware business before starting an ice company. In 1890, he was appointed superintendent of the Trumbull Iron Company in Warren, and in 1897, he took on the same title for the Mahoning Valley Iron Company. By the time Campbell had been promoted to district manager, the company had fallen victim to the consolidation movement and was purchased by the Republic Iron and Steel Company. Like Butler, Campbell had great confidence in his local colleagues and believed that there was still room for another profitable iron and ultimately steel manufacturer in Youngstown. The new plant that Wick and Campbell conceived was projected to have "14 double puddling furnaces, 10 heating furnaces, 6 hot mills, and 2 cold mills."[10]

In 1902, Wick's declining health forced him to step aside as president, and the directors named Campbell to run the company while they searched for a new president. After two years of searching, the Board realized that the best candidate was already running the company, so they officially made Campbell president in 1904. Under Campbell's leadership during the next three decades, the Youngstown Iron, Sheet & Tube Company expanded in size and output making it Youngstown's largest employer and one of the largest independent steel producers in the nation.[11]

The most dramatic and lasting event of the merger movement occurred between the summer of 1900 and the spring of 1901. At this time the largest steel concerns were Carnegie Steel; Federal Steel, controlled by J.P. Morgan; and National Steel (which had absorbed the Ohio Steel Company), controlled by William H. Moore and his brother. A slack market for steel in the summer of 1900 forced greater competition, and Carnegie's rivals announced price cuts. Historian Robert Hessen writes, "In mid 1900 both companies advised Carnegie that they intended to expand their production facilities and would reduce future orders." Hessen adds, "It was widely known in the American business community that Carnegie might be willing to sell if a suitable buyer could be found."[12] But in this clash of steel titans the combative Carnegie was not about to bow out quietly. He countered the Morgan and Moore trusts by announcing plans to construct a new tube mill, a move that would severely undercut Morgan's position.

Despite his combative tone and threats of renewed competition, Carnegie seemed to be inviting an offer from Morgan. Carnegie arranged a dinner in New York City to introduce his protégé and heir apparent Charles Schwab to the industrial and financial elites. In his history of the

Titan of industry Charles M. Schwab was a close friend and admirer of Butler (Library of Congress).

United States Steel Corporation, Arundel Cotter wrote, "Carnegie saw that if the man lived who could convince Morgan to engineer a purchase of the Carnegie Steel Company that man was Charlie Schwab. Carnegie therefore decided to bring together the financier and the president of the Carnegie Steel Company and to let loose on Morgan the flood of Schwab's eloquence."[13]

The dinner, held December 12, 1900, would have a profound effect on the steel industry in the 20th century. Schwab, the guest of honor, gave a speech that outlined the dream of a great American conglomerate that could dominate the world steel market. J.P. Morgan listened attentively and later held a clandestine meeting with Schwab. At the conclusion of their talk, Morgan told him, "Well, if you can get a price from Carnegie, I don't know but what I'll undertake it."[14]

Carnegie's asking price was $480 million, and Morgan accepted; a few weeks later he congratulated Andrew Carnegie on becoming the richest man in the world. On April 1, 1901, the United States Steel Corporation was formally organized as the world's first billion-dollar company. Its size and reach were almost unimaginable. One historian called it a "colossal, titanic, megatherian business." Writing for *The Atlantic Monthly* in June 1901, Charles Bullock stated that "a small group of capitalists wields a power such as has never fallen to the lot of captains of industry in any other age." Proponents of the merger movement, added Charles Bullock, "had no difficulty in showing that a modern combination can produce goods more cheaply than the small enterprises that used to control the field of manufacturing industry."[15] Even President Theodore Roosevelt, the patron saint of anti-trusts, believed that the merger, and a strong U.S. Steel, would bode well for the economy.[16]

With the stroke of a pen, the Ohio Steel Company became the United States Steel Company's Ohio Works. Dozens of subsidiaries across the country awoke to similar news. The announcement was stunning, and it immediately sent a shock wave of uncertainty throughout the industry leaving many to wonder the fate of their firms. This latest development was a threat to Butler's two most important business interests, the new Youngstown Iron, Sheet & Tube Company and the Brier Hill Iron Company.

Butler was concerned with the ability of the remaining independents like Brier Hill to compete against U.S. Steel and the financial consequences to come if they could not. With the help of the Bessemer Pig Iron Association, Brier Hill had managed to compete up to this point against Carnegie Steel, National Steel, Federal Steel, and others. The new United States Steel Corporation, however, in an instant became the largest corporation in the world absorbing these rivals and five others. Though Butler was initially opposed to the combination known as the United States Steel Corporation, that feeling over time would change due in large part to his developing friendship with Judge Elbert Gary, who would become the president of U.S. Steel in 1903. In March 1901, despite his concerns and with the help of his friend and colleague Samuel Mather, Butler quietly purchased a subscription in the United States Steel Corporation valued at $5,000.[17]

Judge Elbert Gary, former president of J.P. Morgan's Federal Steel, played a major role in the formation of U.S. Steel, and he became head of the new corporation's Executive Committee. Gary wasted no time in proposing a revolutionary approach to business competition that would, in time, endear him to the leaders of the iron and steel industry. He believed, as his biographer Arundel Cotter noted, "that a business transaction should be profitable to both parties concerned. Gary went further than this. He believed, and acted this belief, that business should be profitable not only to the parties concerned in any individual transaction but to the whole community."[18]

Gary clashed with Charles Schwab, who had been named president of the new conglomerate. Schwab's biographer Robert Hessen writes, "Gary deplored Carnegie's policy of aggressive price-cutting, and he considered Schwab a co-conspirator in this 'offense' against business stability and harmony."[19]

Schwab's only exposure to business was from the Carnegie school of pillage and plunder. Hessen explains, "Gary strongly opposed some of the policies which Schwab believed had been responsible for Carnegie Steel's leadership in the industry. As Schwab said later 'Judge Gary, who had no real knowledge of the steel business, forever opposed me on some of the methods and principles that I had seen worked out with Carnegie—methods that had made the Carnegie Company the most successful in the world."[20] After two years, Schwab resigned as president of U.S. Steel and was replaced by Judge Elbert Gary.

The ruthless old ways where companies in search of control of certain markets thought it perfectly acceptable to drive competitors out of business were to be supplanted by the new approach. The old survival of the fittest theory, the only known way to do business by most, was now portrayed by Gary as archaic. Unaware of Gary's new proposal on competition and with no way of knowing how many millions of dollars U.S. Steel would eventually mean to the Mahoning Valley in years to come, Butler remained skeptical of the historic deal.

Despite the long shadow cast by U.S. Steel, the growth of Youngstown Iron Sheet & Tube was immediate and substantial. As early as 1902, the new company began its phenomenal expansion by acquiring the "Little Alice" furnace located in nearby Sharpsville, Pennsylvania, with financial assistance from the Cleveland firm, Pickands Mather & Company. It soon purchased the Steel and Tube Company of America in the Chicago district.[21] This purchasing pattern continued unabated. New construction also marked the company's growth.

After experiencing early success in iron production, the new Iron, Sheet & Tube Company decided by 1904 that its future was in steel and in 1905 dropped the word "Iron" from the company name. Butler reported as early as 1904 that "much talk in the past few years of the building of a steel plant in the Valleys which would take care of the product ... has been done." Furthering the cause of continued speculation Butler admitted, "It is probably only a question of time when a step of this kind will be demanded and carried through to a successful conclusion."

There would be other positive effects to this development. In his report "Pig Iron During 1904," Butler wrote "The consumption of pig iron for Malleable purposes, steel castings, coupled with the very great amount needed for general Foundry use, practically uses up the surplus of the independent producers, so that new furnaces will be needed if another steel plant is built in the Valleys." Rather than relying on independent operators for a ready supply of pig iron, the Sheet & Tube Company decided upon a course of self-reliance. By the end of 1906, the company constructed two new Bessemer converters, soaking furnaces, and various finishing mills to its expanding operation.[22]

Nine. Big Steel

During the chaos of the mass consolidation movement, Butler's main concern was the survival of the Brier Hill Iron Company, which relied solely on iron production. As one of the last independent pig iron producers in the Mahoning Valley, Brier Hill continued to be a pig iron supplier for the expanding steel production market. Many of the remaining independents found their role as pig iron supplier to the giant steel producers to be a profitable one. But this was short lived, for even iron producers understood the advantages for steel producers to make their own iron. "It is the avowed intention of the large steel producers," Butler observed in 1904, "to make all their own pig iron, and it is perhaps equally the avowed desire of the independent producers and consumers of pig iron to travel their own road."[23] The steel mill owners learned that it was much more cost effective to produce their own pig iron, especially as increasing steel production raised pig iron demand.

As chairman of the Bessemer Pig Iron Association, Butler saw the growing trend and the inevitable impact it would have on the Brier Hill Iron Company. It could not survive relying on pig iron production alone. Other members of the association unable or unwilling to adapt to the changes taking place grew desperate and looked to their chairman for help in securing orders. Butler expressed frustration with the situation and his own recognition that some of the members were not strong enough to survive the competition. In his "Weekly Letter to the Members of the Bessemer Pig Iron Association," he wrote "My life is being made considerable of a burden, answering the telephone and otherwise giving attention to brokers who are persistent in their demands for recognition. I think if the whole swarm could be eliminated it would be a godsend to the iron and steel business."[24]

In the 1904 presidential race, Butler campaigned for Theodore Roosevelt, though he did not always agree with Roosevelt's policies. He was welcomed at the White House but sometimes found the president hard to reach, especially in the summer when Roosevelt would repair to Sagamore Hill, his summer White House residence in Oyster Bay, New York. In an undated essay Butler humorously recounted a visit he made to Roosevelt. "This part of my letter is not strictly original," he noted, "but I have embellished it somewhat and believe it covers the case.... The driver pulls up at the porch and before you can alight, the President shoots out, with the action of a determined tug-boat bucking the tide. He reaches over and jerks you from the buggy then drags you into the somber library, just inside the door. You breathe a trifle hard as when taking a first plunge into a tumultuous surf. You begin to speak your little piece. The President listens for an instant, in an attitude of tension that is too great to last. With a suddenness that brushes you aside entirely, he seizes the conversational bit in his teeth and you find that you are in a runaway. The desk trembles and the paper weight dances from the blows of his clenched fist, and when you are hurled out on the porch again and into the buggy, you take a long breath, as you might after a little swim through the whirlpool rapids at Niagara Falls. This is the way Mr. Roosevelt rests at Oyster Bay."[25]

Joseph Butler reached his 65th birthday in 1905 but showed few signs of slowing down. The threat from foreign producers and anti-tariff proponents remained persistent, so the need to wave the banner of high tariffs remained a constant necessity. Likewise, promoting and supporting Republican politicians who adhered to this protectionist ideology was a never-ending task for those, like Butler, who were intimately involved in leadership roles within the industry.

He was by this time a director in the Youngstown Sheet & Tube Company, president of the Bessemer Limestone Company, the largest stockholder in the Buckeye Iron Company, an investor in U.S. Steel, chairman of the Bessemer Pig Iron Association, director and general manager of the Brier Hill Iron Company, and member of numerous business and civic organizations. However, Butler's role within his various organizations was changing from a once active agent to a wise counselor, and this shift provided him with more time for lobbying, political campaigning, writing, and travel.

Ten

The Western Adventures

THROUGHOUT HIS LIFE Butler had been a model of efficiency in both his business and personal life. Butler typically was an early riser and usually at his office by 9:00 a.m. He was a familiar figure walking Wick Avenue to and from work or the railroad station. When he was not traveling on business trips, his days were regimented. His life revolved around his business concerns, which left little time for anything else except his growing family.

Butler's daughter Blanche and her husband E.L. Ford had two children, a son, John Willard, and a daughter, Josephine. Daughter Grace and her husband Arthur McGraw of Detroit, Michigan, had one son, Arthur Butler McGraw. Butler's son Henry Audubon had married Grace Heath in 1900, and she gave birth to a son on September 5, 1901. The couple named him Joseph G. Butler III after his grandfather.[1]

By the turn of the century, Butler had logged thousands of miles by rail throughout the Great Lakes regions and the east coast and had traveled through much of the South in the fall of 1890 with members of the British Iron and Steel Institute. But he had yet to cross the Atlantic or travel extensively west of the Mississippi River. Because of his lifelong health habits, he was in excellent physical condition to pursue his dream. Financially, his resources were sound which allowed him to take several journeys.

During his travels Butler habitually kept a journal, and the descriptive narratives of his adventures are evidence of his passion for writing and record-keeping. He consulted these heavily when he prepared his autobiography and other published works. The anecdotes that he recorded offer a further glimpse into his personality and interests. More importantly, the trips tell us that aside from business and leisure, he was collecting impressions and cultivating ideas for his future acts of public generosity.

Butler's first experience in the American West was a business trip he took in 1902. At Colorado Springs he made the acquaintance of an artist, Charles Craig, who shared Butler's fascination with Native Americans. Butler also rode a cogwheel railroad to the top of Pike's Peak. "My lungs were not affected by the high altitude but I was taken with a violent headache and nose-bleeding, and was very glad to return to terrafirma."[2]

In Ogden, Utah, Butler joined up with his good friend and Youngstown business associate Henry H. Stambaugh.[3] They reached California soon after where they visited the usual parks and tourist spots, including San Francisco's Chinatown. Butler recalled, "We next visited a Chinese tenement house almost wholly underground. It seemed as if we went down about five stories before we got to the bottom, and each story contained a lot of little rooms with Chinamen stretched out smoking opium and apparently very happy, but it was a degrading sight to say nothing about the smell."[4]

Departing San Francisco, the friends traveled south to Los Angeles where they spent several days as guests at the Pasadena home of former Youngstown industrialist Tod Ford. On the return trip east Butler and Stambaugh visited the Grand Canyon. "This stupendous gorge," wrote Butler, "is one of the most wonderful sights of the world."[5] The trip was full of excitement for Butler, and it opened his eyes to the country's beauty and natural wonders. He realized that there was much more to see, and he vowed to return.

In 1904 Butler did just that. A speculative business investment necessitated a trip to Nevada. The journey proved more challenging and adventurous than his 1902 trek. Nevada had been luring miners and speculators ever since the discovery of the Comstock Lode in 1859.[6] Prospectors arrived quickly, mines were dug, and investors took notice.

On June 24, 1904, Butler headed to Nevada for two weeks to examine firsthand his recently acquired mining interests. He was accompanied by Frank M. Kirk, president of the Ohio-Tonopah Mining Company in which Butler had invested. Their destination was Goldfield near the Tonopah field. Butler and Kirk traveled aboard the luxurious Overland Limited, advertised as the fastest train in the world. Butler confessed, "I have traveled on all of the best trains of the country ... but this Overland Limited stands at the head."[7] Unfortunately, the railroad did not run all the way to Tonopah, and the last leg was negotiated by stagecoach.

"The stage ride," Butler recorded, "commenced about two o'clock in the afternoon and ended by landing us in Tonopah at Eight o'clock Friday morning. The eighteen-hour stage ride," Butler added, "was enlivened by the howling of coyotes."[8]

The partners inspected various mines as well as the towns of Tonopah and Goldfield, where the superintendent of the Ohio-Tonopah Mining Company property greeted them and secured a tent for their overnight accommodations. Butler wrote, "Before retiring we took a ride around the town, which consisted principally of saloons and what they there

Ten. The Western Adventures

call Floozy Barns." In the days that followed Butler and Kirk visited several claims. They found the whole area filled with characters in search of instant wealth.[9]

After they completed their survey of the Tonopah properties, they headed for Reno. There they caught a night train to San Francisco, arriving in time for breakfast at the Palace Hotel where Butler had stayed two years earlier.

Although Butler may have been a novice at silver mines, he was by no means a stranger to mining. For the past 30 years, Butler had held interests in the iron ore mining industry dating back to the 1870s at the great Mesabi Range, and from that time forward he would be intimately connected with Great Lakes mining.[10]

Butler's involvement in the Nevada mines spanned more than a decade. Unfortunately, it was a period of financial frustration for the successful industrialist. Although Butler had seen some tough business negotiations during his career, the proceedings in Nye County were unlike anything he had experienced, and the conduct of the men involved was an affront to his lifelong straightforward business practices, and it frustrated him deeply.[11]

Butler's autobiography makes little mention of his involvement in the silver mines of Nevada, probably because it was not so fruitful in the end. He took more pains to describe the landscape and the townspeople. The only reference to a financial investment in the Nevada mines was brief; "At Goldfield we inspected the properties of the Ohio-Tonopah Company, in which I was financially interested."[12] His financial status was solid when he first treaded the Nevada foothills, and it remained so afterwards even though his investments there did not yield him the fortune that he, like so many others, had sought.

During his life Butler had grown fond of fairs and expositions. America's world fairs and expositions displayed the latest in the country's technological and agricultural advancements. Each fair was sewn with a thread of patriotism that appealed to Butler. "Beginning with the exposition known as the Philadelphia Centennial in 1876," Butler wrote, "it was my good fortune to see almost every exhibition of this kind held in America subsequent to that time."[13] Not surprisingly, Butler undertook another excursion in 1904, his second in less than six months, with a trip to the Louisiana Purchase Exposition in St. Louis, Missouri. Accompanied by his 16-year-old grandson John Willard Ford, he spent five days entertained by the usual attractions. Naturally, they paid close attention to exhibits with industrial themes. "We visited the Transportation Building and were so fascinated with it that we sort of made that our headquarters," wrote Butler, "and went back to it at least once or twice every day during our entire stay."[14]

The World's Fair of 1904 commemorated the centennial anniversary of the Louisiana Purchase, and Butler noted somewhat wryly, "I may say that the entire price paid for the Louisiana purchase which, as is well known, embraces an empire, is only one-quarter of the expense incurred in this Celebration which I am now writing about."[15]

The duo visited the Lincoln Exhibit, the Philippine Encampment, and many other exhibits as well as the Pike, an area that Butler compared to the Midway at the Chicago World's Fair. In the Palace of Mines and Metallurgy, Butler was happy to see a display of the world's pig iron production, which showed the United States doubling the production of England and Germany. He noted, "I was also very pleased to see at this building a piece of Brier Hill Bessemer pig iron, in fact the only piece I saw on the grounds; there was also an exhibit of both Brier Hill and Struthers cement."[16]

Thanksgiving was spent enjoying dinner at the Tyrolean Alps Café. "The music was fine and the turkey was tough," noted Butler. "The champagne however tasted quite natural." At the Palace of Arts, Butler observed "The art exhibit, as a whole, did not compare with the one in Chicago in the quality of the paintings, the number however was much larger. Quite a number of the noted American artists of whom I have personal knowledge were not represented at all."[17]

President Theodore Roosevelt visited the fair on November 26, where his presence attracted a huge crowd. "His reception was enthusiastic," Butler wrote, "and all danger of his assassination was minimized by the people. Everyone present seemed to consider himself or herself a guard of honor." Butler and John Willard departed for home a day before the Fair closed.[18]

Butler's third trip to the west coast occurred in 1905 with a visit to the Pacific Northwest to commemorate the 100th anniversary of the Lewis and Clark expedition. It was a grand occasion this time with Butler surrounded by his friends of the American Institute of Mining Engineers as well as several family members. The party included Butler's son-in-law E.L. Ford and the by now experienced traveler, grandson John Willard Ford. Butler's wife Harriet met the party in Chicago. Their destination was Portland, Oregon, site of the Lewis and Clark Centennial and American Pacific Exposition and Oriental Fair. By coincidence, the last car of the train on which they traveled was the same one that had carried President McKinley on his last journey from his home in Canton to his fateful encounter at Buffalo. "The room he occupied attracted much attention on the journey," recalled Butler, "and was sort of a shrine to those who happened to know the facts."[19]

The touring party of the American Institute of Mining Engineers separated en route before reconvening in Seattle to finish the leg together to

Portland. Most of the members, including Harriet, decided to take a short trip to Alaska for a more adventurous excursion. Butler decided against the Alaska trip and instead traveled to the Columbia River where he noted the impact of the salmon fishing industry on that region. Harriet's journey gratified her quest for adventure as well. She was able to exude enough excitement and detail of her foray to last a lifetime, and she enjoyed telling friends and family of her Alaskan experience. Her husband playfully chided afterward, "as I say to everybody who asks about it, it is worth a journey to Youngstown to hear her tell the events."[20] Together again, the entire excursion party traveled to Portland on June 30.

The Exposition grounds, built on the banks of Guild's Lake, attracted more than 1.5 million visitors throughout the summer and early fall. Although Butler paid special interest to and spent time in the industrial exhibits housed in the Manufacturers Liberal Arts and Varied Industrial Building and the Industrial and Liberal Arts Palace, he also spent considerable time in the art galleries.[21] One of the featured artists was Edward Sheriff Curtis and his photographic collection of Native American tribes known as the Curtis Indian Prints.

Born in Wisconsin shortly after the Civil War, Curtis had moved westward with his family in the 1880s. The family settled outside of Seattle where the young Edward opened up a photography studio. His interest in photographing the American Indian soon became his passion, which quickly became Curtis's obsession, as over the next four decades he would take tens of thousands of photographs of Native Americans detailing everyday life and culture.[22] In his notes Butler described Curtis's portraits and predicted that if the photographs did not fade over time, they "would be just as valuable as an oil painting for preserving the Primitive race."[23] In time, Butler would collect many of the "Shadow Catcher's" works.

The Exposition's art gallery itself was a huge disappointment to Butler, who by now was considered by many to be a respected art critic. He wrote in his notes, "The building in which the paintings are to be found reminds one of a dungeon. It is a long, low, rambling building.... The light was artificial and ruined the best of the paintings.... On the whole, the art exhibit was a very great disappointment."[24]

His disappointment notwithstanding, Butler would retain from the exhibit a keen interest in Edward Curtis' photographs and the importance of recording Native American images, either by camera or by paintbrush. Butler had been fascinated with Native Americans for years, but the Curtis Collection re-energized his curiosity. Butler would conclude that theirs was a culture worth preserving at least within the framework of an art gallery.

Butler's frequent visits to the country's World's Fairs and expositions were like pilgrimages to pay homage to all that was good and great in America. The many displays of American pride and progress stirred his patriotism. His belief in American ingenuity, creativity, science, and industry reaffirmed his belief in an inherent American leadership role in the world. It was clear that American supremacy was Butler's one true ideology.

Satisfied that he had taken a good look at his own country, the time had come to cross the Atlantic to see Europe. On July 2, 1908, Butler, his wife Harriet, grandson John Willard, and Miss Evelyn Cooper, who had relatives in Great Britain, set sail from Hoboken, New Jersey, aboard the Hamburg-American steam liner *Amerika*. A full schedule of entertainment was offered the first-class passengers to help pass the time. On the second night out, the Fourth of July was observed with a grand ball on the upper deck. While in New York the Butlers had purchased large American flags for the occasion, and they were used to decorate their dinner table that night.

On July 11, the *Amerika* docked at Cuxhaven, Germany, and Butler stepped upon European soil for the first time.[25] After a brief tour of Hamburg, the group headed for Berlin, where Harriet had resided in 1889 and 1890 while children Henry and Grace pursued their studies. She was excited to see many old familiar locations and held her audience spellbound with fond memories of those pleasant times. She delighted in lecturing the group on a drive through the Tier Garten, one of her favorite old haunts. Butler was impressed with Berlin's National Gallery even though the work of only one American artist, Gari Melchers was exhibited. Also displayed was a portrait by the German artist, Heinrich von Zügel. It was of particular interest to the Butlers because one of the artist's works, "Ox and Sheep," hung in their third-floor gallery on Wick Avenue.[26] The next stop was England.

One of the first to call on the Butlers at the Grand Hotel in London was Hilda Kitson, an old friend of Butler's daughter Blanche, and her father, Lord Airedale, the former Sir James Kitson, whom Butler had last seen nearly 20 years ago when Kitson had toured the southern United States as a member of the British Iron and Steel Institute. Lord Airedale and Hilda provided a personal tour of Parliament. It was outside of the House of Commons that Butler was reintroduced to Jenkin Jones who, like Lord Airedale, was once a member of the British Iron and Steel Institute. Butler reminded Jones of their first acquaintance on a visit to Youngstown in the early 1890s.

At Westminster Abbey, Butler noted the graves of many of England's most famous sons and daughters including Charles Darwin. He also saw a monument for the great entertainer Jenny Lind, whom Butler had

Ten. The Western Adventures

observed passing through Niles on a canal boat back in the 1840s. The group also caught a fleeting glimpse of King Edward VII and Queen Alexandra, which inspired a brief stop at Windsor Castle.

The group made three visits to the Franco-British Exposition. Of personal interest to Butler was the McKinley Cottage on display. It was the ancestral home of President McKinley and had been brought to the site from Ballymoney, County Antrim, Ireland. The paintings at London's National Gallery were a disappointment. "The collection was not up to our expectations," Butler lamented as "many of the important paintings have been removed to the Tate gallery."[27]

Because of his love of Shakespeare, one stop that was truly inspirational to Butler was Stratford-on-Avon. The New Dudley Gallery offered many personal belongings of Charles Dickens, another favorite writer. Butler was so taken with the display that he felt the need to purchase a set of champagne glasses that had once belonged to the great writer. Two of the glasses were etched with the initials "C.D.," and Butler suspected that the letters had been inscribed "probably by himself with his diamond ring." He also procured for his personal art collection a set of original watercolor drawings of the leading Dickens characters.[28]

John Willard left the traveling party on July 31 to return home. At 19 the young man was the eldest of the Butler grandchildren, and there was an undeniable bond between grandson and grandfather. John was bright, resourceful, and inquisitive, traits that would serve him well in his future career as an attorney. He was a source of great pride to his grandfather who enjoyed his companionship immeasurably.[29]

The rest of the party arrived home in mid–August completely thrilled with their experience. From childhood Butler had imagined what it would be like to see many of the places and things he had read about, particularly the haunts of Shakespeare and Dickens. Another traveling destination was crossed off his list. But more time, he knew, was needed to further investigate the treasures of Europe.

Life would not be complete without a trip to France, but Butler did not have the time on this excursion to take it in. Arguably, Paris was the art capital of the world and for someone passionate about art and possessed of the means to travel, it would be a grave omission not to undertake a future pilgrimage there. Reflecting years later, Butler said of his first trip to Europe, "I have been abroad a number of times since, but have not enjoyed any other trip so much as this."[30] Butler was content with the revelations of his European literary icons. The experience of seeing the homes and haunts of the larger-than-life figures and their cast of immortal characters was deeply satisfying.

It was Europe's art galleries, however, that he found disappointing.

Although there were countless masterpieces by European artists on display, the noticeable absence of American art troubled Butler. European artists were surely recognized in his personal gallery, and he hated to think that American artists were not given the same esteem overseas. This situation would remain ingrained in his memory.

By the end of the first decade of the 20th century, Butler could claim to be a well-traveled man. He had now seen the western United States from the southwest to the Pacific northwest, and he had nurtured his passion for art, literature, and history with his first trip abroad.

Eleven

The Gary Dinners

On the morning of November 5, 1905, a train pulled out of Youngstown headed for Lorain, Ohio. On board was Joseph G. Butler, Jr., and his wife Harriet. They were joined by children Blanche and Henry and their spouses. Butler's grandchildren, Josephine Butler Ford and Joseph G. Butler III, were also in company. Joining the family were many of Butler's friends, including John Stambaugh, Jr.

The occasion for the trip was the launching of a new bulk ore carrier, the *Joseph G. Butler Jr*. The Youngstown party was joined by many dignitaries from the iron and steel industry and officials of the American Shipbuilding Company. Standing on the Lorain docks of the American Shipbuilding Company that afternoon, Butler's 12-year-old granddaughter Josephine swung a bottle of champagne against the ship, sending the new ore carrier into the cold waters of Lake Erie.

Hutchinson and Company of Cleveland, which managed the Pioneer Steamship Company, had named the ship in honor of Butler because of his longtime involvement in Great Lakes shipping and in recognition of his success and influence in the raw ore industry and shipping in general. Joseph G. Butler III, who attended the launching as a four-year-old, later wrote, "Knowing my grandfather, as I did in later years, I am sure the launching was followed by a lavish dinner with champagne flowing as freely as it had over the bow of the ship when my cousin swung the beribboned bottle saying 'I christen thee *Joseph G. Butler Jr*.'"[1]

In 1907 the nation's economy entered another serious downturn. The Panic of 1907, writes economic historian William Hogan, "was brought on by a number of factors, among them the speculation and over extension of business and the inelasticity of credit and currency." Demand for goods and materials declined, and the steel industry was hit hard. Butler later recalled, "When the panic was at its height, Judge Gary, Chairman of the Board of Directors of The United States Steel Corporation, issued a statement—one of the first of the kind, I believe, ever made public by the head of a large concern in the industry, in which he counseled courage and cooperation on the part of manufacturers, and urged that, instead of trying to save themselves at the expense of other companies, they should so conduct their business that all might survive."[2]

By November the crisis worsened. Gary responded by inviting leaders of the iron and steel industry to meet in New York City for the first of a series of gatherings that became known as the Gary dinners. Butler attended the first meeting on November 20, 1907, held at New York's Waldorf-Astoria Hotel. Gary further advocated cooperation and conciliation. Eventually, writes law professor William Page, sales strategies "for ore and pig iron, pipes and tubular goods, wire products, rails and billets (steel ingots), structural material, plates, steel bars, and sheets and tin plates" were developed under separate committees.[3]

A second Gary dinner was held in January 1908. Butler and J.P. Morgan addressed the gathering. To avoid charges of price-fixing, no agreements or promises were made. What they did share was the prices their companies planned to charge. Butler wrote, "Not a sentence could be construed to even suggest any illegal method of restraining production or maintaining prices at an exorbitant level." However, newspaper coverage of the dinners prompted accusations of collusion. Gary was forced to issue a statement denying any wrongdoing.[4]

That same month, E.W. Oglebay, a Cleveland iron and steel manufacturer, wrote Butler that the "country has had such a terrible set back, and the financial situation having been under such a long continued strain, I fear the revival will be much slower than many expect." Although Oglebay was wary, in general he was confident that the iron and steel industry would ride out the storm. "We are able to await patiently the return to normal conditions," he wrote. "There is no question but what the iron and steel trade, in its entirety, has been handled with unquestioned business ability." Adopting the Gary philosophy, Oglebay felt, would "tend to stimulate activity at a much earlier date."[5] The old guard was slowly buying into the new approach.

By the third dinner in May 1908, prices had stabilized, and the worst days of the Panic seemed to be over. Gary credited the efforts of those present for the improved economic situation. A large fourth gathering was held in December. And in February 1909, a small intimate "luncheon" as Butler called it, was held at Gary's residence. At this meeting Gary announced that U.S. Steel would "withdraw from any meeting at which I am expected to tell you anything about our business, and we will go alone."[6] Gary's change of heart was prompted by evidence that many of the smaller companies were not adhering to the new philosophy.

But a sixth dinner was held nine months later. Page writes, "Suitably chastened, the steel manufacturers held another dinner at the Waldorf on October 15, 1909, not at Gary's invitation, but ostensibly to present him with a 'loving cup' and to praise him for his heroic efforts to save the steel industry during the panic of 1907." Butler described the dinner as "a purely social affair, business being barred, and the evening spent in celebrating the return of business prosperity and the establishment of a genuine neighborliness in the steel industry that had never been known until the Gary dinners began."[7]

A final Gary dinner was held at the Waldorf-Astoria on January 11, 1911. Judge Gary noted that steel orders had fallen to 50 percent of capacity and that any attempts to cut prices even further would be mutually destructive. As always, he claimed this was only advice and not an attempt to fix prices.

Elbert H. Gary, president of U.S. Steel, had introduced a new model of competition to Butler and the leaders of the iron and steel industry. From Joseph G. Butler, Jr., *Fifty Years of Iron and Steel* (Cleveland, Ohio: The Penton Press Co., 1923).

The Gary dinners had two consequences. In the spring of 1909 Gary organized the American Iron and Steel Institute (A.I.S.I.) to be a permanent forum where steel executives could exchange information and promote the industry. Their first official meeting was held in October 1910. Butler was among the founding members and became one of the directors of the American Iron and Steel Institute.

The second consequence was a government inquiry into the legality of the dinners. In May 1911, the same month that the Supreme Court ordered the dissolution of the Standard Oil Trust, a U.S. House of Representatives Committee opened hearings on U.S. Steel. In October 1911, the attorney general filed a suit calling for the dissolution of U.S. Steel.

Butler maintained that "not a single word was said at any of the Gary dinners that Attorney General [George] Wickersham and all Christendom might not have heard." With charges of collusion circulating, Butler remained optimistic, saying, "perhaps the co-operative movement [the Gary plan] has been side-tracked, but it will come back into its own."[8]

It took the courts several years to write the final chapter of the Gary dinners. In June 1915, the U.S. District Court in Trenton, New Jersey, found that the Gary dinners had constituted an illegal combination but also found that U.S. Steel had not monopolized the steel industry, a decision finally affirmed by the U.S. Supreme Court in March 1920.

Joseph Butler embraced the Gary doctrine of competition and became a proponent of the notion that business could indeed work through unpredictable times. The gatherings, according to the attendees, were an attempt to solve the economic crisis at hand without government intrusion. On the other hand, they expected the government to provide them assistance through protective tariffs.

During this period, Butler continued to pursue his many business interests, but he also took on several other projects. Two of his interests were reading and promoting civic improvement, so it was hardly a surprise when he became involved in Youngstown's attempt to build a new public library. Since 1870 the city had provided public access to a modest collection of books originally housed in the office of School Superintendent Reuben McMillan. In 1880, McMillan and a group of dedicated teachers and citizens formed the Youngstown Library Association, and in 1897, the name was changed to the Reuben McMillan Free Library Association to honor the aging superintendent. During the same year, the Association purchased the home of Richard Brown on the corner of Market and Front Streets, and this structure housed the library collection for the next decade.

In 1907, Mahoning County purchased for $141,255 the library property for the site of a new courthouse. In turn the Library Association acquired a lot from W.S. Bonnell on the northeast corner of Wick and Rayen Avenues for $50,000. A prominent local architect, Charles F. Owsley, was hired to design the new library. But well before the building was near completion, the group realized that to finish the job another $50,000 was needed on top of the $96,000 remaining in the building fund.[9]

Butler recommended that Andrew Carnegie be approached to provide the needed capital. By this time, Carnegie had started to fund libraries all over the country. He made the request, but Carnegie turned him down, perhaps because Butler had explained that the new library would be named for Reuben McMillan, not Carnegie. When Butler again saw Carnegie, he renewed the request. "Finally," wrote Butler, "I said to him that a

Eleven. The Gary Dinners

large part of his income was created in the Mahoning Valley and told him that he should do something to offset it." Carnegie again demurred. Butler sent librarian Anna Morse to New York to plead the library's case. Miss Morse, a graduate of the New York State Library School and librarian since 1902, was able to exact a pledge of $50,000 from Carnegie.[10]

In late December 1907, Butler addressed the annual meeting of the Merchant Marine League, an organization he had joined shortly after its founding in Cleveland in 1904. The Merchant Marine was another of Butler's passions. In attendance were Ohio's U.S. Senator Joseph Foraker, New Hampshire Senator Jacob Gallinger, and the Assistant Secretary of the Navy, Truman Handy Newberry. Butler reminded the group that earlier in the year he had led a delegation of 25 businessmen to Washington, D.C., to advocate for a Merchant Marine subsidy bill. The group had met with President Roosevelt, House Speaker Joseph Cannon, and several congressmen. "What we want," Butler told the members of the League, "is a comprehensive bill, something that will do the business. Every country that amounts to a damn has subsidized its merchant marine, and we should do the same."[11]

In the summer of 1908, Merchant Marine League president, Harvey D. Goulder, a Cleveland attorney and counsel for the Lake Carriers Association, resigned due to pressing business concerns. Butler was persuaded to complete Goulder's unfinished term. At the annual meet-

Andrew Carnegie made his fortune through spirited, unrelenting competition. Butler was relentless in pursuing a donation from Carnegie for Youngstown's new library (Library of Congress).

ing in December, Butler was elected to a full term as president. Myron Herrick, who served as Ohio governor from 1904 to 1906, was elected vice president, and Cleveland's John Penton, editor of the *Iron Trade Review*, was elected secretary.[12]

Their goal was to persuade the new 61st Congress to pass the Gallinger Bill, known as the Ocean Mail Act. The bill did not pass in the House of Representatives in the previous Congress. "If the bill can be passed," Butler argued, "it will give an immediate stimulus to the ship building and ship operating interests. They will begin at once to build the largest class of boats, of which this country now has none at all. They will establish at once a line of steamships to South America, which must now be reached by way of Liverpool."[13]

In June, the Republican party nominated William Howard Taft to succeed Theodore Roosevelt in the White House. Butler, the advocate of Republican political candidates, especially one born in Ohio, exercised his political and organizational skills and succeeded in making Youngstown the first city in which a successful presidential campaign both opened and closed.

The 1908 Taft campaign began in Youngstown on September 5. The candidate could not attend the event, but Ohio Governor Andrew H. Harris, New York Governor Charles Evans Hughes, and Indiana Senator Albert Beveridge filled in. Butler escorted the candidate from Cleveland to Youngstown by train. They were entertained at the Youngstown Club. Later, Butler, as chair of the meeting held at the Park Theater, introduced Taft as the next president of the United States. The campaign closed on November 2 with a visit by Taft.[14]

Butler's political activity prompted some Republicans to see him as a possible candidate for United States Senator. The rumors prompted Joseph Foraker, Ohio's senior U.S. senator, to write Butler on December 1, 1908. "I have seen it stated in the newspapers that you intend to be a candidate for United States Senator to succeed me. I do not know of anyone in Ohio whom I would be more pleased to see take my place than yourself, for I would at least know that I was being succeeded by a stalwart Republican of the old school, who has always been a warm personal as well as politican [sic] friend." After speculating on the possible backers of Butler's candidacy, Foraker concluded by asking "if it should turn out that you could not be elected, I would be glad to have their help. If your relations to them are such that you could speak a word in my behalf, dependent on the contingency named, I would be greatly obliged."[15] Butler was not interested in running for office and talk of his candidacy soon died. Foraker, who had served in the Senate since 1897, did lose his seat to a younger and more progressive Republican, Theodore Burton.

Eleven. The Gary Dinners

Later that month, Andrew Carnegie testified before the Tariff Commission of his conversion to an anti-tariff position. "The total abolition of the tariff will leave the steel companies in a better position as far as this country is concerned, than a continuance of the present coddling system."[16] Carnegie's testimony outraged the steel leaders who all knew that steel tariffs had enabled Carnegie to reap his riches.

Carnegie's new anti-tariff attitude, noted his biographer Joseph Frazier Wall, was the Scotsman's "biggest bombshell against the business community." Butler was not alone in his indignation at Carnegie's latest affront. The American iron and steel industry was indeed a powerful global economic force led by the United States Steel Corporation that, at its inception in 1901, controlled more than 60 percent of domestic production.[17] But Carnegie's opinion on such matters always reflected his position as the one-time head of a powerful, giant conglomerate. Butler's perspective, however, was shaped by his experience as a vulnerable independent manufacturer. Carnegie's wealth still held extraordinary influence in politics and business affairs, and his comments were widely circulated. Butler worried over the damage that Carnegie's anti-tariff position could cause and did his best to discredit Carnegie's remarks.

Democratic reformers and progressive Republicans agreed with Carnegie that American industry was indeed strong enough to withstand competition from abroad; therefore, they believed that a reduced tariff was warranted. In addition, they argued that high tariffs resulted in similar responses from overseas competitors that had an adverse effect on American exports.

Butler reminded Senator Charles Dick of Ohio how Carnegie used to appear before Congress "begging for protection, and saying that he could not run his works without it."[18] The independent pig iron manufacturers from Cleveland to Sharon, Pennsylvania, Butler said, could not run their works without the same protection once enjoyed by Carnegie. Butler was also furious over recent comments by Senator Isidor Rayner, a Democrat from Maryland, who had claimed, "This country is filled with tariff liars. There seems to be something about the tariff that seems to make it impossible for a man interested in it to tell the truth." Butler took the senator's comments personally. "I do not like to have my veracity impugned," Butler protested in a letter to Senator Dick. Butler then took aim at Carnegie, who likewise had testified to the Ways and Means Committee. "I may say now that Mr. Carnegie, in his own peculiar way, is one of the great men of the world and in every respect the most unique character born since the Creation of the World. One would almost imagine after reading his testimony that he had a hand in that important undertaking." Butler called Carnegie's testimony jocular and felt that Carnegie was by now too far removed from the industry to be a credible witness. "On the contrary," Butler added, "all that he said would make a fine monologue before a vaudeville audience."[19] Still, Butler tried to restrain his anger, for it was at this time that he needed Carnegie's support to help complete the Reuben McMillan Free Library for the citizens of Youngstown.

The iron and steel industry had benefited from protective tariffs over the course of successive Republican administrations, but by spring 1909 there was a definite shift in the political winds. President Taft had called for a special session of Congress to discuss the matter. The House of Representatives soon passed a bill lowering tariffs sponsored by Sereno Payne, a Republican representative from New York. However, the U.S. Senate passed a substitute bill sponsored by Senator Aldrich, a Republican from Rhode Island, to raise tariffs on many goods.

On April 9, President Taft signed into law the Payne-Aldrich Tariff Act of 1909. The final bill was a compromise that disappointed many on both sides of the issue. Historian Arthur Schlesinger notes, "Taft signs it with no sign of disapproval, and, six weeks later, with clear lack of political savvy, claims it is the best tariff bill ever passed by Congress. Although Taft will sponsor much legislation dear to the Progressive hearts, this lack of political tact helps to lose him the liberal support of his party."[20] This would contribute to Taft's defeat in the 1912 election. The Payne-Aldrich Act reduced tariffs on iron and steel by 50 percent, but the industry, knowing that Congress might have reduced the tariff further, had no choice but to accept the new law.

All of Butler's time was not spent on business and politics. He possessed a keen interest in local history and American history in general. Born in 1840, he was old enough to remember many of Youngstown's early pioneers, and he was aware of the need to gather the historical facts before witnesses like himself were gone. Earlier efforts to preserve local history had faded, and many of those individuals who had founded the Mahoning Valley Historical Society in the mid–1870s had died. Butler hoped to rekindle the organization, so he hosted a dinner at the exclusive Mahoning Golf Club, the predecessor to the Youngstown Country Club, "for the purpose of reviving interest in the Mahoning Valley Historical Society."[21]

The Historical Society was reorganized and incorporated in February 1909. In November, Butler, who had been housing historical records in his home until a suitable location could be arranged, was elected president of the Mahoning Valley Historical Society by the new slate of trustees. It was a post that he would hold for the next 10 years. The Historical Society set up quarters in the city's new library building. Under Butler's leadership, the Society focused on collecting local history, securing mementoes of early Youngstown, and planning a permanent museum. Dorothy Welsh, who became the first paid employee of the Historical Society, credited Butler for "trying to keep the Society alive over the years when people became too involved in making a living and going into industry."[22]

Butler had always kept detailed notes of his experiences and continued to do so. The consummate political observer, Butler was proud of the close associations and friendships he had developed with politicians and statesmen, especially U.S. presidents before and during their terms of office. In addition to McKinley, he had personal relationships with Roosevelt and Taft. He boasted that he had either seen or met every president from Lincoln to Taft. Butler had been elected to membership in Cleveland's Rowfant Club, which provided a venue for the critical study of books and publishing opportunities for its members. In February 1909, Butler was invited to present his presidential memories and research to the members.[23]

His talk on February 27, 1909, included critical observations of each chief executive from Abraham Lincoln to William Howard Taft. Not surprisingly, his remarks favored the Republican presidents. Shortly after, Butler's friend John Penton, a Cleveland publisher who had invited Butler to speak at the Rowfant Club, expressed interest in publishing his remarks, and Butler worked diligently during the next year researching, writing, revising, and editing the manuscript. In addition to the highlights of his own encounters, he made a special effort to provide some historical background of each president. A significant portion was devoted to William McKinley. *Presidents I Have Seen and Known—Lincoln to Taft* became Butler's first book.

In 1909, the Youngstown Chamber of Commerce was in search of a new president. Members believed their organization needed a dose of determination and enthusiasm that the 68-year-old Butler was known for. However, persuading Butler to take the helm of the business organization was no easy task.

The *Youngstown Vindicator* reported, "Being almost overwhelmed with business in connection with the Brier Hill Iron & Coal Company and other private interests, Mr. Butler protested against election but was finally prevailed upon to accept." Public reaction was most favorable. "No better selection could have been made," said the *Youngstown Vindicator*. "Mr. Butler is one of the most public spirited and active citizens of Youngstown and once he becomes interested in an organization can be depended upon to do things and without delay. Under his administration the Chamber will doubtlessly accomplish great things in the interest of the city."[24]

Following Butler's election as president of the Youngstown Chamber of Commerce, he began to shift his priorities more sharply from business to community endeavors, and this truly signified a new direction in his life. On February 4, 1910, Butler addressed the Niles Board of Trade on "The Town Beautiful." In addition to being a proponent of good personal health habits, Butler also believed in the health of a community. This was the objective he set for the Youngstown Chamber of Commerce, and he suggested that Niles make it theirs as well. "We hear so much nowadays about the conservation of natural resources but it is the conservation of the health and lives of our townspeople that is of more importance than the conservation of what is generally classified as our natural resources." The *Youngstown Telegram* reported, "He spoke at length upon the need of an improved water system, a sewage disposal plant and the advantage of an adequate police and fire department."[25] Butler envisioned a large, unbroken city stretching from Warren, Ohio to New Castle, Pennsylvania.

Butler also proposed that Niles should erect a monument to its most famous former resident, William McKinley. The suggestion drew lengthy applause from the crowd, and Butler stated that he would gladly head the list of subscribers to such a project. A bronze tablet commemorating McKinley's birthplace had been placed inside the Dollar Savings Bank of Niles in 1907, where his house once stood.[26] To Butler these gestures were inadequate. After nine years of reflection since McKinley's assassination, Butler finally had the inspiration he needed to honor the memory of his childhood friend. In the next several months, he began to plan a memorial for McKinley.

In April 1910, Andrew Carnegie finally fulfilled his promise made to librarian Anna Morse and sent a check for $50,000 to the Reuben McMillan Free Pub-

Butler in 1910. President of the Youngstown Chamber of Commerce are among many other titles he held during this period (The Butler Institute of American Art Archives, Youngstown, Ohio).

Eleven. The Gary Dinners

lic Library of Youngstown. The library thus opened debt free in the spring of 1910. Butler and the library board felt that Carnegie's contribution should be recognized in some way, so Butler commissioned and donated a bronze bust of the great philanthropist by sculptor J. Massey Rhind, which went on display in the library soon afterward.[27]

Butler once again traveled to England for business reasons in August 1910, but he found some time for a little sightseeing. Always the consummate historian, he decided to tour the ancestral estate of George Washington. The trek, advertised as "A Day in Washington's Country," included a stop in Ecton to view the birthplace of Josiah Franklin, father of Benjamin Franklin. The Althorp House, home of the Spencer family and known for its impressive collection of paintings, was also of special interest to Butler the art connoisseur. "The Earl of Spencer had just died," Butler noted, "and his remains were lying in state at the time of the visit." From here the group made several stops learning of Washington's family history all along the way before they reached their desired destination of Washington Manor.[28]

Lawrence Washington, George's five times great-grandfather, began constructing the home in 1540, and the family occupied the manor until 1659. As he strolled the grounds, Butler could not help but wonder why, though the property was in fine condition, the estate was not owned by American interests. His sense of duty and service, touched off by his patriotic zeal, aroused him to action.

"It seemed strange," wrote Butler later, "that the birthplace of the ancestors of the greatest of all Americans should be in alien hands and used for commercial purposes. The thought occurred to me that the property should at once be acquired by one of our patriotic societies, put in

A carefree Butler enjoying fresh air on the open deck (The Butler Institute of American Art Archives, Youngstown, Ohio).

proper condition and provided with an endowment fund to maintain it for all time to come as a shrine for all patriotic Americans visiting England."[29]

The United States and Great Britain were planning to commemorate a century of peace between the two countries since the end of the War of 1812, and Butler hoped that the commemoration committee would adopt the Washington Manor project to symbolize the shared heritage between the countries. Butler contacted Whitelaw Reid, the American Ambassador to the Court of St. James, who was sympathetic to the plan. Committees were formed, the Sulgrave Institution was created, funds were raised, and the manor was purchased by the British American Peace Committee in 1914 to commemorate 100 years of peace between England and the United States since the end of the War of 1812. On July 25, 1914, in a ceremony attended by representatives from both countries, the deed and the keys to the home were presented as a gift to the American people.

Each country formed a Board of Governors, and the Sulgrave Institution opened offices in London, Ottawa, and New York. Butler, as well as William Howard Taft, Charles Evans Hughes, Herbert Hoover, and Samuel Gompers, joined the board of the American branch. Butler remained a Sulgrave board member for the rest of his life.[30]

Butler attended the fall meeting of the A.I.S.I. in Chicago. Several iron and steel men from England and other parts of Europe were on hand to meet with their American counterparts. The overseas group enjoyed several industrial, historic, and scenic tours and learned much about the American iron and steel industry. Members of the A.I.S.I., Butler felt, gained an appreciation and understanding of their foreign colleagues as well.

The joint convention ended on October 22, 1910 in Washington, D.C., with closing ceremonies hosted by President Taft in the Blue Room of the White House.[31] Gary made a short speech on the importance of the iron and steel industry then led the group through the president's receiving line. Taft gave Butler a warm welcome. Near the end of the ceremony, Butler and Taft were observed together. "I had a few moments' conversation with him relative to the proposed Memorial and monument at Niles, O. to President McKinley," Butler said. "President Taft assured me of his cordial approval of the project, and added that he would be glad to write a commendatory letter respecting the plan." A week later on October 28, Butler received Taft's letter.[32]

On the same day that Butler visited the White House, back home in Youngstown crowds gathered on Central Square to watch smoke pouring from the city's most prominent hotel, the Tod House. No one was injured, but a fire in the basement caused the hotel to be evacuated. The *Vindicator* claimed the loss might reach $10,000.[33]

Eleven. The Gary Dinners

City planners had been talking about the need for a first-class hotel in Youngstown, and with the 40-year-old Tod House now damaged, that talk escalated. Not long after Butler returned to Youngstown, he met with other investors and formed the Youngstown Hotel Company. A charter was secured on November 16, 1910, and a few weeks later the new stockholders met in the Directors' Room of Youngstown Sheet & Tube to elect directors. Elected were Joseph G. Butler, Jr., George D. Wick, L.E. Cochran, Richard Garlick, Porter Pollock, Thomas L. Robinson, and H.H. Stambaugh. These new directors then elected officers of the new company. Butler was chosen as president with George Wick as vice-president and W.B. Hall as secretary-treasurer.[34] It would take more than two years before work on the new hotel began.

Twelve

"The Youngest Old Man We Know"

Butler had survived the turn-of-the-century shift to big steel, and he had helped to keep the local industry relevant during the unpredictable transition. Unlike his peers, Butler also had managed to survive these times with a sound reputation. Others, like Carnegie, Morgan, and Frick, were not as fortunate. They were charged with using ruthless tactics to grow rich. Yet Uncle Joe, as many now affectionately called Butler, was becoming a beloved figure in the Mahoning Valley, and his good reputation continued to grow as his time and energy shifted to the promotion of philanthropic causes. During his remaining years, these various projects would increasingly replace the business matters that once demanded his time as an active industrialist.

During the 1910 congressional election, voters gave the Democrats a majority in the House of Representatives for the first time since 1894. Alabama's Democratic reformer Oscar Underwood was elected majority leader of the House in 1911. As chair of the House Ways and Means Committee, Underwood would become Butler's political nemesis over the next several years.[1]

Butler continued to testify before congressional investigative committees in Washington, especially when talk of more tariff reduction arose. Butler provided a strong pro-tariff voice against the anti-tariff majority in control of Congress.

Butler's 70th birthday fell on December 21, 1910. His friends planned a celebration at the exclusive Union Club in Cleveland. Butler's longtime friend James Hoyt served as toastmaster and host. Hoyt referred to the guest of honor as "the youngest old man we know."[2]

Butler's closest friends from the business world including James Campbell, president of Youngstown Sheet & Tube; Charles Schwab, president of Bethlehem Steel; Samuel Mather, Cleveland ore dealer and a director of U.S. Steel; and John Stambaugh, Butler's longtime friend and

Twelve. "The Youngest Old Man We Know"

business associate gathered with the family. The collective wealth of those in attendance was estimated to be at least $2,000,000,000.

James Campbell introduced the guest of honor. Noting Butler's leadership in civic improvement, Campbell said, "The fact remains that Mr. Butler has done more in two years than all the other people of the town in a decade. He is about to succeed in securing adequate water supply for the city and has worked hard to have grade crossings eliminated in our principal streets, something that should have been done years ago." The enthusiasm and commitment Butler displayed during his chamber tenure contributed to his growing reputation as a concerned and civic-minded citizen. Campbell directed his closing comments to Butler's son and grandson in attendance, telling them, "if they so conduct themselves that in the evening of life they can command such respect, confidence and good will as is enjoyed by their ancestor, they can have no greater honor."[3]

Charles Schwab spoke of his intimate 25-year friendship with Butler. "When I am as old as Uncle Joe," said Schwab, "I shall indeed be proud if my career leaves me with a record as clean and as good as his." John Stambaugh observed, "While some of us are dreaming, Mr. Butler is doing, and when we wake up we find our dreams realities, for he is always wide awake and always finds something good to do."

Industry and political luminaries who could not attend, including Judge Gary and former Ohio Governor Myron Herrick, sent telegrams offering warm congratulations. The speakers and letters of congratulations paid respect to Butler's many accomplishments, but they all made special reference to his many private and personal acts of kindness that only his close confidants would know.[4]

The event received much attention in the press with both Youngstown newspapers noting that Butler had known some of his wealthy guests "before they had the loose change necessary to buy pig iron." Butler's son-in-law, Arthur McGraw, who made the trip from Detroit to attend the festivities, wrote several days later that the dinner was a great success and a fine tribute.[5] At the end of the evening the guest of honor pulled a stack of letters from an inside coat pocket, glanced at them warmly, and expressed his gratitude for all the congratulatory telegrams he received from his friends.

Butler then entertained the crowd with anecdotes about his childhood and eventual entrance into the iron business, his mentors, and the remarkable changes he had seen in the industry during his career. He also announced the completion of his first book, *Presidents I Have Seen and Known*. It was published by Penton Press which also published *The Joseph G. Butler Jr. Testimonial Banquet*, a compendium of the evening's speeches.

Presidents I Have Seen and Known was ready for distribution just in time for Christmas, and Butler sent copies to family members and friends. Arthur McGraw told his father-in-law that the book was "most interesting and the chapter on McKinley is evidently going to throw some new light on his history." Robert Bentley remarked that the book was "one more crowning achievement to the many that mark your rounded out career." President Garfield's widow Lucretia disagreed with Butler's observation that her husband had been "more brilliant than able." For anyone who knew her husband, she said, "the statement should be reversed." Critics of the book were otherwise hard to find since Butler presented copies to friends. James Swank, the aged and respected historian with the American Iron and Steel Association, and Butler's friend, chided the new author saying that although Butler may have seen more presidents, he, Swank, had dined with Zachary Taylor, had seen James Buchanan, and had shaken hands with Franklin Pierce in the White House. In Swank's opinion, he wrote Butler, "This beats your record all to pieces."[6]

In a 1906 letter to his daughter Grace, Butler recalled William Kelly's visit to James Ward's house and confessed that he had considered becoming an author. "I could pretty near write a book myself" about that stopover, he told her. In addition, he had developed a sizable correspondence with the editors of trade journals, having gained experience as a young man as a contributing correspondent for Warren's *Western Reserve Chronicle*.[7] But it was the publication of *Presidents I Have Seen and Known* that would inspire him to write more. The consummate library benefactor, he was glad to present copies of his new books to the many libraries he supported.

With so many business interests, work with the Youngstown Chamber of Commerce and Mahoning Valley Historical Society, political lobbying, travels, and the McKinley Memorial project, Butler stayed engaged with his peers and circle of friends. Much of this work demonstrated his continued commitment to civic improvement. And the McKinley project was motivated by his desire to perpetuate the memory of his boyhood friend.

Butler had earned a reputation for getting things done. Historian John Stewart recorded just eight years after Butler's death, "Mr. Butler was intensely interested in humanitarian work and was identified with every movement of this kind in the community for many years."[8] Community improvement was especially conspicuous during Butler's tenure as president of the Youngstown Chamber of Commerce. It was a gratifying time for him in many ways, but the pattern had been established long before this. He had served multiple terms on City Council, had served six years on the Board of Health, and had spent three years as president of the

Twelve. "The Youngest Old Man We Know"

Youngstown Humane Society. The conclusion of each successful project was followed by a request to aid another.

In July 1911, Butler joined his friends Judge Gary, Charles Schwab, James Farrell, E.A.S. Clarke, Willis King, and others from the A.I.S.I. on a mission to Belgium to meet with European steel representatives. The group, reported the *New York Times*, was looking to establish a "common world code of feeling and practice in steel affairs." The group toured England for about a week and then Belgium, where Butler visited Waterloo. The day after arriving in Brussels he organized an impromptu Fourth of July celebration for the American delegation.[9]

After completing his foreign mission, Butler was back at the helm of the Merchant Marine League. As president of the League, he used every opportunity to promote the expansion of the nation's fleet of merchant vessels. In December 1911, he invited his friend and publisher John Penton, to attend a meeting of the Youngstown Chamber of Commerce. Penton was the secretary of the Merchant Marine League and had been instrumental in getting Butler to head the League. While in town, Penton and Butler made plans to launch a renewed national campaign to build support for the country's Merchant Marine.

Butler was concerned about the disparity of American trading vessels in the Pacific. Japanese trade ships, he noted, numbered more than 500 vessels whereas American ships counted just nine.[10] Butler and Penton made speeches and called for action from Washington. At the same time, the United States was completing work on the Panama Canal, which would open a sea route between the Atlantic and Pacific Oceans.

With such an insignificant American merchant fleet, it stood to reason that foreign nations would benefit once the canal opened. "The truth is that we will have the canal on our hands and no American ships to carry merchandise and the products of our industries through the canal. We are building the canal for the merchant marines of other nations unless we immediately do something to build up a merchant marine of our own," emphasized Butler and Penton. Not only would American industry suffer, but so too would American labor, they said. For the steel industry and the Mahoning Valley, the potential negative effects on the local iron and steel industry were great. "If America will only build its own ships it will be the greatest thing for the steel industry that ever happened."[11] Their message, however, never did garner the political support it needed inside Washington's corridors of power, and as a result, said Butler, the proposal and their lobbying efforts died a natural death.

In the House of Representatives, Congressman Underwood had other ideas and was determined to pass additional tariff reform. He also aspired to run for president and sought his party's endorsement at the Baltimore nominating convention in June.¹² Underwood set out to do what so many Democrats and Progressives had failed to do in the previous Congress—to cut far more deeply into the protective tariffs than the Payne-Aldrich Tariff Act of 1909 had done.

Butler had been suspicious of Underwood because of the iron production capabilities of the congressman's home state of Alabama. There were not many men in the country, aside from Butler and the industry's esteemed historian James Swank, who were familiar with every state's iron and steel production capabilities. Did Underwood intend to assist the much weaker iron producers of Alabama by further tinkering with the tariff? Was he motivated purely by the philosophy of free trade? Or was he motivated by a desire to be president? This anti-tariff fever of 1911–1912 prompted an urgent exchange of letters and strategies among Butler and his colleagues.

The proposed bill was made public on January 22, 1912. When the House debated the Underwood bill, members of the American Iron and Steel Institute decided not to oppose the measure. Instead, advised U.S. Steel's president James A. Farrell to Butler, it "is a matter which should be taken up and considered by those directly concerned, in whatever manner they consider their interests can best be protected."¹³

Farrell also explained that his company, already engaged with the United States government in a historic lawsuit to dissolve U.S. Steel, decided to sit out this fight. The bill had enough support to pass the Democratic-controlled House easily, but it stood little chance of passage in the Senate. Therefore, little or no action was necessary, suggested Farrell. That thinking, argued American Iron and Steel Institute member William Follansbee, was unwise and unfair to those members of Congress and the president who sympathized with their cause. Lawmakers friendly to owners stood unarmed and "without proper argument or protest," to aid their cause, he advised Butler.¹⁴

As the Underwood bill made its way through the legislative process, there stood the tenacious 71-year-old Joseph Butler, who hoped to see its defeat in the Senate. It was Butler, more than any other local industrial leader, who prepared to take on Underwood and the Democrats, men who in his eyes were determined to subdue American industry for their own selfish political and economic rewards.

Against this backdrop, Butler was raising funds for the McKinley Memorial, and he had created renewed interest in the assassinated president, who had been a staunch protectionist. It was as if both causes, tariff protection and memorial building, reinforced the need for the other. Recognizing the combination of timing and opportunity, Butler symbolically connected the two causes and advanced them as best as he could.

Twelve. "The Youngest Old Man We Know"

Butler conferred with the unshakable James A. Campbell, his close friend and business partner. Campbell, president of Youngstown Sheet & Tube, had an appearance that oozed confidence and self-assurance. The two seasoned executives shared a genuine fondness for each other, and in times of trouble knew they could count on the other for sound advice. The two well-known figures lived just a short distance apart and were often in each other's company for business and social functions.

On the afternoon of January 5, 1912, Butler had a long talk with Campbell. The two agreed that the best approach was to have each sector of the steel industry meet and formulate arguments against the tariff bill for presentation to the Ways and Means Committee. Campbell would gather the opinions of the wire and pipe producers, and Butler would consult with his pig iron friends.[15]

Meanwhile, Follansbee discovered that Chairman Underwood was not interested in holding oral hearings. Instead, he asked for written briefs. Some, like Horace Haldeman of Philadelphia's Pulaski Iron Company, thought all efforts to stop the bill's momentum were a waste of time and that its eventual outcome in the House was a foregone conclusion. "I am disgusted with the whole proposition and feel that those controlling legislation in the House have made up their minds as to what they propose doing," Haldeman wrote Butler.[16]

Butler too, was to testify of his contempt for the politics involved. The tariff question should be removed from politics, he said, and should be left to the discretion of the newly created Tariff Board. His wish was not to be. And Haldeman was not alone in his opinion either as letter after letter with the same theme landed on Butler's desk. Leonard Peckitt, of the Empire Steel and Iron Company, like Butler, was most concerned about what effect the bill would have on pig iron. Peckitt thought that the duty on pig iron was already dangerously low and worried that the pending legislation would do more harm.

Butler remained alarmed that the pig iron producers were not yet acting cohesively. His patience had grown paper thin, and shortly after receiving Peckitt's frantic letter, Butler got down to business. On January 13, 1912, Butler wrote a sharp note to Underwood saying, "I flat out protest against any further reduction in the duty on Pig Iron and Scrap. This protest is made on behalf of the Manufacturers of the Mahoning and Shenango Valley, with all of whom I have communicated. We feel that the reductions made by the Payne-Aldrich Bill were all that the Pig Iron industry should be asked to stand."[17]

Always pressing ahead, Butler sought input one last time from 18 major independent pig iron producers located in Pittsburgh, Columbus, Cleveland, the Mahoning and Shenango Valleys, and Kentucky to determine a final course of action. The situation was dire after the Panama Canal opened. William Rogers of Rogers-Brown Iron Company, Buffalo, wrote Butler that the cost of pig iron made in China could be shipped inexpensively to the eastern United States challenging domestic producers there. Already, he said, Chinese pig iron reached California as cheaply as producers in Birmingham, Alabama, could transport pig iron to Cincinnati.[18]

January 1912 was also a pivotal one for the Brier Hill Iron Company as the directors finally decided to take the company into steel production. On the morning of January 28, in the company's downtown office at the Stambaugh Building, the stockholders approved the organization of the Brier Hill Steel Company. It was a $15,000,000 business transaction. Although its strength would continue to be pig iron production over the next decade, with Butler's wholehearted approval, the new Brier Hill Steel Company moved immediately to draw up plans for the construction of open-hearth furnaces. Organizers hoped the new plant could produce between 1,000 to 2,000 tons of steel daily. It would be built just north of the company's current location in Brier Hill.

The Brier Hill directors had acted much like the steel conglomerates that Butler once opposed by enlarging the company through a series of key acquisitions. Their previous purchases included the Biwabik Mining Company, the Thomas Steel Company, the Empire Steel Company, the Western Reserve Steel Company, and the Youngstown Steel Company.

Butler was named a director and second vice president of the restructured Brier Hill Steel Corporation. W.A. Thomas was named president. "I had in mind remaining in a sort of advisory relation to Mr. Thomas," Butler later recorded in his autobiography, "but before deciding finally, I made a candid survey of the situation, with the result that it dawned on me that I was growing old. This I had overlooked, but some of my friends reminded me of it. I therefore withdrew from any connection with the active management of the new company, but continued on the board of directors."[19] Even so, Butler found that he could not remove himself totally from the daily grind, and he remained a common fixture at the office and plants.

Though his days as an active official of two profitable companies lessened after the formation of the Brier Hill Steel Company, Butler's passion would always be the iron and steel industry, and his monetary interests in it would be his chief source of wealth. At the same time, his knowledge and popularity within the iron and steel business continued to secure for him various assignments to committees and delegations to advance the industry. But the time once required of him at his Youngstown enterprises diminished because duties were assigned to up-and-coming younger men.

Twelve. "The Youngest Old Man We Know"

If the absence of daily business matters created a void in his life, he wasted little time in filling it.

Although he occasionally strolled through the grounds of the plants amazed at the stupendous progress that had taken place during his lifetime, it was clear that the energy he kept in reserve could be utilized in other fields. His opinion on business affairs would forever be respected and welcomed by his business friends. He had become an elder statesman by this time, and his colleagues addressed him by the affectionate title, "Uncle Joe." This avuncular nickname, first used by Judge Elbert Gary, would transcend the community at large as his involvement in social affairs and community development increased.[20]

Butler's arguments against the Underwood Tariff Bill were laid out in a February 15, 1912, letter to President Taft. He emphasized them when he appeared before Senator Penrose's Finance Committee hearings held February 21–23. Speaking for the dozen independent pig iron manufacturers he represented, Butler testified that the impact of the reductions established by Payne-Aldrich in 1909 were shouldered by owners instead of passing them on to the thousands of workers employed at their mills.

Part of Butler's concern was that the Underwood bill was an *ad valorem* tariff that figured the duty on pig iron according to the value of the imported iron. Previous tariffs had always calculated the duty according to weight. The proposed new method would put pig iron manufacturers at an even greater disadvantage. Willis King, vice-president of Jones & Laughlin Steel Company, and one of Butler's few allies in opposition of the Underwood Tariff, also testified. King predicted wage cuts, a decline in the standard of living, and "serious financial troubles and economic disturbances."[21]

Compromise of some sort was what Butler and King were hoping for, though he gave no specifics as how best to accomplish it. Anything short of the full measure of the Underwood bill would be a small victory. Despite the Payne-Aldrich Tariff of 1909, Butler knew the Mahoning Valley was a prosperous and growing community. However, the proposed Underwood Tariff, he felt, would have a chilling effect. Production costs were rising, he said. "The decline in iron content of Lake Superior ore, which increases costs of transportation and smelting per ton of pig iron; the rapid exhaustion of the coking coal reserves, which makes it necessary to use supplies mined at greater cost or transported longer distances; the tendency to higher wages which accompanies a rise in general prices—these are some of the causes of increased costs."[22]

Butler's political battles were minor when compared to personal loss. Most recent was the death of George D. Wick with whom Butler had a long-established business and personal relationship. Their ventures together were in the iron and steel trade, but they also tried their hand in other areas by organizing the Youngstown Hotel Company.

Wick, after stepping down as president of Sheet & Tube 10 years before, was still in search of improved health. Many, like Wick, thought that rest, relaxation, and a renewed vigor could be found in Europe. After a trip abroad Wick booked passage aboard the ill-fated *Titanic* for the return home. On its first voyage the luxury liner sank on April 15, 1912, in the frigid waters of the North Atlantic. George Wick perished at sea, though his wife and daughter survived. Wick, co-founder, and first president of Youngstown Sheet & Tube Company was one of the city's oldest and most respected business leaders, and his death was a terrible shock to the community. Butler, James Campbell, and Senator David Tod made the funeral arraignments for the great industrialist.[23]

That same month Butler found himself in the middle of another fundraising campaign to benefit the city. "In nearly every other thing that contributes to the making of a modern up-to-date city," Butler said, "Youngstown has or is preparing to have adequate facilities, except in our hospital accommodations."[24]

St. Elizabeth's Hospital opened December 8, 1911. Although the Youngstown City Hospital also served the community, the area's hospital facilities were found to be insufficient for the growing population, which had increased by more than 30,000 from 1900 to 1910. Hospital beds were in such demand that both facilities kept a waiting list for prospective patients. In addition to the inability of these two systems to provide basic care and services for all who needed aid, Youngstown faced the threat of a catastrophic industrial accident or natural disaster.

After St. Elizabeth's opened, the Cleveland Catholic Diocese recognized the need to expand its mission in Youngstown and hoped to raise $100,000 in private donations from the local community to build a major addition.

Butler, a non–Catholic, was asked to serve as the executive chairman of the campaign, and he agreed despite the ongoing demands of several other projects. He could not deny the need for such a project as the St. Elizabeth expansion, and he quickly set the tone for the campaign. "I feel that when there is an object so worthy as this," he declared, "our people will make a ready response."[25]

After months of planning, a weeklong fund-raising campaign began in April 1912. Of the estimated 700 volunteers, many were hospital employees or members of the diocese, especially St. Patrick's Parish. They would canvass designated areas of the city in search of private donations. A 35-foot thermometer appeared on the public square to track their progress.[26] Fundraising events ran from April 17–25, 1912, starting with

Twelve. "The Youngest Old Man We Know"

a dinner for 500 dignitaries and volunteers at the Elks' Club. The main speakers, Butler and Bishop J. Farrelly, who was head of the Cleveland Diocese, honored the victims of the *Titanic*, in particular George Wick.

Butler called upon a diverse group to come together for the hospital cause. The new building, he said, would tend to the needs of all, discriminating against no one due to race, nationality, creed, or economic status. More than $17,000 was raised that evening.[27] The campaign's headquarters remained open night and day, and donations and pledges came in throughout the week.

For Butler, one of the most poignant moments of the campaign occurred on April 23 as the influential industrialist walked the downtown streets. A young boy peddling newspapers approached the campaign chairman and, as Butler reported, "offered a penny to help in the great work." To inspire others, Butler quickly made the story known to the press. He then made plans to frame the coin for placement in the new hospital. On the night of April 24, the campaign's goal of $100,000 was accomplished. The next day's tabulations showed more than $117,000, and before the campaign ended, the amount totaled more than $130,000.[28]

The *Youngstown Vindicator* heaped enormous praise upon Butler for his role. His influence was the decisive factor in the success of the campaign. On the last night of the campaign, the *Vindicator* reported that long continued cheers rang out at the Elks' Club in recognition of Butler's efforts.[29]

For Butler, the success of the St. Elizabeth's Hospital campaign and the effort put forth by the citizens of his hometown was no surprise. And although he enjoyed the accolades and tributes, he recognized the efforts of the citizens of Youngstown and the Mahoning Valley for their accomplishment. "Nowhere better than in Youngstown is there a response when duty calls," he proclaimed.[30]

When the hospital campaign ended, Butler headed to New York City for the May 1912 meeting of the American Iron and Steel Institute. Competition, Butler told the group, was the foundation of the American capitalistic system, an adage he had learned as a young man. But after half a century in business he had developed a broader view. Titling his address, "Competition—Its Uses and Abuses," Butler denounced the practice of larger companies that sold products below cost to force smaller rivals into merger or bankruptcy. "This form of destructive competition can do no possible good to society; it tends inevitably towards monopoly," he told the group. "As we are endeavoring to abolish war between nations, so we should strive just as earnestly to abolish this form of industrial warfare," he argued.[31] Butler added to this list competition to reduce accidents by adding modern safeguards.

Butler manning the plow at groundbreaking ceremonies for St. Elizabeth Hospital. Butler led the campaign drive to raise over $100,000 to help build the modern facility that was so badly needed for the growing city of Youngstown (The Butler Institute of American Art Archives, Youngstown, Ohio).

The Republican National Convention, held in Chicago in June 1912, was a raucous affair where the Conservatives supported the incumbent Taft, and the Progressives backed former president, Theodore Roosevelt. The Taft supporters gained the upper hand, and the Roosevelt supporters walked out of the convention to form the Bull Moose Party. The result that November was a disaster for the Republicans. The Democratic candidate, Woodrow Wilson, crushed the opposition, winning 435 electoral votes. Roosevelt got 88, and the incumbent President Taft managed only eight.[32]

In the fall of 1912, the federal government continued to take testimony in the lawsuit to dissolve the United States Steel Corporation. Hearings resumed in Pittsburgh on October 29, and witnesses testifying included Henry Wick and Butler, former officers of the Ohio Steel Company. Butler's testimony appeared a week later in the November 7, 1912, issue of *The Iron Age*.[33]

In his inaugural address on March 4, 1913, President Wilson made it clear the voters had elected a progressive reformer. "The great government we loved has too often been made use of for private and selfish purposes, and those who used it had forgotten the people." he thundered. "Our cry has been 'Let every man look out for himself, let every generation look out for itself,' while we reared giant machinery which made it impossible that any but those who stood at the levers of control should have a chance to look out for themselves."[34]

The message was evident to both sides. In the House of Representatives, Oscar Underwood's anti-tariff bill gained momentum. Butler, for his part, wrote a lengthy letter to the *New York Herald*. In attacking the anti-tariff supporters, he drew heavily on the same arguments he had presented to the Senate Finance Committee a year earlier[35] as he looked to "defend every ingot of steel."[36]

Tragedy visited Butler and his wife Harriet in the spring of 1913. Their eldest child, Blanche Butler Ford, had been ill for some time. Treatment in a Cleveland hospital produced no relief, and on the morning of May 3, 1913, she died at the age of 45. "It was my first death-bed scene in all of my seventy years of life," confessed Butler. "The birds were singing in the trees near her residence, and Blanche spoke of them as she held my hand in a last pressure.... We were more like brother and sister than father and daughter. She sympathized with me in all my activities and troubles, and I with her in hers."[37]

In June 1913, the Youngstown Chamber of Commerce published a promotional booklet entitled *Youngstown, The City of Progress*, which touted the city as "a Natural Center of Manufacture and Distribution."[38] In fact, growth had occurred in this decade. Heavy industry continued to be the economic foundation of the city's growth and prosperity with the iron and steel industry serving as its bellwether. The heart of the downtown business district was highlighted with its paved, tree-lined streets, pedestrian traffic, and modern trolley cars. New office buildings reached heights once unheard of.

The scene was very different from the primitive dirt roads and clapboard-sided buildings that dominated the city when Butler first arrived in Youngstown. New schools, libraries, and hospitals further symbolized an unfolding modern city whose population surpassed 79,000 in 1910. Two buildings designed by Youngstown architect Charles F. Owsley, the new Mahoning County Courthouse, and the new Reuben McMillan Free Public Library, were completed in 1910. Also opening in 1910 were the Masonic Temple on Wick Avenue across from the Rayen School and the new Mahoning National Bank building designed by Detroit architect Albert Kahn, who had designed the Stambaugh Building a few years earlier. In 1913, Kahn would add four more stories to the Stambaugh building giving it 12 floors.[39]

Leisure opportunities for adults and children from well-equipped playgrounds to Mill Creek Park were plentiful. "The city of Youngstown," the booklet proclaimed, "is singularly fortunate in the character of the men in charge of and employed in its circle of commercial pursuits." It also spoke of excellent labor conditions and noted that "These conditions have attracted to Youngstown high-class workmen and new enterprises have no difficulty in securing men of the best type."[40]

At the A.I.S.I. banquets, it had become a custom for speeches to be made after dinner, and Butler, a regular speaker, had never failed to inform and entertain the audience. At the October 1913 meeting in Chicago, he referred to the recent ceremonial celebration of the nearly completed Panama Canal. Butler said that Youngstown's mayor, Fred Hartenstein, had approached him looking for input on how to mark the event locally to coincide with President Wilson's ceremony. Butler suggested that the mayor contact the mills and ask that they blow their whistles and ring their bells at the designated time. Hartenstein's request was honored. "The biggest noise was made, as it frequently is, in Brier Hill. (Laughter)" said Butler, who explained that the noise from Brier Hill lasted so long and was so loud that the local citizens soon became alarmed. The noise carried two and a half miles away in downtown Youngstown. Butler added that one elderly woman in the neighborhood was contacted by her daughter who feared some accident had occurred at Brier Hill. "Oh, no, no" her mother reassured her, nothing of the sort. "I think Mr. Butler is dead."[41] The aging industrialist was aware of his increasing years.

President Wilson and the House Democrats in Washington continued to push for reforms. These were meant to curtail the influence of big business, which they felt wielded too much power in running the country. In October 1913, Wilson called the Congress into special session to settle the tariff question. "We must abolish," the president told them, "everything that bears even the semblance of privilege or of any kind of artificial advantage and put our business men and producers under the stimulation of a constant necessity to be efficient, economical, enterprising, masters of competitive supremacy, better workers and merchants than any in the world."[42] Suitably inspired by the president's words, Congress passed the Underwood-Simmons Tariff Act, and Wilson signed it into law.

Butler's displeasure for the president's leadership was increasingly apparent. In a speech to the A.I.S.I., Butler noted that Wilson, via telegraph from the White House, had recently pushed a button that detonated an explosion blowing up a dike in the Panama Canal that completed the waterway passage. In reference to the president's legislative agenda, Butler said the president was "pushing some other things that I wish he would let up on."[43]

His criticism of Wilson's policies became unrelenting. He even went as far as to tell the president in a rare face-to-face White House meeting exactly how he felt. Butler had been in Washington and was invited by his congressman to meet the president. Wilson was very cordial, said Butler of their White House encounter, and the president asked his opinion of the recently passed Federal Reserve Act. Butler assured the president of its good merit; however, Butler, taking advantage of the opportunity, offered the president his unsolicited opinion of the Underwood Tariff. When he concluded his denouncement of the measure, Butler said Wilson's "jaws snapped and the interview was over."[44]

Despite political setbacks, Butler had cause to celebrate in the fall of 1913. The occasion was the opening of the Hotel Ohio. Joseph Butler, known primarily as an iron and steel man, was now the president of the newest and best hotel in Youngstown.[45]

Thirteen

The National McKinley Birthplace Memorial

Joseph Butler would later claim that when he conceived the idea of a memorial to William McKinley, it was simply to honor the memory of his friend and not, at least at the onset, to promote urban beautification. Although he had been contemplating the notion of doing something to honor the fallen president, the idea of a memorial building literally came to him as he spoke to the Niles Board of Trade on the night of February 4, 1910. He may have proposed the McKinley project to cover his limited knowledge of the announced topic. "I delivered an address on 'The Town Beautiful,' a rather broad topic and one on which I found it somewhat difficult to shed much light, since I knew but little of city planning or any such matters."[1] Nonetheless, his impromptu call for a memorial drew an enthusiastic response.

Butler was uniquely suited to take the lead on this project because of his personal, political, and professional connections to McKinley. In addition to the childhood friendship, Butler wrote, "I admired him as the leading apostle of protection during my lifetime, and regarded his work on behalf of this policy as one of the outstanding achievements of American statesmanship." Building the memorial became Butler's personal mission. "Of course I expected to look after the raising of the fund, as well as the innumerable details, for the whole project was from the first my own, and I could not expect others to take the same interest in it felt by me."[2]

He wasted little time setting the idea in motion and quickly solicited input from his colleagues in the American Iron and Steel Institute. It was only natural that this group of industrialists, many of whom were Butler's close friends, would support the project. Like Butler, they recognized the important role that McKinley had played in waving the banner of protective tariffs.

Responses from A.I.S.I. members to Butler's solicitations were overwhelmingly positive from the onset. Willis King, vice-president of the

Thirteen. The National McKinley Birthplace Memorial

Jones & Laughlin Steel Company, gave his hearty support: "I hope you will be successful, as you ought to be in bringing about this recognition of his work, and as the country prospers and grows great in coming years, the monument will keep his memory fragrant in the hearts of a grateful people."[3] King's sentiment was typical from the members throughout the spring and summer of 1910.

Butler expected great support from the citizens of the Mahoning Valley, but he wanted a larger base from which to raise funds. "I had conceived the idea of obtaining a national charter for the movement," Butler informed the *Niles Daily News*. "We desired to make the birthplace memorial a broad national enterprise."[4] That's when he turned to President Taft to obtain a charter.

Presidential and birthplace memorials were not part of the American landscape in 1910, and from a national perspective only the Washington Monument in Washington, D.C., memorialized a president. The memorials to Lincoln and Jefferson, common features today, lay in the future. Burial sites of presidents, like McKinley's mausoleum in Canton, typically served as shrines. The Canton structure where both McKinley and his wife and children are entombed sits atop a high hill overlooking the city. The structure is full of symbolism and is grand in stature but offered nothing on McKinley's life and accomplishments. Presidential birth homes, if in existence and in the hands of good stewards, served as museums but this was rare. McKinley's home in Canton, the site of his famous front porch campaign, would not survive, and his birth house in Niles already had been sold, structurally altered, and moved to a new location.[5]

At a White House meeting, President Taft gave Butler his hearty approval and felt that there would be no difficulty in getting a charter. Butler neither sought nor wanted federal funding but rather national recognition to give the project legitimacy and official endorsement. He took the president's advice and asked the Mahoning Valley's congressman and Niles resident, W. Aubrey Thomas, to submit a bill to the House of Representatives that outlined the organization of an association for the purpose of constructing a memorial to McKinley in the town of his birth. The bill sailed through the legislative process.[6] It was a fine birthday gift for Butler to speak of at his 70th birthday celebration at the Union Club in Cleveland later that month.

Taft's signature on March 4, 1911, created the National McKinley Birthplace Memorial Association.[7] The trustees named were Butler, Myron Herrick, J.G. Schmidlapp of Cincinnati, John Milburn of New York, and former U.S. Representative W. Aubrey Thomas, who had lost his seat in the 1910 election. The charter contained no provisions for federal funding, just as Butler preferred. He was still convinced that the project could be financed through private donations. Armed with the new national charter, Butler quickly went to work.

Judge Gary was one of Butler's first contacts. The U.S. Steel executive did not disappoint by pledging a $1000 donation. Gary advised Butler that he should easily find a hundred men to do the same to reach the goal of $100,000, the amount first estimated to build a modest memorial.[8]

The trustees first met in New York on May 17, 1911, at the office of John Milburn to elect officers. It was to Milburn's Buffalo home in 1901 that the fatally wounded McKinley had been carried and where he eventually died. The trustees elected Butler as the association's president and agreed to seek private donations through a nationwide campaign. "Every American," the association announced, "every lover of the good and true in humanity, every admirer of the man McKinley and every recipient of the benefactions which have followed the adoption of the wise and benevolent policies of the statesman McKinley will feel that he owes it to himself and his country to contribute to the establishment of the proposed memorial." Butler felt that contributions from ordinary citizens from across the country would give the memorial a national character. Before Butler left Milburn's office, he wrote a $5,000 check to the Memorial Association, thus fulfilling the commitment he had made to the city of Niles.[9]

Pledges and donations began to arrive from friends and associates in response to Butler's letter-writing campaign. What he once thought would be a modest structure, he now hoped could be something quite grand. The birthplace memorial would honor McKinley's life work and be a center of education unlike his tomb in Canton. That structure, Butler contended, "was designed solely as a tomb."[10] Butler's other goal was to establish an endowment fund to support the future needs of the memorial. Butler realized that all too often projects like this became burdens to local communities once the financial strain placed upon it by a previous generation became too great. Butler was relentless in seeking donations. For the next four years, and even after the cornerstone was laid in 1915, the campaign continued unabated. Butler shied away from no one in his pursuit of funding.

Butler's efforts to rally support for the McKinley memorial caused much excitement in the Mahoning Valley. It was reminiscent of the two presidential contests, and he was once again in full campaign mode for his old friend.

James Boyle, a former McKinley friend who had been a political correspondent for the *Commercial-Gazette* came to Niles to add his support. He and Butler toured the proposed memorial site. Honoring prominent men associated with McKinley's career, Boyle suggested, would truly gather national support. He also thought that leading industrialists from

Thirteen. The National McKinley Birthplace Memorial

the Mahoning Valley should be honored. Butler announced that Boyle would stay on to oversee the fundraising. His role helped to transform the project from a local and regional campaign to a state and national one. Boyle also provided input on the design and function of the structure. First and foremost, it should be a shrine to McKinley but should also function as a civic center. The *Niles Daily News* wrote that Boyle "painted a beautiful picture of noble architecture."[11] Butler and Boyle realized that in order for the project to garner national support, it required the full backing of the citizens of Niles and the Mahoning Valley. When the McKinley Birthplace trustees decided to seek contributions from the general public, Butler felt that the citizens of the Valley should lead the way. In July, influenced by the success of the St. Elizabeth's campaign held in April 1912, he organized a similar event in Niles for the McKinley project.

The six-day campaign, held on the old school grounds, kicked off on July 25, 1912, and took on a carnival-like atmosphere. The memorial treasury already held $26,500 in pledges with expectations of national pledges that would double that amount. Butler challenged the crowd of 10,000 to raise the final $50,000.

Volunteers were assigned to canvass the community for pledges and donations. Dignitaries from across the Mahoning Valley were on hand each night throughout the week. The highlight was the presence of former McKinley teacher, 82-year-old Maria Kyle. Nightly, the little park was transformed into a rush of good feelings as the community at large came together for a common objective. Each evening they gathered in great anticipation to watch the numbers rise: first to $33,000, to $38,000 by the third, and on the final night an exhilarated crowd erupted when the total of $54,000 was announced. "The ladies," reported the *Niles Daily News*, "had a most important part in the campaign and great credit is due them."[12]

Under Boyle pledges continued to arrive. Pledges steadily arrived on almost a daily basis under the watchful eye of James Boyle. Butler, often with Boyle at his side, made numerous appearances throughout the Midwest and from New York to Washington soliciting contributions. Butler easily charmed the audiences using his sense of humor and easy manner of speaking. He appealed to their hearts, minds, and patriotism for support sprinkling some levity along the way. Butler took advantage of his cordial friendship with outgoing president Taft. Calling on him at the White House in January, Butler thought he "Fired him up thoroughly regarding the McKinley Memorial."[13] Butler attended the October 1913 meeting of the A.I.S.I. in Chicago where he unabashedly interjected the McKinley cause. He expressed his gratefulness to the members for supporting the project from the start and good naturedly acknowledged his unyielding pursuit of their pocketbooks.[14]

The city of Niles and the Board of Trade had donated the property for the memorial on Main Street. The site was the former location of the Old White School House where in the mid–19th century Butler and McKinley had been schoolmates. The schoolhouse had been razed some years earlier, and the location now served as a park. McKinley's birth house had stood a few hundred yards to the south.[15] The site made the most sense because it was in the heart of the downtown district and virtually in the center of town. The original plan called for half a block to be reserved for the memorial, but this was later expanded to a full block. The citizens of Niles approved a $100,000 bond issue to raise funds for land acquisition, the Niles Board of Trade secured several options, and the Weathersfield Township trustees donated a fourth of the needed land.

Public reaction had been so enthusiastic that, in early 1914, Butler could turn his attention to the design of the structure. He wanted the memorial's appearance to be unique. A full-figure statue of McKinley had to be a central feature, and the building had to be functional. A significant section would serve as a library satisfying Butler's wish for an educational component, and there would be an auditorium for public gatherings and a meeting place for the local Grand Army of the Republic post. One section would be a museum to honor the life of the president, and some area, he thought, should be designed to honor McKinley's associates, local pioneers, and titans of industry.[16]

Butler and his supporters had begun a national search for an accomplished architectural firm in May 1914. Six reputable companies had responded to the call. After meeting in John Milburn's Wall Street office in May, the trustees announced their intentions. The building would have a construction budget of $200,000, doubling the original estimate. The design must have the approval of the American Institute of Architects. The building would be constructed of granite with two floors and a basement. Bronze busts of Presidents Roosevelt and Taft as well as Mark Hanna would be featured prominently on the grounds. In addition, Butler insisted that the memory of James Ward should also be honored.

In October, Butler released the names of the six architectural firms that bid on the design of the McKinley memorial. All but one, Philadelphia's Zantsinger, Borie & Medary, were from New York City, and they included H. Van Buren Magonigle, the designer of the McKinley mausoleum in Canton. The trustees did not know who had submitted designs when the plans went before them. By omitting the firms' names, the winner could be chosen solely on merit.[17]

The winning design, submitted by the New York firm of McKim, Mead & White, perhaps the most noted architectural firm of the day, stood out over the others. The firm rose to prominence in the 1880s by

Thirteen. The National McKinley Birthplace Memorial

concentrating on country and summer houses. By the turn of the century their focus shifted to urban design. By the time Butler engaged the firm, two of the three partners were deceased. Only William Mead survived.

Public buildings became the firm's métier and would remain so for the next 20 years. In his book, *The Architecture of McKim, Mead & White 1870-1920 a Building List*, Leland M. Roth writes, "Because of the profusion and dissemination of the firm's work, because of its widespread publication, and because of the firm's influence on the hundreds of young architects who passed through the office, McKim, Mead & White had a pronounced effect on the architecture of their own generation and on that which followed. Most especially, they focused their attention on urban and public buildings and so played a large part in shaping the character of urban architecture during the very years when the city became the dominant element of American life."[18]

The design submitted by McKim, Mead & White met all of the requirements outlined by the trustees: a museum, auditorium, public library and even settings for tablets and busts to honor local figures and associates of the martyred president. The building's exterior would be coated in white Georgia marble, and the structure would face east toward Main Street with the library and auditorium, both at ground level, on opposite sides of a central courtyard and statue. An open colonnade in the Doric style would bridge the two wings. The coffered ceiling would include the ancient Greek color scheme of blue, yellow, red and green.[19]

Construction of the memorial was expected to take about one year with a projected completion date of September 1916. It was a reasonable expectation although in reality two years would pass before the memorial was completed in October 1917.

The most prominent feature of the memorial was to be the statesmanlike statue of McKinley. The immediate and crucial task was to find the right sculptor. Butler most likely knew from the onset who would be well suited to handle such an important task, and that person was John Massey Rhind.

Rhind was born in Scotland in 1860 where his father and brother were both engaged in the craft. At 29 he sailed for America with his new bride and a commitment to the Beaux-Arts styles. For the next 30 years he worked in his New York studio. He had a very broad range of abilities, and his projects adorned a score of public buildings, private estates, and universities and included the likenesses of such figures as John C. Calhoun, Robert Burns, and George Washington. Wayne Craven writes in *Sculpture in America*, "He was mainly a sculptor of architectural decorations and public monuments, and was widely acclaimed in each of these fields."[20]

Butler first met Rhind around 1910 at about the time Andrew Carnegie donated $50,000 to Youngstown's Reuben McMillan Free Library. "I had knowledge that Mr. Rhind had produced a fine bust of Carnegie," he explained. "The result of the visit was the purchase of a duplicate which I presented to our Public Library." When it came time to hire a sculptor to carve the likeness of McKinley, Butler noted, "I knew of no other sculptor aside from Mr. Rhind, and therefore, made a contract with him to create and construct a heroic statue of President McKinley." Butler later hired Rhind to create nearly all the busts and tablets in the McKinley Memorial.[21]

The next task was to hire a contractor to oversee the building phase. Over the years, Butler had overseen many construction projects such as blast furnaces, casting houses, and mills of various sizes and purpose but nothing like the undertaking about to begin.

Since few presidential memorials existed there were not many contractors with the type of experience desired, though there were many who had constructed public buildings, libraries, museums, universities, and schools in general. The site needed to be surveyed and marked, the proper distance and degree from varying points of reference needed to be staked, and the right angles, the proper depth for the foundation, and sight lines all needed careful, expert attention. Such details needed to be determined before any evidence of a building at ground level was even detectable. If any of these prerequisites were off by less than an inch, the integrity of the whole structure could be compromised.

In August 1915, the selection of the John H. Parker Company of New York to serve as contractor was announced. Former president Taft sent Butler his endorsement on the selection. Groundbreaking ceremonies were held the following month.[22] On September 30, Butler called on Henry Clay Frick in New York to support the McKinley project. Butler and Frick had been friends and colleagues in the iron and steel industry for decades, and they also shared a love of art. Frick had amassed one of the finest art collections in the country. As the two walked Frick's gallery admiring the mostly European works, Butler informed him of the memorial's progress. From the start, Frick had been impressed with the plans and, in particular, the inclusion of a public library, and Butler asked him for a major donation payable on some installment plan to help finance the library wing. Frick left Butler momentarily, disappearing into his office that adjoined the gallery. When he returned, he handed Butler a check for $50,000. The amount astonished Butler, who had cautiously hoped for a pledge to be paid overtime. "Subsequent to this I called upon Mr. Frick on my monthly visits to New York and kept him fully posted as to our progress."[23]

The cornerstone laying ceremony was scheduled for Saturday, November 20, 1915. President Woodrow Wilson had been expected to deliver the

Thirteen. The National McKinley Birthplace Memorial

principal address, but two days before the event he wrote Butler a sincere note of apology saying he would be unable to attend and offered praise for McKinley. Traditional courtesy to ex-presidents notwithstanding, the Democrat Wilson was busy rewriting or abolishing many of McKinley's protectionist policies, and his presence at the cornerstone ceremony might have struck some as ironic. Perhaps Butler was not too disappointed considering the frustration he had been experiencing over Wilson's progressive agenda.

A threat of snow flurries that night and the chilly November air did not keep away the thousands of Mahoning Valley residents who turned out for the occasion. Butler arrived well before the 11:00 a.m. start time. Ohio's Governor Frank Willis was on hand; however, the state's newest U.S. Senator, Warren G. Harding, could not attend due to a bout of influenza.

Butler took several minutes to address the overflowing crowd. His remarks highlighted McKinley's life, career, family genealogy, and patriotism, as well as the history of the memorial project. There followed addresses by Governor Willis and former governor, Myron Herrick. After the speeches were concluded, B.F. Perry, Past Worshipful Master of the Great Lodge of Ohio, who was escorted by St. John's Commandry, Knights Templar, conducted the ceremony of laying the cornerstone.[24]

The John Parker Company made much progress by early 1916. Three months after the cornerstone was laid, marble was set around the lower section of the south wing with the use of

Henry Clay Frick shocked Butler with a $50,000 donation to the McKinley Birthplace Memorial. From Joseph G. Butler, Jr., *Fifty Years of Iron and Steel* (Cleveland, Ohio: The Penton Press Co., 1923).

large steam-powered derrick cranes. The marble façade of the north wing nearly reached its full height by late March. In July, steel girders were set in place on the roofs of the two wings, and the horseshoe-shaped rear of the courtyard connected the two structures. With the roof nearly complete, the derrick cranes began standing up the 28 fluted Doric columns in August and September, setting in place the last one on October 3.[25]

By late October, the outside of the memorial was practically complete. The brilliant white marble reflected the sun's rays. There would still be another year of interior work before the memorial was ready for dedication. Some of the project's delay was blamed on the weather and the quarrying process of the Georgia marble.[26] Another campaign underway by this time was the marketing of a commemorative McKinley coin to help raise funds. Earlier in 1916, Butler and his fellow trustees realized that additional funds would be needed to cover rising construction costs as private contributions from Butler's friends had dried up. The price of the coins would be such that most Americans of lesser means could purchase them thereby aiding in the fundraising efforts. Although the idea of selling commemorative coins was not a novel one, the trustees believed a McKinley coin would be a popular item.

The trustees went to Congress seeking authorization for the legal coinage, and after some deliberations a silver dollar commemorative coin was proposed. The thought of a McKinley silver dollar, however, was unthinkable to Butler, who argued before a House committee that a gold coin would be more appropriate since the former President was a lifelong advocate of the gold standard. A one-dollar gold coin displaying a profile of McKinley on the obverse side and the memorial on the reverse was struck at the Philadelphia Mint in 1916 and again in 1917. The coin sold for $3.00. Butler, perhaps letting the promoter's knack for hyperbole get the better of his reason, claimed, "The coinage is unique and rare, exemplifying the unostentatious intelligence of the owner of the souvenir, as well as his or her reverence for the great things in American history." Unfortunately, the design was widely criticized, sales did not meet the expectations of the trustees, and the fundraising project was not successful.[27]

Butler kept at his work for the memorial in other ways throughout 1917. He collected McKinley memorabilia and artifacts, a never-ending task that brought him much enjoyment. He wanted the Memorial Museum to house the best collection of McKinley relics to be found anywhere in the country. Prized among his coveted artifacts were a desk McKinley once used during his days as a practicing attorney and the chair the president used in his office within the executive mansion.[28]

As Rhind worked on the McKinley statue, the trustees commissioned the artist to sculpt 37 busts, all cast in bronze, of various individuals associated with McKinley and his times. After the statue was completed and shipped from New York the first week of July 1917, the artist was able to focus on the busts.[29] The subjects included key figures from McKinley's cabinet, such as his Secretary of State John Hay and Secretary of War Elihu Root; former Presidents Roosevelt and Taft; and pioneers of the iron and steel industry including Sir Henry Bessemer, Andrew Carnegie, and Butler's close friend Elbert Gary. Some of the local figures included Governor David Tod, Frank Buhl, James Ward, and the founder of Niles, James Heaton. Henry Clay Frick's bust would be placed immediately inside the library entrance for patrons to behold. Butler was so appreciative of Frick's generosity that he financed this bust personally.[30] The others would be placed in the Court of Honor, surrounding the statue of McKinley.[31]

The long-anticipated Dedication Day, October 5, 1917, finally arrived. Construction had taken a year longer than expected, but once it was completed the reasons for delay became a distant memory. For an October day in the Mahoning Valley, it was uncharacteristically sunny even though the forecast called for overcast skies. The *Youngstown Telegram* called it "perhaps the most beautiful autumnal day of the year."[32]

A crowd estimated to be 10,000 started gathering on the grounds around the memorial early in the morning looking for a good spot from which to observe the speakers' rostrum where former president Taft, the main speaker of the day would pay homage to his Ohio colleague and predecessor. Twenty thousand more lined the sidewalks to watch the 12:30 p.m. parade. Additional spectators gathered on the nearby rooftops and in windows. The whole town stood ready as city hall, the courthouse, and schools closed for the day. Buildings were decorated with flags and bunting. Several bands were joined by local veterans' groups including the members of the Canton G.A.R. Shortly after 1:00 p.m., Meyer Robertson's Band played "Le Prophet" followed by an invocation from the Rev. E.S. Toensmeier. E.A. Gilbert then introduced Joseph Butler who, before beginning his address, strongly criticized Ohio Governor James Cox for failing to show for the dedication.[33]

The story of McKinley was simple, noted Butler. He was born of humble origins like most in the crowd; he grew up principled and disciplined, and when the call came, he patriotically served his country in war. He continued his service to others as governor of Ohio and president of the United States where, in the end, his life was sacrificed for his beliefs. The best way to pay homage to his sacrifice, therefore, aside from this fine memorial was to live the same way. The people of the Mahoning Valley, said Butler, had done well to erect the memorial.

For Butler, the actual project was seven years in the making, although

The completed National McKinley Birthplace Memorial in Niles, Ohio. From Joseph G. Butler, Jr., *Recollections of Men and Events* (New York: G.P. Putnam's Sons, 1925).

he had wrestled with the idea since McKinley's death. His speech was brief, but he made his points succinctly. He recounted his long relationship with McKinley and told the crowd, "His gentle spirit, his rectitude of heart, his love of country and his wisdom—these things cannot be embalmed in marble. They are to be perpetuated only in our own hearts and in the hearts of our children, and there has never been a time in the history of the world when they should have such meaning for us as now."[34]

Former President Taft delivered his address. His remarks naturally garnered most of the headlines the next day, for his remarks not only honored McKinley but also supported the United States' involvement in the Great War. The other highlight of the day was the unveiling of Rhind's statue of McKinley. With a tug of a cord by Helen McKinley, the president's sister, the flag fell to reveal the stoic figure of McKinley. "The people," reported the *Warren Chronicle*, "stood with bowed and bared heads. Many were in tears…. It was one of the most heart gripping incidents of the day."[35]

After the dedication ceremony was complete, Butler guided a group of friends through the library and auditorium pointing out the many busts honoring the living and the dead. Butler had commissioned Rhind to sculpt a bust of Taft, but it was not ready in time for the day's ceremony. Unbeknownst to Butler, his friends had asked Rhind to sculpt a bust of Butler himself, and they chose to unveil it during this private ceremony. It was a gesture of friendship and an acknowledgment of Butler's efforts in erecting the memorial. Myron Herrick wrote to Butler three months earlier, "It has been rather unusual in years past for men to give so large a part of their time and energy to public affairs as you have done. If there were more men with your public-spirited attitude the country would be vastly better off."[36]

Thirteen. The National McKinley Birthplace Memorial

With the help of Luce's Press Clipping Bureau in New York and the Capitol News Bureau in Columbus, Butler collected reports from across the country, all touting the memorial and the ceremony in a most positive manner. These clippings he neatly placed in a scrapbook. The hometown *Niles Daily News* said it best. "That the beauty and magnificence of the memorial structure was a pleasant surprise to the many who saw it for the first time, was apparent from the many remarks of genuine approval heard on all sides."[37]

In his address at the dedication, Butler said that the McKinley Birthplace Memorial was, "the crowning achievement of his own long and busy life, and the evidence of trust and confidence on the part of a host of generous friends."[38] In truth, his busy life was far from over, and his days of erecting marble buildings were just beginning. The war in Europe was never far from anyone's mind, and Butler continued his work with the Red Cross and the sale of Liberty Bonds as well his support of other charitable causes in the Valley. There was always something to be done with the McKinley Memorial even though the structure was now completed and open. Busts and bronze tablets were added over the years, and Butler headed the Memorial Board until his death.

Fourteen

A Journey to France and the Great War

During the period from 1914 to 1919, Joseph Butler was kept busy supervising the construction of the McKinley Memorial and a new gallery to house his art collection. However, he did not neglect his interests in business, politics, and civic affairs.

A meeting of virtually all the major producers of pig iron in the United States was held in New York City on January 8, 1914. The result of the meeting was the formation of the American Pig Iron Association and the election of Joseph G. Butler, Jr., as its president. The group's goals were to unify contract forms, gather statistics, and standardize pig iron grades.[1]

In the fall of 1914, President Woodrow Wilson signed the Federal Trade Commission Act and the Clayton Anti-Trust Act, both of which affected the way the iron and steel industry operated. John Topping, chairman of the Republic Iron & Steel Company, applauded the prospects of a closer relationship between government and business. Butler protested, "We already have too many commissions. There is too much paternalism in Washington. What the steel business of the country needs is to be let alone and given an opportunity."[2] Butler clearly was no fan of government meddling with business practices unless, of course, the legislation involved setting higher tariffs for iron and steel.

The Liberty Bell was touring the country on a journey from Philadelphia to San Francisco where it would be an attraction at the Panama-Pacific International Exposition. Butler, a member of the Sons of the American Revolution and a man never shy about displaying his patriotism, wanted the bell to make a stop in Youngstown. From 1876 to 1915, the Liberty Bell had been displayed at several expositions, including the 1893 World's Columbian Exposition in Chicago and the 1904 World's Fair in St. Louis. However, the 1915 journey to the west coast would be its final trip away from Independence Hall.

Fourteen. A Journey to France and the Great War

The Bell left Philadelphia in July but did not stop in Youngstown. In November, however, when the Panama-Pacific International Exposition was in its final weeks, the Liberty Bell returned to Philadelphia by a different route, and this time Butler got his wish.

The famous symbol was scheduled to arrive in Youngstown at 1:30 p.m. on November 23, 1915. The *Youngstown Telegram* reported that a crowd of 40,000, including 18,000 school children, viewed the Bell, which arrived by train an hour past schedule. Joseph Butler, who chaired the reception committee, and other local dignitaries, had taken a special streetcar to Niles to meet the train and accompany it to Youngstown. The *Telegram* noted that "all the way down the Mahoning Valley mill men stopped work and lined up along the railroad cheering the train and waving their caps as it steamed by."[3]

In 1915, Butler was elected to the Board of Trustees of the Reuben McMillan Free Library, an honor he must have appreciated given his love of books and libraries and the considerable role he played in getting the funding to complete Youngstown's library.

Of all the community services he would provide, serving as a library trustee was a most fitting and satisfying one for Butler, who valued education and had a passion for reading and writing. He was determined to enrich the diverse population of the Mahoning Valley through the Reuben McMillan Free Library by building up the collection there and elsewhere. As the years passed, he regularly would donate books to libraries around the country and to the Reuben McMillan Free Library in particular. Butler would serve on the Library Board until his death.[4]

Joseph Butler and his wife, Harriet, celebrated their 50th wedding anniversary on January 10, 1916, with a quiet dinner at home. Friends wanted to turn the event into a community-wide celebration, but Harriet's ill-health limited the party to the couple's children and grandchildren. Their daughter, Grace, came from Detroit to celebrate with Henry A. Butler.

The couple had successfully raised three children and was now watching their grandchildren grow up. John Willard Ford, son of Butler's deceased daughter Blanche and her husband E.L. Ford, was an attorney. His sister Josephine married local insurance man Benjamin Agler. Arthur Butler McGraw, Grace and Arthur's son, was a physician in Detroit. Henry and Sarah Grace Butler's children included Joseph G. Butler III, who was a student at Phillips Exeter Academy, and a recently adopted daughter, Mary Grace. Friends, neighbors, and business associates presented the couple with a solid gold loving cup inscribed to mark the occasion.[5]

On the day the Butlers were celebrating their golden anniversary, workers were returning to their jobs at Republic Iron & Steel and the

Youngstown Sheet & Tube Company after a short but violent strike that resulted in the destruction of much of the village of East Youngstown. The origin of the violence has been debated ever since.[6]

The war in Europe had a positive effect on American industry, particularly the steel industry. Countries at war with Germany experienced a decrease in overall economic output due to the siphoning of their able-bodied men for military duty. With their mills lying dormant or operating at diminished capacity, they turned to the United States for help. In Youngstown, the mills increased production to supply the need for steel in Europe. The Mahoning Valley enjoyed a period of prosperity, noted Butler.[7]

The upturn in production and profits also triggered new demands from the mill workers for a wage increase. As the new year began, 300 men at Republic Steel's tube mill plant went on strike, and by January 5, 1916, nearly all of Republic's mills were at a standstill, idling 6,000 workers. "Of this number," the *Telegram* explained, "about 2,500 are day laborers who are actually on strike. Their refusal to work throws skilled and semi-skilled workmen out of employment as operation of the mills without common labor is impossible."[8]

By the following day, several thousand workers at the Youngstown Sheet & Tube Works in East Youngstown had also walked out, forcing the company to suspend operations. The local prevailing rate for common laborers then was $1.95 for a 10-hour day. They were demanding an increase of 25 cents per hour or $2.50 per day.

As Youngstown labor unrest continued, the A.I.S.I. was meeting in New York City. Judge Gary gave the press the following statement: "In view of the prosperous conditions now existing, it was unanimously voted at a meeting of the presidents of our iron and steel companies today to recommend that there should be adjustments of wage rates to take effect Feb. 1st.... It is proposed to increase rates of common labor ten percent."[9] Such a raise had been under discussion, but Butler later admitted that the steel companies had been too slow to announce their plan.

Whatever U.S. Steel did had a ripple effect on the independent steel companies, and the following day the Youngstown Sheet & Tube Company, the Republic Iron & Steel Company, and the Brier Hill Steel Company all announced a retroactive wage increase from 19½ cents to 22 cents per hour for common labor effective January 1, 1916. They also announced that they would match U.S. Steel's planned increases for skilled labor.

This announcement was made at noon on Friday, January 7, which was a day too late to prevent the violence that occurred that night. The striking workers at Sheet & Tube had the previous night begun to use what the papers call "rigorous coercion" to prevent men from crossing their

Fourteen. A Journey to France and the Great War

picket lines. Rocks, clubs, and bottles were being stockpiled, and streetcars bringing men to work were halted by strikers who used poles to pull the trolleys down to disconnect the cars' power.[10]

Other factors contributed to the incendiary atmosphere. Sherry Lee Linkon and John Russo write in *Steeltown, U.S.A.*, "East Youngstown was a rough, undeveloped area with more saloons than grocery stores, and no churches at all. The area was populated almost entirely by recent arrivals, unskilled laborers, many from eastern and central Europe."[11] Many of these new immigrants still used the Julian calendar and were celebrating Christmas on January 7. Officials ignored pleas to close the saloons, though they did ask the governor to send in the Ohio National Guard. By evening, looting and arson were rampant, and by the following morning when the National Guard arrived, most of East Youngstown's business district had burned to the ground. A *New York Times* page one headline succinctly described the situation: "Three Killed, Nineteen Shot, Town Set Afire, Ohio Militia Out."[12] Butler would later call the episode "one of the most remarkable incidents in the industrial history of this country."[13]

A *Youngstown Telegram* editorial laid the blame on the mill owners and community leaders: "When strangers from strange lands are brought in here to contribute by their labor to the advancement of American industry and the upbuilding of American wealth and are permitted to live in such surroundings as those in East Youngstown, the blame for lawlessness lies upon the community that does nothing to prevent it."[14]

A grand jury investigation concluded that liquor and dissatisfaction with working conditions played a role in the riot, but its report also raised the issue of ethnicity. These immigrant laborers, the report argued, "were appealed to and inflamed by the feeling of loyalty for their foreign governments, which governments they considered would be injured by the manufacture and sale of the munitions of war then being made by the industries with which the men were employed...."[15] With the war and the growing influx of European immigrants flooding American cities like Youngstown, there was an ever-increasing call for Americanization. Many in the American establishment, concerned with the foreign influence, grew more nervous and suspicious of foreigners. This theme was particularly concentrated in industrial centers where foreign labor was in such demand.

Even before war broke out in Europe, American industrialists had seen a need to Americanize the foreign-born workers in their employ. Safety was one factor, for language barriers and poor communication skills led to serious injury and even death for workers amid the unsafe conditions prevalent in mills and factories.

Butler acknowledged that the Mahoning Valley's foreign-born population was crucially important to the steel industry but felt that "the severing of home ties and the journey across the seas has a tendency to overturn former conceptions of duty, loosen the bonds which held these immigrants to such standards of life as they may have had, and make them more than ordinarily susceptible to unsound social and political propaganda, which reacts strongly upon their experience with government in the Old World."[16]

Not all immigrants, however, were receptive to efforts aimed at destroying or depreciating their ethnic or religious heritage, especially when those efforts had threatening undertones. In *The Search for Order*, Wiebe writes, "Demanding an immediate transformation, the grim Americanizers fulfilled their own prophesies of doom. Not only did ethnic groups hug to their familiar ways in response to these assaults, but they hastened as well to organize in their own behalf."[17]

Though now 75 years old, Butler continued to maintain an active travel schedule. On May 4, 1916, he went to New York City for the annual meeting of the A.I.S.I. and was re-elected to another term as director. Two weeks later he was in Washington, D.C., for the annual convention of the American Federation of Arts. Following lunch Butler delivered an address on "A Small Museum and Its Value to a Community."

Butler used the first half of his speech to recount several successful exhibitions and lectures held by the newly formed Mahoning Institute of Art. In the second half of the talk, he succinctly articulated his philosophy of the value of art and suggested several ways that art could play an integral role in civic affairs. Public schools and public libraries could be valuable partners with art museums. Schoolchildren would benefit from field trips to museums. "The student of art," Butler argued, "can be helped by providing visual models to correct and form his ideas. In a small community the need of seeing good pictures is greater than in cities where there is actual instruction of art students." He spent the most time explaining how art could be a tool to teach immigrants American values. "Seventy per cent of our population in Youngstown is foreign birth," he noted. "The newly arrived foreigner can be helped by inviting him to see something which will please and interest him before he can read English or enjoy much of anything else in this country. By holding lectures on Art in the various foreign languages, by exhibitions of the art of the foreign people themselves, especially the peasant art which they can contribute themselves, by enrolling some of these people as members of the working committees of the Museum, and sending small exhibits out to their meeting places."

Butler closed his speech with a prophetic wish: "I indulge the hope that Youngstown will some day have an Art Museum that will make the Mahoning Valley as much celebrated as an Art Center as it is now noted as one of the largest steel producing localities in the world."[18]

Fourteen. A Journey to France and the Great War

The Republican National Convention was held in Chicago in June. Former New York governor Charles Evans Hughes gained the nomination for president on the third ballot. Delegate Butler and the other delegates from Ohio had voted for former U.S. senator from Ohio, Theodore Burton on the first two ballots, but all switched to support Hughes on the third and final ballot.[19]

Butler sent Hughes a congratulatory telegram. He also sent a telegram to Theodore Roosevelt, who had split from the Republicans in 1912 to run on the Progressive party ticket. Butler's message read in part: "The Progressive party under your guidance has completed its work. I hope you will immediately make your declination of Progressive Nomination final. This will cement party and bring you back where you belong. We need you."[20]

Butler posing with his son Henry and grandson, Joseph G. Butler III (courtesy the Butler family).

Butler always seemed to find new energy in presidential election years. He intended to spend the rest of the year campaigning for Hughes and overseeing the work on the McKinley Memorial; instead, he would spend two months undertaking what he called "one of the most interesting incidents of a long and busy life."

In late 1915, a French Trade Commission had visited the United States and had toured major industrial centers including Chicago, Pittsburgh, and Youngstown. Now, in the summer of 1916, the American Manufacturers' Export Association of New York was organizing and financing a delegation to visit France.

Butler's long-time friend and president of U.S. Steel, James Farrell, was a member of the association. The main purpose of the industrial commission was to visit France, make recommendations to the French government on post-war industrial recovery, and discuss how to improve trade relations between France and the United States. *The New York Times* reported, "Chambers of Commerce and other organizations have planned receptions, and every facility will be afforded the Americans to learn the needs of France first hand.... The visitors will be taken to the firing line in order that an adequate idea of the war's devastation in an industrial way may be gained."[21]

Farrell, unable or unwilling to make the trip, called upon Butler to represent the iron and steel industry and the American Institute of Mining Engineers. Butler declined citing business interests, but Farrell pressed his request. Butler would later write, "The pressure upon me from numerous friends in the steel business to accept the task was persistent and continuous ... if I did not accept, the great iron and steel industries of the United States would be unrepresented, the matter was settled." Butler agreed to join the American Industrial Commission. One week later he was in New York preparing for departure.

The group was composed of 10 commissioners representing various industries including steel, textiles, chemicals, electrical engineering, railroads, and architecture. William Wallace Nichols, president of the commission, stressed to the group the need to maintain a neutral stand publicly. Neutrality was the official position of the United States in the conflict. Butler said, "I received this admonition with a decided mental reservation ... if the Commission expected to accomplish its object it would be necessary to show a genuine sympathy with the Allied cause, and I acted on this theory during the entire journey." On August 26, the *Lafayette* departed for

Butler at 76 years of age and ready for war-time France (The Butler Institute of American Art Archives, Youngstown, Ohio).

Fourteen. A Journey to France and the Great War

France.[22] Ocean crossings in 1916 were not without risk, and the ship had a French 75-millimeter gun mounted on the stern. It was also escorted by two destroyers to guard against attacks by German U-boats.

The Americans landed on September 4 in the rich wine region of Bordeaux and were greeted by the head of the local Chamber of Commerce. Butler was delighted to see large quantities of steel bars from his own Brier Hill Steel Company and munitions manufactured by Youngstown Sheet & Tube stacked on the docks. They enjoyed a tour of the famous vineyards and vaults holding some of the world's most expensive wines. In Paris, the commission had an opportunity to meet David Lloyd George, and Butler was able to greet the British prime minister in his native Welsh language.

Butler visited the American Ambulance, a hospital and ambulance service staffed by American volunteers who transported injured French soldiers from the front to hospital units in the rear. The scene of dead and wounded French soldiers and the sacrifices of American volunteers left an unforgettable impression on Butler and hardened his opinion that the United States should have entered the war long before.

The commission was warmly greeted in at least a dozen French cities, most of them industrial sites, as well as scores of villages. They made frequent stops at churches, museums, and theaters.[23] Five weeks into their journey, the group stopped near the front lines or "zone of actual hostilities," as Butler called it. At *Besançon* the Americans were asked to sign a waiver in case anyone was harmed or worse.

The American Industrial Commission in Limoges, France where Butler addressed the local chamber of commerce. Butler is standing far left (The Butler Institute of American Art Archives, Youngstown, Ohio).

Butler's disinclination to remain neutral and his public show of support for the French people had been a concern for Commissioner General Nichols, especially at *Besançon* where his fellow members called on him to speak. Nichols finally consented and permitted Butler to address the Chamber of Commerce.

His discourse was laden with Franco-American friendship and loyalty dating back to Lafayette's assistance to the American cause for independence. Now was the time for the United States to return the same assistance to France, he proclaimed. "The commission is in France, first, bearing America's good will, and second, to investigate and render such substantial aid to France as may be in our power."[24]

When the group toured Reims, most members declined the invitation to visit the trenches. Butler and J.R. MacArthur accepted. They were escorted to within 1,000 feet of the German firing lines. Butler had another close call when his guide "drove us across German lines within three minutes ride of the German headquarters."[25]

"The group returned to Paris for a week. They had traveled 3,000 miles in 45 days."[26] They left Paris for Le Havre, and after an uncomfortable crossing of the English Channel, arrived in Southampton on the morning of October 19. They were then off to London and Liverpool for the voyage home. During the crossing Butler made good use of his time getting help in translating some documents and writing an account of the trip for the *Iron Age* and the *Iron Trade Review*.

The ship arrived in New York on October 28. Butler took the morning train to Youngstown and arrived home on Monday, October 30. He had been away for two months.[27]

The Iron Age published Butler's report of his observations in France in its November 2, 1916, issue. "I think that when the war ends," Butler predicted, "the imports to France from the United States of iron and steel will be confined to special forms and that France will be able to compete with the United States, but also with other countries in the matter of exports of general iron and steel products." He noted that the French plants paid their workers much less than American workers received. "There are very few disturbances," Butler added, "and dictatorial labor unions such as we have in the United States are unknown in France."[28] By the summer of the following year, Butler's article had grown into a book—*A Journey Through France in War Time* published by his friend, John Penton of the Penton Press.

Butler had returned home just in time to vote in the presidential election on November 7, 1916. Woodrow Wilson's policy of neutrality had become his campaign pledge, and a small majority of Americans supported his position and re-elected the president to a second term, much to the chagrin of Butler.

Fourteen. A Journey to France and the Great War

However, world events made it impossible for Wilson to keep the country out of the European conflict, and on April 6, 1917, the United States declared war on Germany. As the conflict in Europe raged on, America transformed itself into a country at war. Butler's focus had to shift from his work on the McKinley Memorial to the current struggle abroad. Everyone, even men in their 70s, had a duty to do.

The Mahoning Valley mobilized its people and its economy for war. Many members of Butler's family volunteered in some capacity. Butler himself sold Liberty Bonds and chaired the local Red Cross chapter's Canteen Committee. Butler secured the vacant Pennsylvania Railroad Station for use as a canteen for the soldiers.[29]

Butler's son, Henry, chaired the Red Cross's Military Relief Committee while his wife, Sarah Grace, chaired the Mahoning County Committee of the Women's Council of National Defense. Butler's granddaughter, Josephine Ford, served as vice-chairwoman of the Mahoning County chapter of the Red Cross, while her brother, John W. Ford, became a captain in the U.S. Air Service.[30]

Soon after America entered the war, the government's war needs triggered a total re-direction of industrial production. Local mills ramped up production, but the call for young and able-bodied men like those who worked in steel plants posed a challenge to production. Butler recalled those steel workers who remained exceeded expectations.

A measure of the war's effect on the local mills is seen in a comparison of pig iron prices in the Mahoning and Shenango Valleys. In July 1915, the price of pig iron per gross ton was $12.74; in July 1916 the price rose to $18.00, and in July 1917 to $52.50.[31]

To help finance the war the federal government issued Liberty Bonds and encouraged sales through local bond drives. Long time Congressman and Speaker of the House, James "Champ" Clark, Democrat of Missouri, criticized American industrialists during the war charging that they discouraged the sale of Liberty Bonds. The criticism stung Butler, who knew that local owners and workers had responded generously to the Liberty Bond campaign. Every major city was given a goal to sell a certain amount of bonds. Youngstown, for example, was asked to sell $5,000,000 worth and easily exceeded its target.

At the annual A.I.S.I. meeting Butler condemned Speaker Clark's remarks (which Clark later retracted), and he was backed in his rebuke by Elbert Gary. Butler and Charles Schwab delivered intensely patriotic speeches. James Campbell summed up the prevailing attitude succinctly when he said, "There is not much worth while in this world today except to win the war."[32] Later at this meeting, Butler gave one of his most memorable speeches, a life's review of more than 60 years in the iron and steel business. He had become the unofficial historian of the industry.³³

The speech was published a week later in *The Iron Age*. Penton Press of Cleveland published a much-expanded version in book form, titled *Fifty Years of Iron and Steel*, before the end of the year. The book would go through seven editions in the next six years.

At the third annual meeting of the American Pig Iron Association, held in February 1918, Butler retired as president of the organization. The group elected Butler the association's chairman for life and offered numerous tributes.³⁴

For some time, Butler had been grooming his son Henry to take his place as head of several business enterprises that he owned. By the time the United States entered the Great War, Henry was 44 years old with a wife and two children. By 1918, it was unlikely that he would be drafted, but he wanted to serve in some capacity. In October, Henry Butler took a leave of absence from Youngstown Sheet & Tube and sailed for London as a Red Cross volunteer. On November 12, the day after the Armistice was signed, he was ordered to Paris where he connected with his nephew, Captain John W. Ford. In December, Henry was commissioned by the Red Cross as the chief of the Home Service Section in France.³⁵

In the summer of 1919, when the Red Cross ordered the section to wind down operations, Henry resigned his post and sailed for New York City where he was

Butler with grandson and namesake, Joseph G. Butler, III, probably at the family vacation spot at Squirrel Island, Maine (The Butler Institute of American Art Archives, Youngstown, Ohio).

Fourteen. A Journey to France and the Great War

met by his wife, children, and father. The following day, July 23, 1919, the Red Cross officially released Henry, and the Butler family traveled to their frequent vacation destination on Squirrel Island, Maine, where Henry was reunited with his mother. In the fall of 1919, Henry resigned his position as manager of the order department at the Youngstown Sheet & Tube Company and became president of Valley Investment and the Mahoning Valley Mortgage Company. He also served as a director of the Bessemer Limestone Company and the Portage Silica Company, two companies of which Joseph G. Butler, Jr., served as president.[36]

Henry Stambaugh, Butler's best friend. *Portrait of H.H. Stambaugh*, 1919, by Ivan Gregorovitch Olinsky. Oil on canvas (The Butler Institute of American Art, Youngstown, Ohio; Gift of the Estate of H.H. Stambaugh, 1919 © Ivan Gregorovitch Olinsky or Estate).

Early in 1919, the Mahoning Valley received shocking news that Henry H. Stambaugh, aged 60, had died unexpectedly on January 4 in New Orleans while on his way to California. Stambaugh was one of Joseph Butler's closest friends. They had been business partners for decades in the old Brier Hill Iron and Coal Company and the current Brier Hill Steel Company. They had traveled together and had enjoyed many adventures. In his autobiography Butler wrote, "Any account of my experiences at Brier Hill without including Henry Stambaugh would seem like the play Hamlet with Hamlet left out." His death surely must have shaken Butler badly.[37]

When the American Iron & Steel Institute held their annual meeting in New York on May 23, 1919, Butler gave another major address to the group. His topic was the record of the steel industry in the world war. "This was a war of steel" he said.

Butler noted that the United States and Germany were the leaders in steel production, but none of the European powers could match America's economic might. "It was reserved for America, and above all, American steel to win the Armageddon of the modern world," Butler said. "Blast furnaces, open-hearth furnaces, plate mills, rolling mills, and by-product coke plants costing millions of dollars were hurried into existence long before their time and without regard for cost, in order that the steel and benzol needed might be made available." Butler proudly concluded his speech by saying that the steel industry had sent more than 77,000 men to active military service and that the steel companies and their individual workers had purchased more than $484,000 in Liberty Bonds to aid the war effort.[38]

FIFTEEN

Pro Bono Publico

FOR MOST OF JOSEPH BUTLER'S ADULT LIFE, beginning when he first sat for a portrait in Chicago in 1863, he had cultivated an appreciation for art. For the next 50 years that interest led him to accumulate a fine personal collection of paintings. His actions were part of a larger trend taking place among America's wealthy elite, particularly among industrialists who enjoyed newfound wealth at the turn of the century.

Some of Youngstown's stores displayed paintings in their windows, and the small number of local citizens who collected art, including Butler, would hold private showings in their homes. In time, the local exhibitions grew requiring larger showrooms such as those offered at the Reuben McMillan Library. Only personal friends, honored guests, and family were given a tour of Butler's private third floor gallery, but the time was approaching when he would need a larger space to display his collection.

At the dawn of the 20th century, Youngstown did not have what one might call an art community; however, that would change within a decade. In the spring of 1911, the Fellowship of the Pennsylvania Academy of the Fine Arts mounted an exhibition that traveled to several cities in Pennsylvania and Ohio. On April 25, 1911, the show opened in the auditorium of Youngstown's Reuben McMillan Free Library. The *Vindicator* reported the event as "the first exhibition of paintings which has ever been held in Youngstown" and noted that the show was divided into four categories: oil paintings, watercolors, pastels, and black and whites.[1]

In the fall of 1914, the Ohio Federation of Women's Clubs met in Youngtown. In conjunction with this statewide gathering, an exhibition of Ohio artists was held, which prompted the local artists, collectors, and art devotees to consider forming an organization. The group initially promoting the formation of the Youngstown Art Association was largely made up of women, most of them wives of local businessmen and industrialists. It also included Joseph Butler.

A meeting was held with Butler presiding. The keynote speaker was Mrs. Nina Stevens, assistant director of the Toledo Museum of Art. Her

Butler's third-floor private gallery. Shown here is his collection of Native American art (The Butler Institute of American Art Archives, Youngstown, Ohio).

goal, she told the press, was "to awaken interest in this city toward the founding of a museum such as Toledo has."[2] Within a few weeks papers were filed with the Ohio Secretary of State, and the Youngstown Museum of Art was incorporated. Though there was not yet any actual museum, the name change clearly reflected the intended goal of the new organization.

The five incorporators were Butler, James Porter, Sara Baker (all part of the organizing group), Charles F. Owsley, and Mellicent Wick. The Articles of Incorporation listed the goal: "to erect, establish and maintain a hall and academy for advancing and improving all the arts."[3]

The officers were Butler, president; Jonathan Warner, vice-president; Mellicent Wick, treasurer; Owsley, corresponding secretary, and James Porter, recording secretary. These five were joined by 10 others to form a 15-member Board of Trustees.[4] The formation of the Youngstown Museum of Art was a giant step toward organizing an art community, and Butler was clearly the leading force in the movement.

Unfortunately, the fledgling organization began to unravel almost immediately. The two secretaries found they could not work together. Porter was a painter and photographer who had a studio on North Phelps

Fifteen. Pro Bono Publico

Street. Owsley was a gifted local architect who had recently designed the Mahoning County Courthouse, the Reuben McMillan Free Library, South High School, and Youngstown's City Hall. Butler, in a letter to Nina Stevens, summarized the problem. "Mr. Owsley," he wrote "is of an arrogant, dictational temperament accustomed to having his own way, like a spoiled child." Butler explained that the nominating committee had made a mistake in originally ignoring Porter, and then had split the secretarial position into two offices naming Porter to one and Owsley to the other.

Both men had agreed to this plan. Owsley, however, changed his mind and ordered stationery with himself named recording secretary. When challenged, he threatened to resign. "I promptly wrote him a letter," continued Butler, "asking him to send in his resignation in writing. He again changed his mind and refused to resign."

Faced with this friction and the unpleasantness of the situation, Butler informally contacted the other trustees who agreed that the Youngstown Museum of Art could not function under these conditions. Since Owsley would not resign, nearly all the other trustees, including Butler, tendered their resignations, and by December the group petitioned the secretary of state to dissolve the short-lived corporation. Butler added, "Both the newspapers handled the matter most discreetly."[5]

Butler and most of the trustees quickly organized the Mahoning Institute of Art, "reducing the Trustees," Butler noted, "to eleven leaving Mr. Owsley out and strengthening the organization by adding Mr. Henry H. Stambaugh." The new organization was incorporated on February 22, 1915.[6] Owsley was left off the new board. The newly elected trustees then elected Butler as president. The new name suggested a broader appeal. The first exhibition was held in the Reuben McMillan Free Library and displayed 65 paintings by American artists such as John Singer Sargent, William Merritt Chase, Childe Hassam, and J.H. Twachtman.[7]

Thanksgiving found Butler with much to be thankful for. His business interests were doing well because of the war, the McKinley Memorial project was a complete success, and he had quietly started planning the most important project of his life, an art museum for Youngstown.

In early December, the Mahoning Valley was hit by an unexpected storm that left considerable hardship in its wake. The temperature in the business district fell to -3. "Never in the history of the city has such an extreme cold wave caught Youngstowners in such a state of unpreparedness," it was reported.[8]

By December 11, the temperature was starting to make its way out of single digits and the Butler household was comfortably warm due to a recently installed wood-burning furnace in the basement. Butler was scheduled to catch the afternoon train to New York, and as he headed downtown, he carried with him several photographs and autographed letters, which he put in his office.[9]

In late afternoon, some hours after Butler had departed for the train station, his wife Harriet discovered the house was on fire when, as the *Vindicator* reported, "flames suddenly sprayed through a register in the library where Mrs. Butler was sitting. Mrs. Butler and two maids rushed to the basement and found flames shooting in every direction about the furnace pipes." Calls immediately were made to the fire department and to her son-in-law, Edward L. Ford, who lived just two doors away.

The efforts of the firemen to extinguish the basement blaze appeared at first to be successful. In the meantime, Mrs. Butler's two maids and concerned neighbors removed first floor valuables for safe keeping. Harriet's jewelry and the family's silverware and china were removed, and valuable rugs collected from around the world were rolled up and handed out through windows. Neighbors began removing their own valuables fearing that the flames would spread to their homes.

Finally, someone looked up to notice smoke coming from the third floor where Butler's art collection was housed. "A rush was made for the gallery," said the *Vindicator*, "and opening a door a sea of flames was encountered. Every one of the half hundred pictures seemed to have leaped into flames simultaneously."[10]

The third-floor gallery did not stand a chance. When the fire burst through the gallery's skylights, the cold air acted like a giant flue. A crowd of curious onlookers and concerned neighbors watched the fiery destruction, and the *Telegram* reported that "Millmen returning from work declared it looked as tho [sic] the whole North Hill was ablaze."

According to the *Telegram,* "The third floor and roof were burned away, the second floor heavily damaged when the roof and third floor fell and the first floor suffered from water and some fire. The basement was much damaged by fire and water."[11]

A telegram reached Butler in his drawing room of an oil city sleeper on the Erie Rail line near Meadville, Pennsylvania, 45 miles from home. The concise message was stunning, "Return home at once—your residence destroyed by fire."[12] One can only imagine the horror and uncertainty Butler felt, not only by what the telegram said but what it did not say, as no mention was made of Harriet's wellbeing.

Butler returned home to assess the destruction. The losses were devastating. In addition to his personal effects and family portraits, most of his art collection was destroyed. About a dozen paintings from the first floor had been saved, and nearly all of Butler's collection of Native American portraits was spared because it was on exhibition at the public library. But the 50 paintings that he had planned to display in his new gallery going up across the street were gone. The most valuable paintings lost were *The Old Homestead* by Joe Jefferson, *The Eton Boy* by William Merritt Chase, and *The Golden Wood by* Francis Murphy. An immediate assessment of the damage was set at $100,000. The insurance estimate of the damage was $40,000 with $10,000 alone attributed to the house. For Butler, the cost was beyond calculation because a true price tag could not be placed upon original art works. The following morning Butler told a *Vindicator* reporter, "no use to fret about it. They're gone and that's all there is to it."[13] His calm public demeanor surely masked the anguish he felt for the loss of a collection that had taken years to assemble.

One needed only to look across Wick Avenue to note the irony of the situation. Already under construction was Butler's new gallery to display and protect the art collection that had just been incinerated.

Butler and his wife moved in temporarily with their son Henry A. Butler, who lived across the street at 444 Wick Avenue, while their home was being rebuilt. Butler continued to monitor the construction of the museum.

Nothing could have better demonstrated the need for a properly equipped building than the tragic December 1917 fire that destroyed Butler's home art gallery. An enduring popular misconception is that the loss of his collection was the catalyst that led Butler to decide to build an art museum. Despite many sources that report this version of events, the notion is demonstrably false, for Butler had begun planning his museum a year and a half before the fire.[14]

Plans were completed and construction was underway well before the fire on December 11, 1917. The news accounts of the fire clearly mention the museum's construction taking place across the street from the Butler home. A small notice in the December 20, 1917, issue of *The Iron Age* noted, "The irony of the loss is in the fact that Mr. Butler was just completing, opposite his home, a fireproof museum, which was soon to house the treasures."[15]

Many sympathetic letters noted the irony of the misfortune. Son-in-law, Arthur McGraw, wrote from Detroit, "What a pity it is that the fire could not have been delayed until you had transferred your pictures to the new gallery." Grandson and former travel companion, John W. Ford, wrote of the "terrible destruction ... just before the completion of a building to contain the pictures." Publisher John Penton wrote to his close friend "Just as you were preparing to house it for posterity, that it [the art collection] should have been wiped out."[16]

Others, like friends from the American Iron and Steel Institute including Willis King, who had known Butler intimately for more than two decades, knew full well how he would respond to the adversity. "You will take this loss philosophically," King wrote, "and go about repairing it." For Butler, there was no other option but to move forward as he indicated in a December 17, 1917, letter to J.J. Turner. "Since the destruction of my home and its contents," he wrote one week after the event, "I am more than ever anxious to complete this building."[17]

Butler's thoughts of financing and building an art museum on his own originated during the construction of the McKinley Memorial and his discussions with McKim, Mead & White and sculptor, J. Massey Rhind. Butler and the other trustees of the Mahoning Institute of Art had been aware of the need for a larger exhibition space, including Henry K. Wick, who left his country home, "Alnwick," and 400 acres to the citizens of the Mahoning Valley upon his death "to be used as an Art Gallery."[18]

Butler's intentions are revealed in a January 8, 1917, letter to a neighbor: "This letter is, for the present, written … in strict confidence…. I have purchased the H.K. Wick property at 524 Wick Ave. It is my intention to erect on this lot a model Museum or Art Gallery, in which to house my collection of paintings."[19]

Pleased with their work on the McKinley Memorial, Butler chose McKim, Mead & White to design his art museum. William Mitchell Kendall, one of McKim, Mead & White's premier architects, was selected to draw the plans for the museum. Kendall had worked on the McKinley Memorial, so Butler was confident in his abilities. Butler also chose local architect, Paul Boucherle, of the firm Owsley and Boucherle, to provide on-site supervision. By fall 1916, plans for the art museum were progressing rapidly.

When Butler returned from France in late October, some of the finer details of the plans had already been decided, including a terra-cotta ceiling for the portico. It complimented the Beaux-Art design that the firm was known for. Capitalizing on the Italian Renaissance theme, Kendall suggested the use of portrait heads in the ceiling of the portico to honor the patron of Michelangelo, Giuliano Della Rovere, who became Pope Julius II, and the patron of Brunelleschi and Donatello, Cosimo de' Medici. It was a feature Kendall borrowed from the National Museum in Florence.[20]

On December 13, 1916, Kendall sent Butler a detailed letter and sketches of the proposed museum. "The building is in the style of the early Italian Renaissance," wrote Kendall, "a style which lends itself to great beauty of treatment—less severe than the style of the McKinley Memorial, but depending just as much upon beauty of proportion and detail." McKim, Mead & White paid close attention to the positioning of the building upon the lot, which measured 200 feet along Wick Avenue by 400 feet to the rear. Kendall explained, "We consider the landscape treatment of the western part of the lot as one of the museum uses to which the land could be put, and should be considered just as much a part of the exhibits as the objects in the museum proper; landscape gardening being one of the most important arts, and one as yet comparatively unrecognized as an essential part of a museum." Kendall further suggested a carriage approach to the building from the broad avenue.[21]

The building would consist of three parts with the main section running north and south parallel to Wick Avenue and two wings running west. A courtyard was planned for the back of the building between the two wings. At Butler's request, the drawings also contained plans for future expansion. A staircase led to the second-floor gallery over the main section. In all, the galleries offered more than 4,575 square feet of exhibition space.

Butler envisioned the exterior treatment of the museum to be white marble, a natural complement to the Italian Renaissance style.[22] He engaged his sons-in-law, E.L. Ford and Arthur McGraw, to scout buildings of varying façade treatments before he decided. Ford was to examine buildings locally while McGraw was instructed to do the same in his hometown of Detroit.[23] After the general design was settled, attention turned to the technical details including ventilation and heating systems. In a March 1917 letter, Butler told Kendall, "it will be necessary to forget about having the city heat put in the building. There has been scarcely a day passed this winter but that a number of the public institutions, located in various parts of the city have been closed for want of heat."[24] In addition to the heating system, a modern ventilating system was designed that would collect and filter the air from the outside before introducing it into the galleries. The hours that Butler had invested in poring over designs, lighting and heating systems, landscape suggestions, marble colors, and more were known to only a few of his most intimate associates as he kept his plans strictly confidential.

When the plans were completed in June 1917, Butler revealed his project to a curious public in a *Vindicator* article. There had been much speculation about what was taking place on the old Caleb Wick property.

The new $250,000 Italian Renaissance–style gallery would be cased with white marble. The front of the building would be 124 feet wide by 32 feet high with an entrance highlighted by three arches supported by two polished monolithic columns. A copper roof would cap the structure, and skylights would light the exhibit rooms in the daytime. The building would be constructed using the unit plan method so that additions could be added later without modifying the original architectural design. A portable stage was planned for lecturers. And the most important feature of the museum was that it would be built with fireproof construction.[25]

J. Massey Rhind would play a significant role as advisor and sculptor for the new gallery. Rhind was a frequent visitor at the office of McKim, Mead & White and inquisitively pored over the drawings, giving Butler his opinion on various aspects of the plans. Such collaboration between architects and sculptor was a common theme of the turn-of-the-century American Renaissance movement.[26]

Kendall's design called for two large niches cut into the façade on each side of the front entrance. These niches, according to Rhind, were perfect for statues, writing Butler, "Needless to say, it would give me great pleasure to be the sculptor of these figures." He admitted his request may have been premature but added, "My experience has been that the sculpture should be started at the same time as the building."[27] Rhind received the commission.

With plans secured, the John H. Parker Company, the same company that erected the McKinley Memorial and the Minneapolis Institute of Art (also designed by McKim, Mead & White), arrived the first week of July 1917 to begin the long-awaited project. Lindsay Watson, fresh off the McKinley work site, would serve as the Parker Company's superintendent on the Butler museum project.[28] Work began in earnest and progressed steadily through the summer.

Before the fall season arrived, however, signs of trouble developed when marble deliveries ran behind schedule. Butler had chosen the same supplier he had used on the McKinley Memorial, the Blue Ridge Marble Company of Nelson, Georgia, to furnish material for the museum.[29] By late November, the situation worsened. The Parker Company showed no surprise at the delays and reminded Butler that because of the Blue Ridge Marble Company's procrastination, the McKinley Memorial project had been completed a full year later than originally planned. "They seem to be under the impression," Parker wrote, that "because you selected their marble they can deliver this marble any time they see fit."[30] Butler was furious with the delay and made every attempt to pressure the Blue Ridge Marble Company into getting his marble delivered. By the time of the December 1917 Butler house fire, the museum's shape was evident, but the building was only minimally clad in marble.

The fire did not slow the museum's construction in any way; only the lack of marble had done that. By January 1918, the first-floor walls of the gallery were up almost to the level of the second tier of beams. Without a roof overhead there was no protection from the elements; therefore, electrical, and other interior work could not proceed. With construction well underway, Butler turned his attention to the acquisition of new paintings to replace those he had lost.[31]

For the next 19 months Butler's patience was tested by construction delays. Much of this was directly caused by America's participation in the world war. A proponent of America's involvement in the war from the start, Butler could not have predicted that the nation's war mobilization would slow construction of his museum. But that was exactly the message sent to Butler from McKim, Mead & White in early 1919. War work on the home front significantly slowed productivity of domestic goods and services and crippled many nonessential industries like marble quarrying. More important matters took precedent, particularly when it came to rail transportation. In early March 1919, Butler's impatience with construction delays reached a boiling point, and he wrote some testy letters to McKim, Mead & White demanding some improvement and questioning the abilities of Lindsey Watson, the Parker Company's superintendent on the gallery site.

The architectural firm responded on March 15 with a long letter explaining that "The John H. Parker Company collapsed financially. At present there is no one in that office who can follow up the work in the proper manner." As for Watson, he was "a great disappointment to us."[32] Watson was soon replaced, and the John Parker Company declared bankruptcy. Distressed over construction delays, Butler shifted his attention toward building a new collection of art.

Knowing that what he collected henceforth would be the foundation for his new art museum, he concentrated on three identifiable national themes that included western, marine, and genre pieces of American art. Butler still had an outstanding body of work upon which to build. His collections of Native American and western paintings escaped the house fire because they were on display at the library.

The first of his major acquisitions of art that interpreted the Native American scene occurred in 1902 with a purchase of 118 works by famed portrait painter, Elbridge Ayer Burbank. Two of Burbank's portraits featured the famous Chief Joseph and Geronimo. His second major Burbank purchase in 1912 symbolized his understanding that the artist was capturing a record of traditional tribal customs and culture before their inevitable fade from the American landscape. Butler also purchased Joseph Henry Sharp's *Ration Day at the Reservation*. Known widely for his protest of government interference in the daily lives of Native Americans, Sharp expressed his sentiments in his works like *Ration Day*.[33]

Butler's desire to collect artistic impressions of Native Americans and scenes from the West would continue. There is no better symbol of this passion than the bronze *Indian Scout* statue by J. Massey Rhind that Butler purchased for the new museum for $1,875. Both Butler and Rhind wanted the sculpture installed by the time of the opening, but some issues over the cost and quality of the casting pushed the delivery past the opening. The *Indian Scout* was first installed inside but was later moved outdoors to its present location on the lawn in front of the main entrance.[34]

As he set about replenishing his collection, Butler decided to collect works by American artists. "It should also promote American pride and loyalty for American ideals and help to encourage cultivation and development of artistic genius in the New World," he wrote. The American Association of Museums Directory notes that Butler's museum was the first in the country built specifically to house American Art.[35]

To help create his new collection, Butler did not hesitate to employ the knowledge and experience of his many friends in the art world. Men like William Rogers, a director of the Art Institute in Buffalo; Robert McIntyre from the Macbeth Gallery in New York; and J. Massey Rhind, his friend and sculptor, were all enlisted to help build the collection.[36]

One painting that Butler had coveted for years, and which had eluded his grasp, was *Snap the Whip,* painted by Winslow Homer in 1872. Butler first saw the painting at the Centennial Exhibition in Philadelphia in 1876 but could not afford the $1,000 asking price. The painting, an action scene of barefoot schoolboys hard at play, reminded Butler of his youth, and the schoolhouse in the background was reminiscent of his Old White School House in Niles. His grandson, Joseph Butler III, later recalled that Butler saw the painting again in Paris in 1900 but still could not afford it. Now, in his post-fire, accelerated state of collecting, he employed the William Macbeth Company, a New York dealer specializing in American artists, to track down Homer's work. The firm succeeded, and Butler purchased the painting for $2,755.[37]

As the collection came together, he began looking ahead, anticipating the museum's opening and long-term operation, knowing the museum would require professional leadership if it was to be regarded with credibility. In October 1918, he hired 29-year-old Ethel Quinton Mason, whose sister-in-law was Cornelia Sage, director of the Albright Gallery in Buffalo. She began to work with McKim, Mead & White on design details and began preparing a catalog for the opening. She wrote Rhind in February 1919: "Work on the gallery goes on slowly but ... I love my work and my association with Mr. Butler."[38]

In the months preceding the opening, for reasons unknown, Butler let Mason go and hired Margaret Evans, an art teacher in the local schools who had studied at the University of Chicago and Columbia University. Evans would go on to serve as the museum's director for the next 16 years. Butler, who wanted the new museum to be an institute of learning as well as an exhibition gallery, may have felt that Evans's classroom experience made her better suited to develop the education department. Within two

The art museum, Youngstown's new "Lighthouse of Culture," nearing completion (The Butler Institute of American Art Archives, Youngstown, Ohio).

years, Evans advanced Butler's mission by developing four areas of study for local artists of varying degrees of talent.[39]

Slow but steady arrivals of marble and new supervision brought the construction phase to a successful, albeit, overdue ending. First, Ethel Q. Mason, and then Margaret Evans, along with Butler himself, worked on the exhibit layout with help from J. Massey Rhind. Most of the works were oils except for a few watercolors. Highlights included Robert Vonnoh's *In Flanders Field*, Winslow Homer's *Snap the Whip*, and George Inness's *Tragedy at Sea*. Butler paid a whopping $25,000 for the Inness, by far the highest price of any work in his collection. The Native American collection was on display, and a fresh portrait of Butler's late friend Henry Stambaugh by Ivan Olinsky was hung in the south gallery.[40]

On October 15, 1919, The Butler Art Institute held a private opening for 400 invited guests. Butler and his wife Harriet received guests throughout the afternoon. The *Vindicator* reported, "Joseph G. Butler Jr. was the happiest man in Youngstown Wednesday.... Mr. Butler, himself, art devotee, philanthropist, steel magnet [sic], traveler, author, and progressive and public-spirited citizen of Youngstown, very informally and genially

The happiest man in Youngstown astride the steps of his newly completed art museum (The Butler Institute of American Art Archives, Youngstown, Ohio).

welcomed everyone and with characteristic modesty waived all congratulations for himself and urged everyone to enjoy the paintings."[41]

On the following day the museum, dubbed by one reporter as the "lighthouse of culture" was "thrown open to the public." More than 1,000 people showed up.[42] The visitors were greeted by Rhind's two massive sculptures, Apollo, and Minerva, which stood guard in their respective niches on the front of the building. Inscribed on the frieze above the front doors was the Latin phrase, *Pro Bono Publico*, meaning "For the Public Good." Butler had decided upon it just one week after his house fire two years before. The cost of the completed museum, its property, and paintings was estimated to be $500,000.[43] Joseph Butler served as president of the board for the rest of his life.

Sixteen

Writing the Final Chapters

HENRY CLAY FRICK, supporter of the McKinley Memorial Library, traveled to Niles on October 29, 1919, to see firsthand the project to which he had contributed so generously. In late November, Frick suddenly took ill and died on December 2, 1919.[1] Butler traveled to Pittsburgh to attend the funeral. The train ride home from Pittsburgh to Youngstown had been made so many times over the years that Butler probably could see the passing scenery with his eyes closed. After arriving at the downtown train depot, Butler started the familiar walk home up Wick Avenue.

Maneuvering his automobile through the traffic that Friday afternoon was H.H. Winfield, who brought his vehicle to a stop at the intersection of Wick and Rayen avenues. Butler began to cross the street just as the cars started to move again. Although Winfield's auto moved slowly, he struck the 78-year-old Butler, knocking him to the pavement. Butler was brought home unconscious with a noticeable scalp wound. Further examination revealed a broken rib and multiple contusions. He was tended to throughout the night. Henry reported the next morning that his father was in much pain but "resting as comfortably as could be expected."[2]

It became evident that most of the harm was done to Butler's legs, and the pain he experienced was at times excruciating. The early prognosis was positive with doctors expecting the spirited patient to be much improved in a matter of weeks.[3] The injuries, however, proved far more serious than anyone could know and would compromise Butler's health for the rest of his life. Though slowed by the unfortunate accident and lengthy recuperation, his determination was not diminished. Rather, he displayed extraordinary energy and courage to get through some painful days. Butler occasionally would seek respite in the therapeutic air of the seaside town of Atlantic City, New Jersey. Fortunately, many of his projects and business interests were physically less strenuous and required little travel.

In the 1920s, despite lingering pain from his auto accident and his ongoing therapy, Butler would focus his energy in four areas: continue to buy paintings to expand the collection of the Butler Art Institute; write books and articles, use his political contacts and influence to promote his favorite Republican candidates; and spend time with his family.

The ensuing winter months found Butler in bed with pen and paper nearby. His reputation as an author was also growing. By 1920, he had produced five books including his latest, *Fifty Years of Iron and Steel*, an expansion of a speech he gave to the American Iron and Steel Institute in 1917. In Butler's estimation it was the most important book he had written.[4]

There were many other positive developments in 1920 that were extremely gratifying to Butler. One was the U.S. Supreme Court's long-awaited ruling in *United States v. United States Steel Corporation,* that the United States Steel Corporation was a legal organization, not an illegal trust. Butler praised the high court's decision and credited Elbert Gary for his vision and guidance. The decision, Butler said, meant that industry could proceed "unhampered by the menace of vindictive legislation."[5]

Butler was also gratified to see new support for the Merchant Marines, a cause for which he and Myron Herrick had been advocating for much of the previous decade. The original intent was to boost the sale of domestic exports through the construction of private shipbuilding, but in the early years of the movement the proposal failed to gain the necessary funding from Congress. After witnessing the importance of the Merchant Marine in carrying out wartime auxiliary naval duties, Congress favored a new level of support resulting in the passage of the Merchant Marine Act of 1920.

With President Wilson's second term ending, conservatives hoped that a Republican would replace the ailing Democrat. Butler was asked by local leaders to attend the convention in Chicago that June as a delegate for Warren G. Harding.[6] He had first touted Harding's presidential candidacy in 1914 when Harding had come to town to speak to the Youngstown Chamber of Commerce.

Days before the nomination, Harding expressed doubt as to his chances against his rivals, who included General Leonard Wood, Governor Frank Lowden of Illinois, Senator Hiram Johnson of California, Columbia College President Nicholas Murray Butler, and Governor Calvin Coolidge of Massachusetts. Harding would need a stalemate to occur. Much like Abraham Lincoln's strategy in 1860, Harding would have to wait patiently in the background and make himself everyone's candidate of second choice.[7]

The Ohio delegation was led by former Ohio governor Myron T. Herrick as chairman and Butler as vice-chairman. Butler's trip to the Chicago Republican Convention was done against the wishes of his physician, but he was not to be denied a chance to engage in one more political battle.

Sixteen. Writing the Final Chapters

Butler also had been elected one of the vice-chairmen of the convention. Will H. Hays, Republican National Committee chairman, asked him to sit on the convention platform, but, as the *Youngstown Telegram* reported, "the Youngstown man refused, saying he could do more for Harding sitting in the midst of the delegates on the floor of the convention." The convention opened with a hint of uncertainty, but on the second day Harding gained support.[8]

After the first several ballots, the delegates behind Wood and Lowden would neither concede nor swing their support to the other. Instead, neither candidate approached the required 680-plus votes. But Harding's dark horse candidacy was still considered a long shot. Butler addressed the Ohio delegates, "I said that if Harding went into the Convention [the next day] with less votes than he had on the last ballot, his chance for nomination was gone; that if he showed the same strength on the first ballot the following day, his chances were good."[9]

Harding's role as a compromise candidate improved as his vote tally slowly increased. On the ninth ballot, the *Telegram* claimed, it was Butler who "succeeded in inducing Wyoming to cast its solid vote for the Ohio senator, and on the tenth and last ballot it was his influence that induced Pennsylvania to swing 60 votes to Harding clinching his hold on the nomination."[10]

The last order of business was to select a vice-presidential running mate for Harding. When the convention's chairman called for vice presidential nominees, Ohio's Chairman Myron Herrick proclaimed his state's entire vote for Wisconsin Senator Irvine Lenroot. Surprised by Herrick's motion, Butler rose in protest as quickly as he could to proclaim his support for Coolidge. Butler learned later that Harding had asked Herrick to place Lenroot's name for a vote. At the time, however, Butler believed Coolidge to be the right choice. The *Youngstown Telegram* again reported with some exaggeration that Butler's "influence with surrounding delegations was sufficient to sweep the governor into nomination."[11]

The press reported, "Few if any of the delegates and visitors withstood the grinding work of the convention and the stifling heat as did the venerable Butler. He was not absent once from the convention floor during the whole convention period and none worked harder for Harding's nomination."[12]

Butler said that the 1920 Convention was one of the most worthwhile endeavors he had participated in. How much he was able to influence other delegates is debatable, but he did his best to sway opinions and believed that his efforts helped to advance Harding's name. But the effort took a physical toll on Butler, who confessed in a letter to ex-President Taft, "The Convention ... was too much for me. I came home a physical wreck."[13]

The next three months found him confined to his home under the care of his doctors and nurses. He continued to write and address legal issues concerning both business and pleasure. He employed the services of his lawyer, William W. Zimmerman, a trusted legal adviser for many years. Zimmerman handled his client's personal and business interests including his will, the McKinley Memorial, his silver-mining venture in Nevada, and his ore-mining interests in Michigan. Butler also needed Zimmerman during that summer to help prepare the legal instruments that would transfer the Butler Art Institute to the city of Youngstown and to purchase additional adjoining property for the museum grounds before the re-dedication ceremony in September.

Butler never intended to retain ownership of the art museum and in 1920 donated the structure and its contents to the city of Youngstown. The museum had been the dream of so many Mahoning Valley art enthusiasts for so long it was only fitting, he reasoned, for the museum to belong to the people and the city whereby it should remain forever free for their enjoyment.

The ceremony was held on September 10, 1920. Butler was in "considerable physical discomfort" and remained seated when he delivered his address. Assembled in the south wing, Butler announced he was transferring the museum's deed from his name to that of the Butler Art Institute under the control of a self-perpetuating board of trustees that included Butler, his son Henry, grandson John Willard Ford, John Stambaugh, and Jonathan Warner. It would no longer belong to Butler. He also announced the purchase of property behind the gallery extending the boundary of the grounds westward to Bryson Street to accommodate plans for future expansion. Cognizant that such well-intended gifts could strain city finances, Butler created an endowment fund of $200,000. An emotional Butler concluded his remarks by saying the gift to the people of his community was "a token of my affectionate regard and my earnest desire for the betterment of conditions of our community."[14]

Butler continued to add to the permanent collection of the Butler Art Institute as he sought out the best works of American artists that he could afford. He had hoped to expand the museum as early as 1921, but he and the other trustees concluded that the Institute could not afford such an undertaking at present.[15]

The Niles Chamber of Commerce declared October 23, 1920, Butler Day in the city. The event was marked by a parade to the delight of the 5,000 spectators who attended. Butler was presented a silver loving cup, and there was talk of making the event an annual celebration.[16]

In November, Butler's physicians decided upon surgery to help the now disabled benefactor. Following the procedure, Butler sent nearly

Sixteen. Writing the Final Chapters

identical messages to many of his friends informing all that a "serious operation" had taken place; however, he provided no specific details. Unfortunately, the operation did little to alleviate the pain or improve his strength and mobility.[17] He returned home for another period of prolonged confinement in time to observe the first anniversary of the accident and celebrate his 80th birthday.

On January 10, 1921, Butler and Harriet marked their 55th wedding anniversary. The occasion was bittersweet for the aging couple. He was in constant pain, and Harriet's health was even more perilous due to a deteriorating heart condition. She died of heart failure on the morning of April 27, 1921. Harriet was failing for some time, and her passing came as no surprise.[18]

Henry Audubon Butler in 1922. An aging and invalid Butler increasingly relied on his son to look after his business and personal affairs (The Mahoning Valley Historical Society, Youngstown, Ohio).

Harriet's funeral took place two days later at St. John's Episcopal Church, just a few doors down Wick Avenue from the Butler residence. Her husband was too weak to attend, so a private ceremony was held inside the Butler household before the officiants proceeded to the church. Interment followed at Belmont Park Cemetery where Butler had previously purchased a large family plot and had erected a memorial. The large square slab had two larger than life statues standing on each side. The angel-like figures sculpted by J. Massey Rhind symbolize art and industry, the passions of the man who would someday lie beneath their shadow.[19]

Despite his physical afflictions and the loss of Harriet, Butler moved forward with many ongoing projects. The trustees of the McKinley Memorial purchased property for the museum grounds, accepted artifacts related to McKinley, and ordered busts and bronze tablets for worthy honorees. A bust of President Harding was added in June 1921 with Vice-President Calvin Coolidge on hand for the unveiling. Afterward the vice-president stopped at the Butler Art Institute before calling on Butler at his residence.[20]

At the request of the American Historical Society, Butler had been compiling the *History of Youngstown and the Mahoning Valley*, a far more laborious undertaking than any of his previous books. As he noted in the preface, "Writing local history is always a difficult and usually a thankless task.... To ascertain the true facts requires painstaking investigation, which often discloses the frailty of human memory." At age 80, he was personally acquainted with many of the people and events he was chronicling. He also was considerably aided by two men, Raymond J. Kaylor, publicity director for Youngstown Sheet & Tube Company, who had helped him with *Fifty Years of Iron and Steel*; and Albert A. Reilly of the *Telegram* staff, who gathered much of the information and helped Butler to organize it. Volume 1 covered the local history; volumes 2 and 3 included biographical sketches of those who had contributed to the development and growth of Youngstown.[21]

The last chapter of volume 1 was titled "Personal Reminiscences." Here Butler took the opportunity to write 31 pages of his own memories of events from his youthful days in Niles, his involvement in the evolution of the Valley's business scene, his participation in presidential elections, and other personal stories.

History of Youngstown and the Mahoning Valley was published by the American Historical Society in 1921. Butler considered the three-volume work to be "the most complete history of Youngstown and the Mahoning Valley written up to the present time."[22] More than a century later it remains the Mahoning Valley's most in-depth historical account and often the first stop for many students of local history.

In the summer of 1921, Butler spent five weeks in Atlantic City, New Jersey, at the advice of his physician. In a letter to President Harding, Butler provided a health update: "I am slowly recovering but it looks as if my ultimate recovery is a long way ahead.... I am able to walk a short distance with the aid of a cane, but it is difficult."[23]

After completing *History of Youngstown*, Butler began writing a travel book. In late 1921 he privately printed 200 copies of *My First Trip Abroad*, an account of his first trip to Europe in 1908. In 1922, Penton Press of Cleveland published the book, which gave it a much wider circulation.

In January 1922, *The Blast Furnace & Steel Plant*, a trade publication, published a lengthy profile of Butler, whom the editors called the "most beloved citizen of the Mahoning Valley." The article concluded, "No other man has rendered such energetic and unselfish service to his country and his community, and he stands out among the historic figures of which northeastern Ohio has produced so large a number."[24]

Butler pored over several daily newspapers and had recently installed a radio to stay informed. Henry and the grandchildren frequently stopped in to check on him. Friends and old business acquaintances often came to visit. And he continued to write. When he tired, a stenographer was available.[25]

On April 1, 1923, the Youngstown Sheet & Tube Company purchased the Brier Hill Steel Company along with the Steel and Tube Company of America in the Chicago district. Butler, who remained vice-president of Brier Hill Steel, later wrote, "The price fixed for the absorption of the Brier Hill Steel Company properties by the Youngstown Sheet & Tube Company was first agreed upon between Mr. Campbell and myself. Throwing the name 'Brier Hill' into the discard was a bitter pill for me to swallow, but I swallowed it with the best possible grace." It was a lucrative deal for stockholders of both companies. Brier Hill, wrote Butler, was now "cherished as a memory and Sheet & Tube is a successful reality."[26]

In the summer of 1923, Butler was back in Atlantic City for several weeks of recuperation. While there, he and the rest of the country received the shocking news of the death of President Warren G. Harding. Butler described the loss of their nearly 30-year friendship as "a severe blow."[27] More hard news would soon arrive.

For some time, his daughter Grace's husband, Arthur McGraw, had been ailing and was in New York receiving medical treatment. After several months it became apparent that the Detroit businessman's health was dire. Suffering one final bout of depression over his condition, McGraw committed suicide. The *Youngstown Vindicator* reported, "Friday morning while taking his usual walk, accompanied by his nurse, he suddenly dashed from her side, hurdled two iron railings, and leaped through an air shaft to the tracks of the New York Central Railroad, 80 feet below. Death was instantaneous."[28] His death on August 31, 1923, and how it occurred was a tremendous shock to the Butler family.

Such unexpected, tragic events like McGraw's and Harding's deaths gave Butler reason for reflection. Time was running out to keep a promise he had made to his daughter, Blanche, before her death in 1913. Butler had never been a member of an organized religion. He was a professed Christian and attended many services of various denominations. In fulfilling his promise to Blanche, Butler, surrounded by family at home, was baptized in the Episcopal Church on Easter Sunday, 1924.[29]

Butler was working on, or at least thinking about, writing several books at the same time. He had begun to record his life story during the previous decade. Many of those accounts were recalled in letters to friends and families. Butler's first attempt at an autobiographical sketch had occurred in 1910 at his 70th birthday celebration where he read from a speech that he had taken great care to prepare. The greatest of his civic contributions as well as his post–McKinley era political campaigns had not yet occurred, nor had the historic war time trip through France. By the mid–1920s, Butler decided that these and other stories needed to be told. He again depended on the assistance of the trusted and reliable Kaylor. While working on his autobiography, he decided to publish an updated account of his McKinley biography and the history of the National McKinley Birthplace Memorial, highlighting the building's successful development since its opening in 1917. In October 1924, he sent Kaylor a 24-page memo outlining a possible biography of Governor David Tod. He also considered doing an updated and greatly expanded version of his *Fifty Years of Iron and Steel*. Ultimately, Butler did not pursue either of these projects.[30]

One project that still interested Butler was Sulgrave Manor, the ancestral home of George Washington in Northamptonshire, England, which he had first visited in August 1910. By 1921, the restoration of Sulgrave Manor was completed, and the house was opened to the public. That same year Butler reprinted his essay, "A Day in Washington's Country," as the final chapter of his latest book, *My First Trip Abroad*. In 1924, the National Society of the Colonial Dames of America raised $112,000 to be used for perpetual care of the site.[31]

By 1925, the cordial relationship between the American branch and the British branch of the Sulgrave Institution had soured. W. Lanier Washington, a descendant of the first president, wrote to Butler on February 22, 1925, to apprise him of the current situation. He told Butler of British plans to create a new corporation to take title of the Manor. "A most preposterous proposition," Washington wrote, "and to forestall any such attempt it is proposed to send to England, Mr. Charles Stewart Davison, one of the ablest lawyers in New York, who is a graduate of Cambridge, and who first practiced law in England, to act in our behalf." Butler later received a copy of a scathing letter written by Attorney Davison to a British law firm condemning most strongly a document produced by the British branch.[32] The matter was eventually resolved, though Butler played no role in the resolution. Sulgrave Manor remains today a tourist site just as Butler envisioned. The project in its infancy was conceived by Butler, yet he received very little credit for the idea.

Butler spent much of 1924 working on his own autobiography. His earlier books all contained autobiographical elements, and Butler had long been accustomed to writing extensive memos about his travels. He tended to keep copies of his correspondence, providing him with a variety of sources from which to draw. Butler noted that Youngstown's history was less than 125 years old, and he had lived in the city for half that time and had witnessed much of its development.

Butler's *Recollections of Men and Events, Being Some Account of Activities, Experiences, Observations and Personal Impressions During a Long and Busy Life*, was published by Penton Press in the spring of 1925 in a limited edition. Butler had looked to his dutiful son to write the book's introduction. That decision was as much practical as it was poignant. Henry had faithfully attended to his father over the years and more so after the accident. The introduction was a tribute to the legacy his father hoped to leave behind. He gave special notice to the commitment his father made to the improvement of his community, which he regarded as Youngstown, the Mahoning Valley, and the United States in general.

As the title announced, the book was a recollection of the most popular business and political figures, and world leaders that Butler had encountered in a lifetime of constant activity. He expounded upon the components essential to success: namely, industry, good judgment, and the courage to act.

Recollections was well received in the local papers and trade journals. The *Ohio History Quarterly* said Butler's effort was, "a distinct contribution to state and local history with interesting excursions into wider fields." Butler would later write to his friend, John Penton, after his company published three editions, "The book was brought to the attention of G.P. Putnam's Sons. I made a contract for one thousand copies."[33]

More signs of the community's affection came his way. The Veterans of Foreign Wars asked Butler for the second year in a row to be the general chairman for Youngstown's Defense Day celebration on July 4, 1925, a sure sign that his beloved city had not forgotten its most popular citizen or his legendary patriotic zeal.[34]

As the end of 1925 approached, Butler relied on the assistance of a nurse to move about. His house was like a hospital, and he was coming to understand that his nurses, Ann O'Brien and Delia Concricote, were providing more than rehabilitation exercises and in fact were rendering assistance with everyday needs.

Aside from writing, Butler took great pleasure in compiling letters, articles, news clippings, invitations, menus, poems, ticket stubs, White House passes, and convention tickets into organized scrapbooks. When Butler would send out complimentary copies of his books to friends, libraries, and colleges, he would get thank you notes in return, and these would sometimes fill an entire scrapbook. Eventually these ephemera would fill more than 50 large scrapbooks.[35]

Butler devoted much of 1926 to turning his extensive collection of autographs and photographs into what would become his final book. *Autographed Portraits* consists of 221 biographical profiles; 40 are of women, a remarkable number given Butler's collecting targets: U.S. presidents; presidents of leading universities, railroads, and steel companies; the entire roster of the American Iron and Steel Institute; and a few leading clergy—all categories that included very few women in Butler's day. Of the 40 women, 30 are first ladies, and two others acted as White House hostesses.

Butler wrote most of the short biographies. In his preface, he gives credit to 10 other authors. The foreword was written by Butler's friend, former U.S. Supreme Court Justice John H. Clarke. *Autographed Portraits* was published in honor of Butler by his friends at the Butler Art Institute.[36]

In the spring of 1926, the M.A. Hanna Company of Cleveland bought the entire stock and holdings of the iron ore-mining firm known as the Tod-Stambaugh Company. The men of the Hanna Company, a shipping and ore-mining company with holdings throughout the Great Lakes region, hoped to enlarge their interests by acquiring the Youngstown-based operation that was founded in 1901 by Butler, David Tod, and John Stambaugh. Howard M. Hanna, Jr., one of the new owners, apologetically wrote Butler informing him that because of the purchase, "it is with great regret that I have to report that it seems necessary for us to discontinue your salary along with the discontinuing of the company's active existence."[37] However, as a stockholder of the Tod, Stambaugh Company, Butler would have been well paid for the sale.

Butler's days and activities continued to be simple yet productive. When he felt strong enough, and when the weather permitted, Butler would ask his chauffeur, Richard Evans, to take him on two-hour automobile rides. That December, family and friends gathered for a Christmas dinner and to celebrate Butler's 86th birthday. It was the last gathering for these members of the Butler clan as death, in the months ahead, continued its arbitrary assault on Butler's family and colleagues.[38]

The following summer on July 4, 1927, Edward L. Ford, widower of Blanche Butler Ford and Butler's loyal son-in-law, died at the age of 71. He had been stricken suddenly at home by an undetermined cause, possibly a stroke, and was hospitalized for three weeks before dying. Butler hardly had time to mourn Ford's death, for five weeks later he received the news that his friend Elbert Gary, host of the Gary dinners and the founder of U.S. Steel, had died. Gary was the head of U.S. Steel from its inception until his death on August 15, 1927. He also founded the American Iron and Steel Institute and served as its only president until his death. *The Iron Age* said of Gary, "Within and without the steel trade he is adjudged its greatest leader.... Commonly he is credited with doing much to bring in a new era

Sixteen. Writing the Final Chapters

in industry, marked by the principle of cooperation." By inviting Joseph Butler to each of the exclusive Gary dinners and by seeing that Butler was elected to the board of directors of the American Iron and Steel Institute, Gary played a significant part in elevating Butler to national prominence in the industry.[39]

Charles Schwab, first president of U.S. Steel and now head of Bethlehem Steel, had been elected to replace Gary as president of the A.I.S.I. On November 10, Schwab arrived in Youngstown to pay his respects to Butler. Schwab had once written Butler a touching letter describing his affection for the older man. "I think of you much more dearly than one would of a friend," wrote Schwab. "You seem like a brother or like a father or like an uncle to me, so dear have you grown to me in our years of friendship." The old companions visited for two hours exchanging memorable tales of their "olden days and golden days together."[40]

It was evident to the Butler family that they should make every effort to gather again to celebrate Butler's birthday in December. The endearing and beloved figure to his family, would turn 87 on December 21. His daughter, Grace, left Detroit by train with her son Dr. Arthur B. McGraw giving themselves plenty of travel time to arrive in Youngstown before the day of celebration. Butler received a telegram from Grace notifying him that she was en route.

Even though Butler's overall health was clearly in decline, there were no outward signs that death was imminent. On December 19, after dinner he spent the evening in quiet relaxation signing checks, writing, and reading. Adhering to his scheduled bedtime, he retired with the aid of his nurse at around 10:00 p.m. As the nurse turned to leave his bedside, she noticed that his breathing had suddenly grown heavy. He was unconscious in the instant it took her to return to his bedside. A physician and Henry were summoned immediately. With Henry seated at his father's bedside, Butler lingered in a state of unconsciousness until just after midnight when heart failure finally brought his life to a close one day short of his 87th birthday. "Father," Henry Butler reported, "died peacefully."[41]

As tributes to Joseph G. Butler, Jr., began to pour into Youngstown newspapers, in Niles, his bust at the National McKinley Birthplace Memorial was draped with a black cloth as a sign of mourning. It would remain for 30 days as a symbol of the profound grief and respect that the citizens of Butler's boyhood town felt toward him.[42]

The funeral was held on December 22, 1927, at St. John's Episcopal Church where Harriet had been eulogized six years earlier. Mourners gathered outside the church before the scheduled 3:00 p.m. services. People and flowers overflowed the inside of the church, a scene unequaled in its history. Butler's surviving siblings, James Butler and Mrs. Edwin

Clarke, arrived from Cleveland as did John Penton. Others from near and far made the trip during the busy holiday season to hear the eulogy delivered by the Rev. W.A. Leonard, Bishop of the Protestant Episcopal Diocese of Ohio. He was assisted by the Rev. L.W.S. Stryker, rector of St. John's. After the church service ended, the longest funeral procession in the city's history followed the hearse carrying Joseph G. Butler, Jr., to Belmont Park Cemetery to lay Youngstown's First Citizen to rest alongside his wife under the two statuary figures carved by J. Massey Rhind that symbolized art and industry.[43]

Epilogue

A WEEK AFTER BUTLER'S DEATH, Attorney John W. Ford filed his grandfather's will in Mahoning County Probate Court. The size of Butler's estate was estimated to be $1,500,000; however, three weeks later appraisers increased its value to $2,233,884.

Butler signed his will on July 8, 1924, but he continued to amend it with codicils added on November 20, 1924, May 14, 1926, November 1, 1926, and July 1, 1927—evidence that he was thoughtful about his bequests.

As he had been in life, Butler was generous in death. The largest gifts to local institutions were $100,000 each to the endowment funds of the Butler Art Institute and the National McKinley Birthplace Memorial. He also gave $50,000 to Youngstown Hospital, $10,000 to St. Elizabeth's Hospital, and $5,000 to Christ Mission.

To his brother James, Butler gave $2,000 plus a $100 per month allowance for life and a residence in Cleveland. Butler's sister, Emma Clarke, received $1,000 plus a $100 per month allowance for life.

His son, Henry, received $100,000 with an additional $5,000 going to Henry's wife. Butler's widowed daughter, Grace McGraw, received $50,000. The five grandchildren received varying amounts with $10,000 to Josephine Ford Agler, $7,500 each to John W. Ford and Arthur B. McGraw, $25,000 to Joseph G. Butler III, and $2,500 to Mary Grace Butler, Henry's adopted daughter. Butler's eight great-grandchildren each got $2,500 in trust accounts.

Butler's housekeeper Margaret McElhaney and his personal attorney W.H. Wulf each received $5,000. His nurses, stenographers, secretary, chauffeur, and some staff members of the Butler Art Institute got smaller amounts.

Control of the Butler Art Institute was left in the hands of a five-person board of trustees made up entirely of Butler's family; his son Henry served as president, his grandsons John W. Ford and Joseph G. Butler III, and his grandson-in-law Benjamin Agler were also appointed. Several valuable paintings were left to the gallery while some were distributed to family members.

Another of Butler's legacies was that he imbued his children and grandchildren with the same spirit of philanthropy that had characterized his life. John W. Ford, his sister Josephine Agler, and their uncle, Henry Butler, erected a maternity wing at Northside Hospital as a memorial to their families.

Henry, who received the largest bequest, had been groomed for years to take his father's place as head of a number of organizations and companies. He also took his father's place on the board of trustees of the Rueben McMillan Free Library. The *Youngstown Telegram* noted that "During the depression to aid skilled workmen of the city in providing for their families, he took funds from the estate and built a wing at the institute at a cost of $150,000, providing work for some 50 men over a period of several months." In 1932, Henry and Phillip Wick merged their brokerage firms, Butler, Beadling and Wick & Company, to form the Butler-Wick investment firm.

Unfortunately, Henry outlived his father by only seven years. He died of a heart attack on April 26, 1934, following his usual Thursday round of golf with friends. Following Henry's death, Joseph G. Butler III became the third generation of the Butler family to run the Butler Art Institute. However, instead of becoming president of the board, he became director of the gallery, replacing long-time director, Margaret Evans.

Joseph G. Butler III directed the Butler Art Institute for 47 years until his death in June 1981. Under his tenure, the art collection grew from 100 works of art to more than 5,000. He created what is now known as the National Midyear Show, an exhibition of national importance.

Joseph G. Butler, Jr., should be remembered for many things. He should be credited for helping to nurture and guide the iron industry during the competitive era of the late 19th century. The success of that industry surely brought wealth to owners, but it also gave employment to thousands. The growth of the iron and steel industry helped the Mahoning Valley grow in importance.

Of course, he was not a perfect man and critics could cast dispersions on his hard business approach and his negativity toward organized labor. Although he was quick to condemn the rioters of the East Youngstown strike, he made no effort to really understand the cause of their anger and grievances when he wrote the history of that event. Instead, he inaccurately blamed their violent reaction on alcohol and immoral Euro-ethnic values at a time when major industrial cities were flooded with tens of thousands of immigrants who spoke different languages, adhered to ethnic and old familial customs, held different values, and worshipped in unfamiliar ways.[1] Still, he reached out to them indirectly, if not directly. Unsurprisingly, he tried through the medium of art, the one universal commonality among all peoples. Some of the art institute's first shows invited the city's ethnic groups to participate and showcase their talents. He wanted all to enjoy the museum.

Butler was not shy about promoting America's values and supported the "Americanization" efforts taking place during the World War I era. But much of this movement was rooted in safety. Attempts to educate and teach English to recent immigrants was as much about workplace safety as it was about becoming loyal Americans.

Most of Butler's efforts were attempts to improve the quality of life for the citizens of the community. The Mahoning Valley can list its fair share of benefactors over its long and fruitful history, but Butler was one of the first to emerge. His contributions were certainly the most diverse. His fundraising efforts to expand St. Elizabeth Hospital surely improved the lives of countless residents over the decades long after his own death. Butler should also be remembered for the gifts he gave the community that continue to enrich the lives of generations of citizens and will continue to do so long into the future.

The memorial to honor William McKinley's birth and his art museum are the most visible and strikingly beautiful gifts. His work to secure a modern library for Youngstown, his donations to many other libraries, his fundraising efforts and donations to local hospitals, his work to save Sulgrave Manor, his patriotic service to sell bonds during World War I, his work for animal welfare, and his efforts to preserve and collect local history are a few contributions. Hopefully, this work will cause a new appreciation for the efforts he made to improve the quality of life for so many.

He lived by a few simple beliefs which guided him throughout his life, a life that was as surely self-made as any other. He achieved success in a variety of arenas throughout a very busy and useful life. He garnered the honorary title, "Youngstown's First Citizen," not because he carried himself in an arrogant and pretentious manner above and in front of others but rather, because by and large he put the interests of the citizens of Youngstown first.

Chapter Notes

Preface

1. "The Joseph Butler, Jr. Testimonial Banquet," December 21, 1910, and, *The Youngstown Telegram*, December 22, 1910.

Introduction

1. Clayton Ruminski, *Iron Valley, The Transformation of the Iron Industry in Ohio's Mahoning Valley, 1802–1913* (Columbus, Ohio: Trillium, an imprint of The Ohio State University Press, 2017), 115.
2. See John Higham, *Strangers in the Land* (New York: Rutgers University, 2002) and Susan F. Martin, *A Nation of Immigrants* (New York: Cambridge University, 2011).
3. Steve Fraser, *The Age of Acquiescence: The Life and Death of American Resistance to Organized Wealth and Power*. (Boston: Little, Brown and Company, 2015) and Sean Dennis Cashman, *America in the Gilded Age: From the Death of Lincoln to the Rise of Theodore Roosevelt*. (New York: New York University Press, 1984).
4. Charles William Calhoun, *The Gilded Age: Perspectives on the Origins of Modern America* (Washington, D.C.: Rowman & Littlefield, 2007).
5. "The Joseph Butler, Jr. Testimonial Banquet," December 21, 1910, and, *The Youngstown Telegram*, December 22, 1910.
6. Michael Hiltzik's *Iron Empires, Robber Barons, Railroads and the Making of Modern America*, (New York: Houghton Mifflin, Harcourt, 2020), is the most recent study of the spirited competition among the industrial leaders of the post–Civil War era whose drive to succeed enriched their fortunes and propelled the industrial advancements of the United States.

Chapter One

1. The term comes from the 1873 satirical novel *The Gilded Age: A Tale of Today* by Mark Twain and Charles Dudley Warner.
2. Joseph G. Butler, Jr., *History of Youngstown and the Mahoning Valley, Ohio*, vol. 1 (Chicago: American Historical Society, 1921), 14.
3. William David Butler, John Cromwell Butler, Joseph Marion Butler, *Butler Family in America*. (St. Louis, Missouri: Shallcross Printing Co., 1909), 13. Joseph Marion Butler of Chicago was the principal author of the section of this book dealing with the direct ancestry of his uncle, Joseph G. Butler, Jr. Joseph Marion Butler, born August 18, 1858, was the oldest child of Ithamar Marion Butler, who was Joseph G. Butler Jr.'s oldest brother.
4. William David Butler, John Cromwell Butler, Joseph Marion Butler, *Butler Family in America*, 25–27.
5. William David Butler, John Cromwell Butler, Joseph Marion Butler, *Butler Family in America*, 38, 41–43. In *Reflections of Men and Events*, his autobiography, Joseph G. Butler, Jr., erroneously claims his grandfather, Joseph Butler (first) sired eight children, four each by his two wives. In fact, Esther Green, his first wife, bore him eight children before she died; Rachel Parker, his second wife, produced five more children. *The Butler Family in America*, 41–42, lists the names and birth, death, and marriage dates of all 13 children.

6. Butler, *Recollections*, 4; *Butler Family in America*, 43.

7. William David Butler, John Cromwell Butler, Joseph Marion Butler, *Butler Family in America*, 44.

8. Dale E. Shafer, *Salem, A Quaker City History, The Making of America Series*, (Charleston, S.C.: Arcadia Publishing, 2002), 8; George D. Hunt, *History of Salem and the Immediate Vicinity*. Originally published by the author in 1898. Reproduced by Unigraphic, Inc., 17.

9. William David Butler, John Cromwell Butler, Joseph Marion Butler, *Butler Family in America*. 47.

10. Butler, *Recollections*, 6.

11. Bining, "The Rise of Iron Manufacture," 243.

12. Joseph Riesenman, Jr., *History of Northwestern Pennsylvania, Comprising the Counties of Erie, Crawford, Mercer, Venango, Warren, Forest, Clarion, McKean, Elk, Jefferson, Cameron and Clearfield*, vol. I (New York: Lewis Historical Publishing Company, Inc., 1943), 390; Joseph G. Butler, Jr., places the birthplace of his older brother Miles Green Butler at Temperance Furnace. The authors of *The Butler Family in America* say Miles was born in Centre County, Pennsylvania. There are other discrepancies in the spellings and birth dates of other siblings. Compare Butler, *Recollections*, 16, with *The Butler Family in America*, 47. We regard the latter as more carefully researched and thus more accurate.

13. J.G. White, *A Twentieth Century History of Mercer County, Pennsylvania*, vol. (Chicago: The Lewis Publishing Company, 1909), 80.

14. Hughes, "The Pioneer Iron Industry in Western Pennsylvania," 218–19.

15. McKnight, *A Pioneer Outline History of Northwestern Pennsylvania*, 584; *Youngstown Vindicator*, August 9, 1942; *Combination Atlas of the County of Mercer and the State of Pennsylvania, From Actual Surveys and Official Records*, (Philadelphia: G.M. Hopkins and Company, 1873), 73. In 1851, Sandy Creek Township was sub-divided into four new townships. The section Joseph Green Butler had settled in was renamed Mineral Township and later again renamed Perry Township.

16. For a recent history of the Panic of 1837, see Alasdair Roberts, *America's First Great Depression: Economic Crisis and Political Disorder After the Panic of 1837* (Ithaca, NY: Cornell University Press, 2012).

17. White, *A Twentieth Century History*, 80; *History of Mercer County, with Illustrations* (1877), 129.

18. The ad that Butler place in the *Mercer Luminary* on January 24,1838, is reproduced in its entirety in an article by John L. Morrison in the *Youngstown Vindicator*, August 9, 1942.

19. John L. Morrison, "Butler, McKinley Were Partners in Project." *Youngstown Vindicator*, August 9, 1942; *A Pictorial History of Niles, Ohio*, Bicentennial Edition (Niles, Ohio: Niles Historical Society, 1976), 9; Charles S. Olcott, *William McKinley*, (Boston: Houghton Mifflin Company, 1916), 6.

20. Joseph G. Butler, Jr., "Wonderful Development of the Iron Business," *Iron Age* 100, no. 18 (November 17, 1917), 1043; *History of Mercer County, with Illustrations* (1877), 128.

21. Butler, *Recollections*, 5–6; Riesenman, *History of Northwestern Pennsylvania*, 384.

22. White, *A Twentieth Century History of Mercer County*, 351.

23. Walker, *Hopewell Village*, 165, 120.

24. Joseph G. Butler, Jr., *Recollections of Men and Events, An Autobiography, Being Some Account of Activities, Experiences, Observations and Personal Impressions During a Long and Busy Life* (New York: G.P. Putnam's Sons, 1927), 8.

25. *Combination Atlas of the County of Mercer*, 73.

26. *A Pictorial History of Niles, Ohio*, 222.

27. *A Pictorial History of Niles, Ohio*, 11, 66; Marc Harris, "James Ward." *Iron and Steel in the Nineteenth Century*, ed. Paul F. Paskoff, 353; Marilyn R. Lown, *The Pennsylvania and Ohio Canal: A Brief History*, I, 4–6. Lown provides a good account of life on the canal and the types of boats that used the canal.

28. *Combination Atlas of the County of Mercer*, 73; Mulkearn and Pugh, *A Traveler's Guide*, 283; William Butler, *Butler Family in America*, 61. The new owners renamed the furnace, "Harry of the West," after statesman Henry Clay.

29. Morgan, *William McKinley and His America*, 5; Olcott, *William McKinley*, 10–11.

Chapter Two

1. *Bicentennial History Book* (Warren, Ohio: Warren-Trumbull County Bicentennial Commission, 1976), 27; *Pictorial History of Niles*, 6. In his autobiography Joseph G. Butler, Jr., says his family arrived in Niles in 1841. The authors of the *Butler Family in America* say it was in 1842, the same year that James Ward began operating his rolling mill. We consider 1842 to be a more reliable date.

2. Marc Harris, "James Ward," *Encyclopedia of American Business History and Biography, Iron and Steel in the Nineteenth Century* (New York: Bruccoli Clark Layman and Facts on File, 1989), edited by Paul F. Paskoff, 353–54; Butler, *Recollections*, 38. See also, Clayton J. Ruminski, *Iron Valley, The Transformation of the Iron industry in Ohio's Mahoning Valley, 1802–1913* (Columbus, Ohio: The Ohio State University Press, Trillium, 2017, 56.

3. Stewart, *History of Northeastern Ohio*, vol. I, 244; William David Butler, John Cromwell Butler, Joseph Marion Butler, *Butler Family in America* (St. Louis, Missouri: Shallcross Printing Co., 1909), 61. Most sources say the Ward brothers' partner was Thomas Russell, not William.

4. United States Steel, *The Making, Shaping and Treating of Steel, Ninth Edition*, edited by Harold E. McGannon (Pittsburgh: Herbick & Held, 1971), 13.

5. Butler, *Recollections*, 9.

6. William David Butler, John Cromwell Butler, Joseph Marion Butler, *Butler Family in America*, 47–48; Joseph G. Butler, Jr., *Recollections*, 16. Joseph G. Butler Jr.'s list of siblings carried different birth dates for Emma and William, both of whom died in infancy. We have followed the dates listed in *The Butler Family in America*.

7. Butler, *Recollections*, 15–17.

8. Butler, *Recollections*, 19; Butler, *History of Youngstown*, vol. I: 824.

9. Butler, *History of Youngstown*, vol, I: 823–24.

10. Butler, *Recollections*, 33, 255; J.G. Butler to Josephine DeMott Robinson, January 10, 1927, MVHS; *Joseph G. Butler, Jr. Testimonial Banquet, December 21, 1910* (Cleveland: Penton Press, n.d.), 26.

11. Butler, *Recollections*, 10; Butler, *History of Youngstown*, vol. I: 822–23.

12. Butler, *Recollections*, 13.

13. Butler, *Life of William McKinley*, 5; Butler, *Recollections*, 10–11; Butler, *History of Youngstown*, vol. I: 822.

14. Butler, *Recollections*, 341.

15. "Reminiscences of Mrs. Eliza Ward Morris, October 12, 1915," Butler Scrapbook on the McKinley Memorial, MVHS.

16. Butler to Grace Butler McGraw, August 11, 1919, MVHS; Butler, *Recollections*, 27.

17. Butler to Grace Butler McGraw, August 11, 1919, MVHS.

18. Butler, *Recollections*, 27–28. Sixty-five years later in 1919, Butler made a nostalgic trip back to the Tremont Furnace site, which he described in a letter to his daughter, Grace. "The house where we lived is still standing and in good condition. The ruins of the furnace and surroundings are quite picturesque. I picked from the cinder dump a piece of pig iron, … and brought it home." Butler to Grace Butler McGraw, August 11, 1919. Butler Scrapbooks, vol. 4, page 115, MVHS.

19. Butler, *Recollections*, 28–29.

20. *Pictorial History of Niles*, 6.

21. Butler to James W. Butler, May 20, 1927, MVHS; James M. Swank, *History of the Manufacture of Iron in All Ages, and Particularly in the United States for Three Hundred years from 1585 to 1885* (Philadelphia: Allen, Lane and Scott, 1884), 248.

22. Butler, "Raw Materials," *Congratulatory Addresses Delivered at a Complimentary Dinner Tendered to Judge Elbert H. Gary*, Waldorf-Astoria, New York, October 15, 1909 (souvenir compliments of Iron Trade Review), 14; Butler, *Recollections*, 29.

23. Butler, *Recollections*, 31–32; *Joseph G. Butler, Jr. Testimonial Banquet, December 21, 1910*, 26.

24. Butler, "Wonderful Development." *Iron Age*, vol. 100, no. 18 (November 1, 1917): 1042.

25. Butler, *History of Youngstown*, vol. I: 821.

26. Hardy Green, *The Company Town: The Industrial Eden's and Satanic Mills That Shaped the American Economy*. (New York: Basic Books, A Member of the Perseus Books Group, 2010), 5. Green's study provides a fascinating sketch of the complex, dynamic, and exploitive relationship between owners and their employees.

27. Butler, *History of Youngstown*, vol. I: 820; Butler, *Recollections*, 37–38; *Joseph G. Butler, Jr. Testimonial Banquet, December 21, 1910*, 26.
28. Butler, *Recollections*, 32; *Joseph G. Butler, Jr. Testimonial Banquet, December 21, 1910*, 26.
29. Stewart, *History of Northeastern Ohio*, vol. I, 420–421; Butler, *Recollections*, 49–50.
30. Butler, *Recollections*, 35.
31. *Joseph G. Butler, Jr. Testimonial Banquet, December 21,1910*, 53–54.
32. Butler, *Recollections*, 51–52; *Joseph G. Butler, Jr. Testimonial Banquet, December 21, 1910*, 30.
33. Butler, *History of Youngstown*, vol. I: 834; Butler to Grace Butler McGraw, June 20, 1906, MVHS; Butler, *Presidents I Have Seen*, 1.
34. Butler, *Recollections*, 22, 37; Butler has a short profile of James Ward in Butler, *Autographed Portraits*, 174.
35. Butler, *Fifty Years of Iron and Steel*, 50; *Joseph G. Butler, Jr. Testimonial Banquet, December 21,1910*, 26; Butler, *Recollections*, 38.
36. Butler, *Recollections*, 39.
37. Clayton J. Ruminski, *Iron Valley, The Transformation of the Iron Industry in Ohio's Mahoning Valley, 1802–1913* (Columbus: The Ohio State University, Trillium Press, 2017), 116.
38. Duff's Business Institute file, Pennsylvania Department, Carnegie Library, Pittsburgh, PA; Butler, *Recollections*, 39.

Chapter Three

1. Butler, *Recollections*, 7.
2. Butler, *Recollections*, 40.
3. "Reminiscences of Mrs. Eliza Ward Morris," October 12, 1915, Butler Scrapbook on the McKinley Memorial, MVHS.
4. Butler, *Recollections*, 16, 107; *Joseph G. Butler, Jr. Testimonial Banquet, December 21, 1910*, 27.
5. Butler, *Recollections*, 16.
6. Ruminski, 104.
7. See Lester V. Horwitz, *The Longest Raid of the Civil War, Little-Known & Untold Stories of Morgan's Raid into Kentucky, Indiana & Ohio* (Cincinnati, OH: Farmcourt Publishing, Inc.), 2001.
8. *Joseph G. Butler, Jr. Testimonial Banquet, December 21, 1910*, 28.
9. Butler, *History of Youngstown*, vol. I: 819; Butler, *Recollections*, 46.
10. *Joseph G. Butler, Jr. Testimonial Banquet, December 21, 1910*, 28–29; Butler, *History of Youngstown*, vol. 1: 819; Butler, *Recollections*, 46. Also, see Horwitz, *The Longest Raid*.
11. Butler, *History of Youngstown*, vol. I: 198.
12. Swank, *History of the Manufacture of Iron in All Ages*,44.
13. Butler, *Recollections*, 53; *Joseph G. Butler, Jr. Testimonial Banquet, December 21, 1910*, 29.
14. Butler, *Recollections*, 343.
15. *Joseph G. Butler, Jr. Testimonial Banquet, December 21, 1910*, 29.
16. Butler, *Recollections*, 53.
17. Butler, *Recollections*, 69.
18. Blue, et al., *Mahoning Memories*, 66. The successor company to Hale & Ayer gained full control of the Brown, Bonnell Company in 1879 and operated it until 1899 when it was sold to the newly formed Republic Iron and Steel Company. See Butler, *History of Youngstown*, vol. 1,672; *Joseph G. Butler, Jr. Testimonial Banquet, December 21, 1910*, 29.
19. Butler, *History of Youngstown*, vol. I: 674; *Youngstown Vindicator*, March 27, 1938.
20. *Youngstown Vindicator*, May 8, 1867.
21. Butler, *Fifty Years*, 8; *Youngstown Vindicator*, December 20, 1977. Cogswell would go on to become a renowned portrait artist and paint many national figures including Abraham Lincoln and Ulysses Grant. See Peter E. Palmquist and Thomas R. Kailbourn, *Pioneer Photographers of the Far West, A Biographical Dictionary, 1840–1865* (Stanford University Press, 2000), 180. Some of his works will become part of the collection of the Butler Institute of American Art.
22. *Western Reserve Chronicle*, August 3, 1864; *Recollections*, 54, 56. For another account of the murder of James Ward, Sr., and the apprehension of the murderer, see Linda Freeman, "Case Study: A Ruthless and Savage Murder." *Western Reserve Historical Society Genealogy Bulletin*, vol. 35, no. 4 (Winter 2016): 1, 8–11; and vol. 36, no. 1 (Spring 2017): 4–6.
23. Ruminski, 117.

24. William T. Hogan, *Economic History of the Iron and Steel Industry in the United States, vol. I* (Lexington, Massachusetts: Fordham University, Lexington Books, 1971), 14.

25. Alvin W. Skardon, *Steel Valley University, The Origin of Youngstown State* (Cincinnati: C.J. Krehbiel Co., 1983), 9; Butler, *History of Youngstown*, vol. I: 200.

26. Butler, *History of Youngstown*, vol. I: 201; *Joseph G. Butler, Jr. Testimonial Banquet, December 21, 1910*, 30.

27. *History of Trumbull and Mahoning Counties with Illustrations*, vol. I: 172; *Biographical History of Northeastern Ohio, Embracing the Counties of Ashtabula, Trumbull, and Mahoning* (Chicago: The Lewis Publishing Company, 1893), 160.

28. *Joseph G. Butler, Jr. Testimonial Banquet, December 21, 1910*, 30.

29. The agreement signed by David Tod, William Ward, William Richards, and Joseph G. Butler, Jr., to form the Girard Iron Company is reprinted in Butler, *History of Youngstown*, vol. I: 686–87.

30. *History of Trumbull and Mahoning Counties with Illustrations*, 190; Popenoe/Popnoe/Poppino &Allied Families. Genealogy-Sylvanus Seely's Family, www.popenoe.com/Diary/Seely Diary2htm.; Butler, *Recollections*, 58.

31. National Society of the Daughters of the American Revolution, volume 39, page 251, Dar.htm.

32. Butler, *Recollections*, 57–61.

33. Henry Audubon Butler's middle name, according to Henry's own son years later, was given due to his father's admiration for the naturalist, John James Audubon. See "Butler Art Institute, Personal Experience," Joseph G. Butler, III interviewed by Paul Bick on December 10, 1975. Youngstown State University Oral History Program. The Butlers lived at 32 West Rayen Avenue for 24 years before moving to Wick Avenue.

34. Ruminski, 147.

35. *Youngstown Vindicator*, April 25, 1947.

Chapter Four

1. *Mahoning Courier*, February 28, 1866.

2. J. Lesley, *The Iron Manufacturer's Guide to the Furnaces, Forges and Rolling Mills of the United States with Discussion of Iron as A Chemical Element, An American Ore, and A manufactured Article, in Commerce and in History*, (New York: John Wiley Publisher, 1859), 110; Harriet Taylor Upton, *History of the Western Reserve*, vol. I (Chicago-New York: The Lewis Publishing Co., 1910), 619; Butler, *History of Youngstown*, vol. 1: 687.

3. Butler, *Recollections*, 71, 216.

4. *Joseph G. Butler, Jr. Testimonial Banquet, December 21, 1910*, 30.

5. Butler, *Recollections*, 71; Butler, *History of Youngstown*, vol. 1: 688.

6. Butler, *History of Youngstown*, vol. 1: 688.

7. Butler, *Recollections*, 108; Butler, *Autographed Portraits*, 124.

8. *History of Trumbull and Mahoning Counties with Illustrations*, 365; Butler, *History of Youngstown*, vol. 2: 202.

9. Wiebe, *Search for Order*, 13.

10. *Mahoning Courier*, December 16, 1868, carried an advertisement for the new bank. The officers and directors were listed, but the name of the president was left blank. David Tod's death had occurred so recently that the directors had not yet filled his position; Butler, *History of Youngstown*, vol. 1: 360. The original directors of the Youngstown Savings & Loan Association were David Tod, Chauncey H. Andrews, W.J. Hitchcock, F.O. Arms, T.K. Hall, Joseph G. Butler, Jr., T.H. Wells, John Stambaugh, David Theobald, Richard Brown, A.B. Cornell, B.F. Hoffman, and William Powers.

11. *Joseph G. Butler, Jr. Testimonial Banquet, December 21, 1910*, 30.

12. Butler, *Recollections*, 107.

13. See Ruminski, 137–140.

14. Butler, Autographed *Portraits*, 326.

15. Butler, *Recollections*, 73.

16. Butler, *Fifty Years*, 30; Kenneth Warren, *The American Steel Industry, 1850–1970. A Geographical Interpretation* (Oxford: Clarendon Press, 1973), 168; Ruminski, 139.

17. Butler, *History of Youngstown*, vol. 1: 678–79 (interests of William Ward and William Richards), 731–32 (brief profile of A.M. Byers Company), and Butler, *Autographed Portraits* (profile of A.M. Byers),108; Butler, *Recollections*, 72.

18. Warren, *The American Steel Industry*, 56.

19. Wiebe, *Search for Order*, 13; *Joseph G. Butler, Jr. Testimonial Banquet, December 21, 1910*, 32.
20. Butler, *History of Youngstown*, vol. 1: 732; Butler, *Autographed Portraits*, 124.
21. *Youngstown Vindicator*, January 7, 1870.
22. Theodore Clarke Smith, *The Life and Letters of James Abram Garfield*, vols. 1 & 2 (Yale University Press, 1968), 454–456; *Youngstown Vindicator*, January 7, 1870.
23. Kennon and Rogers, *House Documents* no. *100–244*, 197.
24. "The Tariff, English and American interests. Rejoicing in England. English iron masters jubilant over the downfall of American iron industry. The treason of Congress to American interests," *Miners' Journal*, May 14, 1870, *An American Time Capsule: Three Centuries of Broadsides and Other Printed Ephemera*.
25. Memorandum from Butler to Kaylor, October 11, 1924, 22. In 1876 after a decades-old legal battle with the village of Canfield, the city of Youngstown was finally made the county seat. See Butler, *History of Youngstown*, vol. I: 844, for an account of the dedication of the Soldiers Monument. Blue, et. al, *Mahoning Memories*, 59, has a photograph of the newly installed monument.
26. *Reifsnider & Gardner's Youngstown Directory*, Cleveland, OH: Reifsnider and Gardner, 1872. The three local newspapers and their political affiliations are listed on page 114. The Cleveland papers are advertised on a colored insert following page 72. The *Mahoning Register* was a Republican paper, the *Mahoning Vindicator* was Democratic, and the *Youngstown Courier* was Prohibitionist.
27. Butler, *History of Youngstown*, vol. 1: 184, 202–205.
28. Butler, *History of Youngstown*, vol. 1: 477, 206.
29. Theodore C. Smith, *Life and Letters of James Abram Garfield*, 515, 517, Butler, *History of Youngstown*, vol. 1: 206, 477.
30. Butler, *History of Youngstown*, vol. 1, 502, 686; Victor S. Clark, *History of Manufacture in the United States, Vol. II, 1860–1893* (New York: McGraw-Hill Book Co., Inc., 1929), 251.
31. Butler, *History of Youngstown*, vol. 1: 181, 771.
32. Kennon and Donald, *House Documents* no. 100–244, 187; J.H. Weirick to Butler, undated Scrapbook of *Presidents I've Seen & Known*," MVHS.
33. Butler, *Recollections*, 110. The investors were Emanuel Hartzell, Simon Hartzell, Allen Hellawell, Josiah Reamer, Wesley Wilson, and Joseph Butler.
34. *Youngstown Vindicator*, March 27, 1938.
35. *Youngstown Vindicator*, August 3, 1877.
36. Wiebe, *Search*, 10. For an interesting contemporary account of the railroad strike of 1877, see "The Strikes," *Harper's Weekly*, August 18, 1877, which strongly condemned the strikers.
37. Butler, *Recollections*, 238–239. See also Samuel Richey Kamm. *The Civil War Career of Thomas A. Scott: A Dissertation* (University of Pennsylvania), 1940.
38. *Toledo Review* reprinted in *Youngstown Vindicator*, August 24, 1877.
39. Wiebe, *Search*, 2.

Chapter Five

1. Butler, *Autographed Portraits*, 124.
2. Butler, *Recollections*, 71.
3. "Stockholders Meeting of Brier Hill Iron and Coal Company including contract between Brier Hill Iron and Coal Company and Joseph G. Butler, Jr., and Thomas H. Pollack, May 9, 1878," MVHS.
4. *Joseph G. Butler, Jr. Testimonial Banquet, December 21, 1910*, 30; Butler, *Recollections*, 74.
5. "Stockholders Meeting of Brier Hill Iron and Coal Company including contract between Brier Hill Iron and Coal Company and Joseph G. Butler, Jr., and Thomas H. Pollack, May 9, 1878," MVHS. The stockholders of the Brier Hill Iron & Coal Company were John Stambaugh, William Pollock, Grace Tod Arrel, Sallie Tod, Mrs. David Tod, Executors of David Tod, George Tod, Henry Tod, George T. Perkins, Nelson Crandall, and William Tod. Butler's salary of $2,000 per year would be the equivalent of $50,577 in 2018 dollars.
6. "Stockholders Meeting—Brier Hill, May 9, 1878"; Butler, *Recollections*, 73.
7. Butler, *Recollections*, 73.
8. Joseph Butler's years with the Girard Iron Company are recounted in Butler,

Recollections, 70–73, and Butler, *History of Youngstown*, vol. 1: 686–88.
 9. Butler, *Autographed Portraits*, 335.
 10. *Directory to the Iron and Steel Works of the United States, Embracing the Blast Furnaces, Rolling Mills, Steel Works, Forges, and Bloomaries in Every State and Territory* (Philadelphia: The American Iron and Steel Association, 1880), 64.
 11. *Youngstown Vindicator*, July 26, 1878.
 12. *Youngstown Vindicator*, July 26, 1878.
 13. Butler, *Recollections*, 74.
 14. *Youngstown Vindicator*, September 13, 1878; *Youngstown Vindicator*, July 26, 1878, September 27, 1878.
 15. Butler, "Wonderful Development." *Iron Age*, vol. 100, no. 18 (November 1, 1917): 1043.
 16. *Youngstown Vindicator*, December 13, 1878.
 17. OHS Fundamental Documents, David Tod, 43.
 18. *Youngstown Vindicator*, April 9, 1878; *Youngstown Vindicator*, June 6, 1878.
 19. Bodnar, *Transplanted*, 96.
 20. Butler, *Recollections*, 73; *Youngstown Vindicator*, September 5, 1879.
 21. Butler, *History of Youngstown*, vol. I: 212.
 22. *Youngstown Vindicator*, January 9, 1880.
 23. *Youngstown Vindicator*, January 16, 1880; Butler, *Recollections*, 75.
 24. *Youngstown Vindicator*, January 23, 1880; Butler, *Recollections*, 75.
 25. Raymond Boryczka and Lorin Lee Cary, *No Strength Without Union, an Illustrated History of Ohio Workers, 1803–1980* (Columbus: The Ohio Historical Society, 1982), 79.
 26. Butler, *History of Youngstown*, vol. 1: 675.
 27. *Youngstown City Directory, 1880*, 216.
 28. Butler, *Fifty Years*, 24, 37, 38, 40, 41; Swank, *History of the Manufacture of Iron*, 251.
 29. Swank, *History of the Manufacture of Iron*, 250.
 30. Warren, *The American Steel Industry*, 168.
 31. Warren, *The American Steel Industry*, 168.
 32. Hatcher, *Western Reserve*, 281.
 33. Butler, *Fifty Years*, 70.
 34. Butler's opinion of T.W. Kennedy is recorded in his autobiography, *Recollections*, 112. For his comments on Captain Bill Jones, see Butler, *Fifty Years of Iron and Steel*, 67.
 35. Butler, *Recollections*, 112, 114; *Youngstown Vindicator*, March 27, 1938.
 36. *Youngstown (OH) Weekly News and Register*, January 25, 1882, and February 22, 1882.
 37. *Youngstown Weekly News and Register*, June 21, 1882.
 38. Butler, *Recollections*, 75; Butler, *History of Youngstown*, vol. 1: 711.
 39. Butler, *Recollections*, 76; *Joseph G. Butler, Jr. Testimonial Banquet, December 21, 1910*, 31.
 40. John N. Ingham, *The Iron Barons, A Social Analysis of an American Urban elite, 1874–1965* (Westport, Connecticut: Greenwood Press, 1978), 67; *Youngstown Weekly News and Register*, December 6, 1883.
 41. Butler, *History of Youngstown*, vol. I: 727. The Bessemer Limestone Company's origins are difficult to sort out. In his *History*, vol. I, Butler says on page 513 that the company was organized in 1887; on page 727 he says it was organized in 1885. The Bessemer Limestone Company added a brick plant in 1901, expanding this addition in 1903, 1906, and 1911. In 1919, the Bessemer Limestone & Cement Company was organized. According to the *Biographical History of Northeast Ohio*, page 467, Bessemer Limestone Company (presumably of Pennsylvania) was incorporated on April 26, 1888, for $60,000. The history of the Bessemer Limestone Company of West Virginia, including a copy of the incorporation certificate, list of stockholders and their shares, and minutes of their meetings, is deposited in the archives of the Mahoning Valley Historical Society, Accession number 87.73.10A through 10K, Ledger Book 1 and 2.

Chapter Six

 1. *Youngstown Vindicator*, March 14, 1888.
 2. Butler, *Autographed Portraits*, 124.
 3. *Youngstown Vindicator*, April 29, 1893; *Biographical History of Northeastern Ohio, Embracing the Counties of Ashtabula, Trumbull and Mahoning*, (Chicago: The Lewis Publishing Co., 1893), 467.

4. Butler, *Autographed Portraits*, 298; Butler, *Recollections*, 84.
5. Warren, *American Steel*, 169–170.
6. *Youngstown Vindicator*, October 4, 1889, and March 27, 1938.
7. Blue, et. al, *Mahoning Memories*, 66.
8. Butler, *Recollections*, 131, 346.
9. Butler, *History of Youngstown*, vol. 1: 217, 674.
10. Stephen E. Ambrose, *Nothing Like It In The World, The Men Who Built the Transcontinental Railroad, 1863–1869* (New York: Simon & Schuster, 2000), 133.
11. *Youngstown Vindicator*, April 13, 1892.
12. *Youngstown Vindicator*, April 21, 1892.
13. *Youngstown Vindicator*, September 3, 1892.
14. Butler, "Competition—Its Uses and Abuses," *Iron Age*, vol. 89, no. 21 (May 23, 1912): 1270.
15. Butler, "Competition—Its Uses and Abuses," *Iron Age*, vol. 89, no. 21 (May 23, 1912): 1270; Butler, *Fifty Years of Iron and Steel*, 91–92. By 1917, when Butler praised him in an address to the American Iron and Steel Institute, Meissner had become the head of the Coke Committee of U.S. Steel.
16. Joseph G. Butler, Jr., *Testimonial Banquet, December 21, 1910*, 31.
17. Roy Rutherford, "Rollin C. Steese Rose to Superintendency Of Brier Hill Iron & Coal in Six Months," *Youngstown Vindicator*, April 13, 1947. Rutherford's two-part profile of Rollin Steese, now 80 years old, includes biographical information and Steese's memories of the early days of steel in the Mahoning Valley. Part Two ran in the *Vindicator's* April 20, 1947, issue.
18. Roy Rutherford, "Rollin C. Steese, Key Man in Valley's Growth," *Youngstown Vindicator*, April 20, 1947.
19. Joseph G. Butler, Jr., *My First Trip Abroad* (Youngstown: Joseph G. Butler, Jr., 1921), 29, 38. Kitson's daughter, Hilda, was a good friend of Butler's eldest daughter Blanche.
20. Butler, "Mr. Butler's Report of His Southern Trip in October, A.D. 1890." The quotes are from pages 5, 9, 17, and 21. MVHS 66.56.01.09.
21. "Joseph G. Butler, Jr., 1854," file, Mahoning Valley Historical Society Collection. (MVHS)
22. *Youngstown Telegram*, April 27, 1934; 6-6 *Youngstown Vindicator*, September 4, 1923; *Youngstown Vindicator*, June 19, 1954.
23. P. Ann Gillespie, "Wick Avenue 1940–1967: Millionaire's Row and Youngstown State University" (Master's thesis, Youngstown State University, December 2006), 3.
24. Butler to Editor of *Iron Age*, March 14, 1885.
25. Warren, *American Steel*, 170.
26. *Youngstown Vindicator*, May 26, 1892.
27. *Youngstown Vindicator*, April 30, 1892.
28. Higley, *Youngstown, Intimate History*, 125.
29. *Youngstown Vindicator* May 30, 1892.
30. *Youngstown Vindicator*, May 18, 1892; April 30, 1892; May 25, 1892; Butler, *Fifty Years*, 50.
31. Thomas J. Misa, *A Nation of Steel: The Making of Modern America, 1865–1925*, (Baltimore: Johns Hopkins Press, 1995), 266.
32. Les Standiford, *Meet You in Hell: Andrew Carnegie, Henry Clay Frick, and The Bitter Partnership That Transformed America* (New York: Three Rivers Press, 2005), 132.
33. Paul Krause, author of *The Battle for Homestead, 1880–1892: Politics, Culture, and Steel*, is quoted in Thomas J. Misa, *A Nation of Steel: The Making of Modern America, 1865–1925*, 267. Numerous other books have been written about the Homestead strike. See also Peter Krass, *Carnegie*, Chapter 21 "The Homestead Tragedy": 275–303, and Kenneth Warren, *Triumphant Capitalism: Henry Clay Frick and the Industrial Transformation of America*, Chapter 3 "Carnegie Company Growth and the Homestead Crisis": 56–112. Les Standiford provides a detailed account of the violent confrontation between the Pinkertons and the locked-out Homestead workers in *Meet You in Hell: Andrew Carnegie, Henry Clay Frick, and the Bitter Partnership That Transformed America*, 163–76.
34. Standiford, 137.

Chapter Seven

1. Higley, *Youngstown, Intimate History*, 125.

Notes—Chapter Seven

2. *Youngstown Vindicator*, July 28 and September 10, 1892.
3. *Youngstown Vindicator*, August 11 and 31, 1892.
4. *Youngstown Vindicator*, August 30, 1892.
5. *Youngstown Vindicator*, September 14, 1892.
6. *Youngstown Vindicator*, September 14, 1892.
7. *Youngstown Vindicator*, January 21, 1893.
8. *Youngstown Vindicator*, December 29, 1892, and January 21, 1893.
9. *Youngstown Vindicator*, October 15, 1892.
10. Lamoreaux, *Great Merger Movement*, 33.
11. *Youngstown Vindicator*, December 9, 1892.
12. *Youngstown Vindicator*, December 9, 1892, and January 12, 1893.
13. Butler's quote comes from his autobiography, *Recollections*, 116–118; a less personal and slightly different account of the monument controversy is recorded in Butler, *History of Youngstown*, vol. 1: 843–44.
14. *Youngstown Vindicator*, February 2, 1893, and Butler's *Recollections*, 120–121.
15. *Youngstown Vindicator*, April 20, 1947; Butler, *Recollections*, 122.
16. Sarah Cart, Paul Jagnow, Robert McFerren, *These Hundred Years: A Chronicle of the Twentieth Century* (Youngstown, Ohio: Vindicator Printing Company, 2000), 9; Butler, *Recollections*, 121.
17. *Youngstown Vindicator*, May 29, 1893.
18. Joseph J. Korom, *The American Skyscraper, 1850–1940: A Celebration of Height* (Boston: Braden Books, 2008).
19. Charles Hoffman, *The Depression of the Nineties: An Economic History* (Westport, CT: Greenwood Press, 1970), 63. For an interesting week-by-week contemporary account of the Panic of 1893, see Albert C. Stevens, "Analysis of the Phenomena of the Panic in the United States in 1893," *Quarterly Journal of Economics*, Vol. 8, #2 (January 1894): 117–48 (accessible at JSTOR).
20. H. Roger Grant, *Self-Help in the 1890s Depression*. (Ames, IA: Iowa State UP, 1983): 7,8.
21. *Youngstown Vindicator*, March 27, 1938. One of the outside investors in Ohio Steel was James Parmelee, president of the Cleveland Electric Illuminating Company, treasurer of the Cleveland Electric Railway, and a director of the Euclid Avenue National Bank of Cleveland and the First National Bank of Youngstown. This issue of the *Vindicator* is a particularly rich source for local history. To commemorate the newspaper's 70th anniversary and its move into a new building, it ran a special 224-page issue on the history of Youngstown, its industries, churches, and other institutions. See also Butler, *History of Youngstown*, vol. 1: 692–93.
22. Butler, *History of Youngstown*, vol. 1: 221; Victor S. Clark, *History of Manufacture in the United States, Vol. III, 1893–1928* (New York: McGraw-Hill Book, Co., 1929), 94–95.
23. Butler, *History of Youngstown*, vol. 1: 221.
24. Naomi R. Lamoreaux, *The Great Merger Movement in American Business, 1895–1904* (New York: Cambridge University Press, 1985), 62.
25. Butler, "Competition—Its Uses and Abuses," *Iron Age*, vol. 89, no. 21 (May 23, 1912), 1270.
26. A detailed, contemporary account of the Bessemer process and the steel industry written for a general audience is Bowker, R.R., Ed. "Great American Industries: XL—A Steel Tool," *Harper's New Monthly Magazine* (March 1894) Vol. 88, No. 526: 587–602. The quote describing the Bessemer process is from page 594.
27. *Youngstown Vindicator*, February 2, 1893.
28. Butler, *History of Youngstown*, vol. 1: 693; *Youngstown Vindicator*, February 2, 1893. Thomas McDonald mentioned the expected number of employees. Henry Wick optimistically told the same reporter he expected the mill to be in operation by January 1, 1894.
29. Butler, *History of Youngstown*, vol. 1: 694.
30. Butler, *History of Youngstown*, vol. 1: 693.
31. Butler, *History of Youngstown*, vol. 1: 693.
32. *Mahoning Courier*, February 21, 1866.
33. Lamoreaux, *Great Merger Movement*, 27.
34. Henry Passavant to J.G. Butler, November 18, 1922, MVHS.

35. *Youngstown Vindicator*, April 20, 1947.

36. Kenneth Warren, *The American Steel Industry, 1850-1970* (Oxford: Clarendon Press, 1973), 172.

37. Baldwin is quoted in Butler, *History of Youngstown*, vol. 1: 694. Baldwin replaced Butler as secretary when Butler assumed the vice-presidency of Ohio Steel following the death of H.O. Bonnell.

38. Peter Krass, *Carnegie* (Hoboken, NJ: John Wiley & Sons, 2002), 366.

39. Butler, *History of Youngstown*, vol. 1: 695.

Chapter Eight

1. Margaret Leech, *In the Days of McKinley*, Chapters 4 and 5 provide a useful account of McKinley's run for the White House. See also, Robert W. Merry, *President McKinley, Architect of the American Century* (New York: Simon & Schuster, 2017), 130-146.

2. Butler, *History of Youngstown*, vol. 1:262.

3. Butler, *Recollections*, 89.

4. Butler, *Fifty Years of Iron and Steel*, 74.

5. National McKinley Birthplace Memorial Association, *Proposal to Build a Monument and Memorial to William McKinley at Niles, Ohio, the place of his birth*. (Cleveland: Penton Press, 1911), 9.

6. Leech, *In the Days*, 47; Krass, *Carnegie*, 254, Merry, *President McKinley*, 78-81, 166-7.

7. Butler, *Recollections*, 315.

8. Butler, *Recollections*, 315; Butler, "Proposal to Build a Monument"; Leech, *In the Days*, 66-67.

9. Butler, *Recollections*, 325-27.

10. Butler, *Recollections*, 231.

11. Wiebe, *Search for Order*, 103; Leech, 87.

12. *Youngstown Vindicator*, October 20, 1896.

13. Butler to William McKinley, October 23, 1896, MVHS.

14. Butler to McKinley, October 23, 1896, MVHS.

15. Krass, *Carnegie*, 254.

16. Butler to McKinley, Oct. 23, 1896, MVHS.

17. Butler, *Life of William McKinley*, 7.

18. Butler, *Recollections*, 314; Butler, *Life of William McKinley* and *Presidents I Have Known*, 39. The correct spelling of Butler and McKinley's rescuer is Shelar.

19. Butler, *History of Youngstown*, vol. 1: 838.

20. *Youngstown Telegram*, November 19, 1896, and, November 9, 1896.

21. Leech, 181. Leech's Chapter 7 covers McKinley's attempt to avoid war in Cuba and the aftermath of the *Maine* explosion. See also, Merry, 258-268.

22. *Youngstown Vindicator*, October 15, 1900.

23. John A. Porter to Butler, May 5, 1897; Butler to McKinley, October 16, 1898, MVHS; George B. Cortelyou to Butler, June 15, 1900, MVHS.

24. JGB Sr. to JGB, August 15, 1895.

25. JGB to McKinley undated, Butler Scrapbook, MVHS.

26. Butler to William McKinley, August 30, 1899, Papers of William McKinley, Youngstown State University Archives.

27. Youngstown *Vindicator*, January 6, 1900; *Directory to the Iron and Steel Works of the United States*, vol. II (1901), 256-259.

28. Edmund Morris, *The Rise of Theodore Roosevelt* (New York: Coward, McCann & Geoghegan, Inc., 1979), 718.

29. Butler, *Recollections*, 217-18.

30. *Youngstown Vindicator*, October 7, 1900.

31. *Youngstown Vindicator*, October 3, 1900.

32. *Youngstown Vindicator*, October 3 and October 15, 1900.

33. *Youngstown Telegram*, October 15 and 18, 1900.

34. Butler to George B. Cortelyou, November 6, 1900, MVHS; *Youngstown Telegram*, November 8, 1900.

35. *Youngstown Vindicator*, November 9, 1900.

36. Butler, *Life of William McKinley*, 9-10.

37. Leech, *In the Days of McKinley*, 592, and Merry, 478-481

38. Butler, *Life of William McKinley*, 10.

Chapter Nine

1. *Youngstown Telegram*, November 8, 1900.

2. Butler, *Fifty Years*, 82.

3. Robert Hessen, *Steel Titan, The Life of Charles M. Schwab* (New York: Oxford University Press, 1975), 113–14; Bryan, William Jennings, "The Election of 1900." *North American Review*, vol. 171, Issue 529 (December 1900): 788–801. Bryan analyzes his loss to McKinley and lists many more monopolies in addition to the two examples cited.

4. *Youngstown Telegram*, November 12, 1900.

5. Asael Adams is quoted in the *Youngstown Telegram*, October 29, 1900; Republic's improvements are listed in the *Youngstown Telegram*, November 23, 1900.

6. Blue, et.al., *Mahoning Memories*, 115.

7. Butler, *History of Youngstown*, vol. 1: 697. Butler's concern that the outsiders would destroy the Valley did not materialize until 50 years after his death when on September 19, 1977, out-of-state owners abruptly closed the former Youngstown Sheet & Tube Campbell Works. Five thousand workers lost their jobs.

8. *Youngstown Telegram*, November 1, 1900.

9. The list of the 55 original investors is found in Kaylor, *In Thirty Years*, 13; Butler describes the incorporators and his election to the board of directors in *Recollections*, 283.

10. The origins of the Youngstown Sheet & Tube Company are recorded in many sources. See Larry N. Sypolt and Bruce E. Seely, "Youngstown Sheet and Tube Company," *Encyclopedia of American Business History and Biography: Iron and Steel in the Twentieth Century*, ed. Bruce E. Seely (New York: Bruccoli Clark Layman and Facts on File, 1994), 499; *50 Years in Steel, The Youngstown Sheet and Tube Company, 1900-1949* (Youngstown: The Youngstown Sheet and Tube Company, 1950), 5. For biographical profiles of James Campbell, see Larry Sypolt, "James Anson Campbell," in *Encyclopedia of American Business History and Biography*, ed. Bruce Seely, 76; Butler, *History of Youngstown*, vol. 2: 4; Butler, *Autographed Portraits*, 312.

11. *50 Years in Steel*, 9; Hessen, *Steel Titan*, 269.

12. Robert Hessen, "Charles M. Schwab," in *Encyclopedia of American Business History and Biography: Iron and Steel in the Twentieth Century*, ed. Bruce E. Seely (New York: Bruccoli Clark Layman and Facts on File, 1994), 381; Krass, 396.

13. Quoted in Cotter, *History*, 14–15.

14. Quoted in Krass 409.

15. Leech, *In the Days of McKinley*, 545; Merry, 477; "Trusts and Public Policy," *The Atlantic Monthly: A Magazine of Literature, Science, Art, and Politics*, vol. LXXXVII, no. DXXIV, June 1901, Cornell University Making of America. See also Ron Chernow's *The House of Morgan, An American Banking Dynasty and The rise of Modern Finance* (New York: Atlantic Monthly Press, 1990), 83–86.

16. Nathan Miller, *Theodore Roosevelt, A Life* (New York: William Morrow and Company, Inc., 1992), 477–478.

17. Samuel Mather to Butler, March 21, 1901; Samuel Mather to Butler March 4, 1901, MVHS.

18. Cotter, *The Gary I Knew*, 15.

19. Hessen, *Steel Titan*, 127.

20. Hessen, *Steel Titan*, 127.

21. *50 Years in Steel*, 7, 13.

22. Butler, "Pig Iron During 1904." Bessemer Pig Iron Association, Typed draft, 3, MVHS; Butler, *History of Youngstown*, vol. 1: 701.

23. Butler, "Pig Iron During 1904." Bessemer Pig Iron Association, Typed draft, 3, MVHS.

24. Butler, "Weekly Letter to the Members of the Bessemer Pig Iron Association." October 26, 1904, MVHS.

25. Butler, "Opposition to Roosevelt." Undated typed draft. Joseph G. Butler, Jr., files. Scrapbook 70.51.27, MVHS.

Chapter Ten

1. *Youngstown Vindicator*, July 22, 1973, and June 17, 1981; Butler, *Recollections*, 63.

2. Butler, "A Trip Across the Continent, August 23, 1902," 3–4, MVHS.

3. Henry's father, John Stambaugh, hired Butler to be general manager of Brier Hill Iron and Coal Company in 1878. Henry joined the company the following year and eventually rose to be president. In their long careers, Butler and Henry Stambaugh would both serve as directors of Brier Hill Steel Company, Youngstown Sheet & Tube, and the Bessemer Limestone Company (which Butler founded). Captain Frederick Kohler was appointed chief of

police the following year and was elected mayor of Cleveland in 1922.

4. Butler, "A Trip Across the Continent, August 23, 1902," 6, MVHS.

5. Butler, *Recollections*, 162.

6. P.E. Keeler, "Nye County," in *The History of Nevada*, Vol. II, ed. Sam P. Davis (1912).

7. Butler, "A Second Trip Across the Continent," 1, MVHS.

8. Butler, "A Second Trip Across the Continent," 5–6, MVHS.

9. Butler, "A Second Trip Across the Continent," 12, 3, MVHS.

10. Butler papers, "Everett Iron Company statement filed July 1, 1875," MVHS.

11. Joseph G. Butler, III, *A Venerable Vessel. A Short Story of the Bulk Carrier Joseph G. Butler, Jr., 1905–1971* (privately printed, Poland, OH, 1972), 1.

12. William M. Veith to Butler, April 7, 1910, and W.C. Lamb to William Zimmerman, April 8, 1910, MVHS.

13. Butler, *Recollections*, 167.

14. Butler, *Recollections*, 174.

15. Butler, "Impressions of the World's Fair, 1904," 3, MVHS. The Louisiana Territory was purchased for $15 million.

16. Butler, "Impressions of the World's Fair, 1904," 4, MVHS.

17. The Ferris Wheel Butler saw (and perhaps rode) in St. Louis was, in fact, the same great wheel that George Washington Gale Ferris, Jr., had built for Chicago's World's Columbian Exposition in 1893. The two engines that ran the Ferris Wheel in both Chicago and St. Louis were built by the William Tod Company of Youngstown, Ohio. See Norman Anderson, *Ferris Wheels: An Illustrated History* (Bowling Green, OH: Bowling Green State University Popular Press, 1992), 84; Butler, "Impressions of the World's Fair, 1904," 4, MVHS.

18. Butler, "Impressions of the World's Fair, 1904," 6, 9, MVHS.

19. Butler, "Impressions of the World's Fair, 1904," 9, 11, MVHS.

20. Butler, "Notes of a Third Trip to the Pacific Coast—The Lewis & Clark Centennial Exposition and Oriental Fair, 1905," Collection #209, Box 2, Joseph Green Butler, Jr. Papers, Accession #66.56.01.12, MVHS, 8.

21. Butler, "Notes of a Third Trip to the Pacific Coast—The Lewis & Clark Centennial Exposition and Oriental Fair, 1905," Collection #209, Box 2, Joseph Green Butler, Jr. Papers, Accession # 66.56.01.12, MVHS, 21.

22. See Timothy Egan's, *Short Nights of the Shadow Catcher, The Epic Life and Immortal Photographs of Edward Curtis* (New York: Houghton Mifflin Harcourt, 2012), for an excellent biography of Curtis.

23. Abbott, Carl. "Lewis and Clark Exposition." *The Oregon Encyclopedia* (a project of the Oregon Historical Society). https://oregonencyclopedia.org/articles/lewis_clark_exposition/ (Accessed October 27, 2018).

24. Butler, "Notes of a Third Trip to the Pacific Coast—The Lewis & Clark Centennial Exposition and Oriental Fair, 1905," Collection #209, Box 2, Joseph Green Butler, Jr. Papers, Accession # 66.56.01.12, MVHS, 13.

25. Butler, "Notes of a Third Trip to the Pacific Coast—The Lewis & Clark Centennial Exposition and Oriental Fair, 1905," Collection #209, Box 2, Joseph Green Butler, Jr. Papers, Accession # 66.56.01.12, MVHS, 19–20.

26. Butler, *Recollections*, 129. Chapter 10 of his autobiography covers this first European trip. In 1922, Butler published an expanded account as a separate book titled, *My First Trip Abroad*.

27. Butler, *My First Trip Abroad*, 20–21.

28. Butler, *My First Trip Abroad*, 48.

29. The visit to the New Dudley Gallery's Dickens exhibit is recounted in Chapter 13 of Butler's *My First Trip Abroad*.

30. Butler, *My First Trip Abroad*, 55; Butler, *Recollections*, 142.

Chapter Eleven

1. *Youngstown Telegram*, November 4, 1905; Joseph G. Butler III, *A Venerable Vessel* (Privately printed, Poland, Ohio, 1972), 1.

2. William T. Hogan, *Economic History of the Iron and Steel Industry in the United States*, vol. I (Lexington, Massachusetts: Fordham University, Lexington Books, 1971), 503; Butler, *Recollections*, 152; Chernow, *The House of Morgan*, 121–130.

3. William H. Page, "The Gary Dinners and the Meaning of Concerted Action." *SMU Law Review* 62 (2009): 603.

4. Butler, *Recollections*, 154.
5. E.W. Oglebay to Butler, January 9, 1908, MVHS.
6. Butler, *Recollections*, 55; Judge Gary's quote is found in the same source, 606.
7. Page, *SMU Law Review*, vol. 62:606; Butler, *Recollections*, 156.
8. *New York Times*, November 11, 1911.
9. Blue, *Mahoning Memories*, 72–73; Butler, *History of Youngstown*, vol. 1: 374–377. W.S. Bonnell and his wife contributed $5,000 toward the $50,000 purchase price for their property.
10. Butler, *Recollections*, 278.
11. *Detroit Free Press*, July 13, 1908.
12. *Youngstown Vindicator*, December 4, 1908; *Bulletin of the American Iron and Steel Association*, vol. 42, no. 12 (Philadelphia, September 1, 1908): 90.
13. *Youngstown Telegram*, December 4, 1908.
14. Butler, *Presidents I Have Seen and Known*, 65.
15. Joseph Foraker to Joseph G. Butler, Jr., December 1, 1908, 70.51.30: 93, MVHS.
16. Krass, *Carnegie*, 479.
17. Wall, *Andrew Carnegie*, 960; Foner and Garraty, *Reader's Companion*, 575.
18. Butler to Senator Charles Dick, May 19, 1909, MVHS Accession # 70.51.27: 29.
19. Butler to Senator Charles Dick, May 19, 1909, MVHS Accession # 70.51.27: 29.
20. Schlesinger, *Almanac of American History*, 417.
21. Aley, *Heritage to Share*, 187.
22. *Youngstown Telegram*, February 8, and 10, 1909; Butler's *History of Youngstown*, 3 vols., I: 395–396; Dorothy Welsh, "Mahoning Valley Historical Society," interview by Hugh G. Earnhart, tape recording, (Youngstown, Ohio, November 4, 1975), Youngstown State University Oral History Program.
23. Rowfant Club: Printed Ephemera and Associated Items, 1901–1997. www.grolierclub.org/Libraryamc.rowfantclub.htm; Butler, *Recollections*, 252.
24. *Youngstown Vindicator*, May 26, 1909; *see also* Butler, *Recollections*, 284.
25. "Niles Board of Trade Banquet Great Success," *Youngstown Telegram*, February 5, 1910.
26. "Niles Honors Memory of William M'Kinley," *Youngstown Telegram*, August 26, 1909.
27. Butler, *History of Youngstown*, vol. 1: 378.
28. Butler, *Presidents I Have Seen and Known and A Day in Washington's Country*, 79–80.
29. Butler, *Recollections*, 145–46.
30. Butler, *Presidents I Have Seen and Known and A Day in Washington's Country*, 77–85; *Recollections* 145–47; Letters from John Stewart to Butler, February 18, 1922, and August 8, 1927, include letterhead lists of the Sulgrave Institution Board of Governors, Butler Scrapbooks, MVHS, 70.51.5: 74 and 117. There is considerable confusion over the date of Butler's first visit to Sulgrave Manor, the home of George Washington's ancestors. At a testimonial banquet held for him on December 21, 1910, Butler says he visited Sulgrave Manor "while I was in Europe last year," which would imply 1909. In his autobiography, *Recollections of Men and Events*, Butler has a chapter on Sulgrave Manor [Washington Manor] and places his initial visit in August 1909. In his essay "A Day In Washington's Country," published in December 1910 as part of his first book *Presidents I have Seen and Known*, he says the visit was made "while I was in England during the month of August last," which is ambiguous but implies August 1910. The correct date must be August 1910. Butler first visited Sulgrave Manor as part of a day excursion that also carried him to Althorp House, the home of the Spencer family. In "A Day In Washington's Country," Butler comments on the Earl of Spencer's recent death and notes that he was lying in state at the time of Butler's visit. The 5th Earl of Spencer died August 13, 1910. Butler made frequent trips to England, and he appears to have confused the dates of the initial Sulgrave visit. [Note: the 5th Earl of Spencer, John Poyntz Spencer, died childless. His half-brother Charles became the 6th Earl of Spencer whose great-grand-daughter Diana became the Princess of Wales.]
31. "Steel Men at White House," *New York Times*, Oct. 23, 1910; Butler, *Recollections*, 176.
32. Butler's account of the White House visit and the text of Taft's letter are found in *Presidents I Have Seen*, 72.
33. "Fire At Tod House Results In Panic," *Youngstown Vindicator*, Oct. 23, 1910.
34. "Hotel Is Greeted With Open Arms

by Youngstown," *Youngstown Telegram*, Sept. 30, 1913.

Chapter Twelve

1. James S. Fleming, "Oscar W. Underwood: The First Modern House Leader, 1911-1915." in *Masters of the House: Congressional Leaders Over Two Centuries*, eds. Roger H. Davidson, Susan Webb Hammond, and Raymond W. Smock. (Boulder, Colorado: Westview Press, 1998), 96. Fleming's chapter provides a useful summary of Underwood's rise to power and his role in Woodrow Wilson's administration.
2. *Joseph G. Butler, Jr. Testimonial Banquet, December 21, 1910*, 1.
3. *Joseph G. Butler, Jr. Testimonial Banquet, December 21, 1910*, 20-21.
4. *Joseph G. Butler, Jr. Testimonial Banquet, December 21, 1910*, 38, 49.
5. *Youngstown Telegram*, December 22, 1910. *Youngstown Vindicator*, December 22, 1910. Both papers print a nearly identical report that contains the unattributed quote; Arthur McGraw to Butler, December. 24, 1910, MVHS.
6. Arthur McGraw to Butler, December 24, 1910; Robert Bentley to Butler, December 27, 1910, Butler Scrapbooks, vol. 1: 28; Lucretia Garfield to Butler January 24, 1911. All three letters are in the Joseph Butler scrapbooks, Mahoning Valley Historical Society. James Swank to Butler, December 28, 1910, MVHS.
7. Butler to Grace Butler McGraw, April 8, 1906, MVHS. His first literary efforts are recounted in Butler, *Recollections*, 251.
8. Stewart, *History of Northeastern Ohio*, Vol. II: 559.
9. *New York Times*, July 7, 1911; Butler, *Recollections*, 177-182.
10. Butler, *Presidents I Have Seen*, 68.
11. "Launch New Movement to Build Up Merchant Marine," *Youngstown Vindicator*, December 4, 1911.
12. James S. Fleming, "Oscar W. Underwood: The First Modern House Leader, 1911-1915." in *Masters of the House: Congressional Leaders Over Two Centuries*, eds. Roger H. Davidson, Susan Webb Hammond, and Raymond W. Smock, 101.
13. James A. Farrell to Butler, January15, 1912, MVHS.
14. James A. Farrell to Butler, January 15, 1912, MVHS; William Follansbee to Butler, January 3, 1912, MVHS.
15. Butler to William Follansbee, January 5, 1912, MVHS.
16. Horace L. Haldeman to Butler, January 8, 1912, MVHS.
17. Butler's wish to separate the tariff question from politics is expressed in "Against Lower Duties," *Iron Age*, vol. 89, no. 9 (February 29, 1912): 533-33. Leonard Peckitt wrote to Butler on January 8, 1912, and Butler replied on January 10. The letters are in the Butler Scrapbooks, MVHS; Butler to Oscar Underwood, January 13, 1912, MVHS.
18. Butler's letter to the Pig Iron Manufacturers is dated January 16, 1912; William A. Rogers to Butler, January 17, 1912, MVHS.
19. "New Steel Co. Organizes," *Youngstown Vindicator*, January 29, 1912; Butler, *History of Youngstown*, vol. 1: 710-714, provides a history of the Brier Hill Steel Company; Butler, *Recollections*, 126-27.
20. Bruce E. Seely, "Joseph Green Butler, Jr.," *Iron and Steel In the Twentieth Century, Encyclopedia of American History and Business*, 1994, 70-71. Seely is also the editor.
21. "Against Lower Duties on Iron and Steel." *Iron Age*, vol. 89, no. 9 (February 29, 1912): 532-33. The companies Butler represented in his appearance before the Senate Finance Committee were: Ashland Iron & Mining Company, Ashland, Kentucky; Columbus Iron & Steel Company, Columbus, Ohio; Perry Iron Company, Erie, Pa.; Girard Iron Company., Girard, Ohio; Andrews & Hitchcock Iron Company, Youngstown, Ohio; Pickands, Mather, and Company, Cleveland, Ohio; Toledo Furnace Company, Toledo, Ohio; Stewart Iron Company, Ltd., Sharon, Pa.; M.A. Hanna & Company, Cleveland, Ohio; Belfont Iron Works, Ironton, Ohio; Kittanning Iron & Steel Mfg. Company, Kittanning, Pa; and the Brier Hill Steel Company, Youngstown, Ohio.
22. "Against Lower Duties on Iron and Steel," *Iron Age*, vol. 89, no. 9 (February 29, 1912), 532.
23. Butler, *History of Youngstown*, vol. 3: 646; *Youngstown Vindicator*, April 14, 1937.
24. "Rousing Opening Of Big Hospital

Campaign Is Held," *Youngstown Telegram,* April 18, 1912.

25. Butler's comments were reported in "Rousing Opening Of Big Hospital Campaign Is Held," *Youngstown Telegram,* April 18, 1912. For an account of the origins and early history of St. Elizabeth's Hospital, see Melnick, John C, M.D. *History of Medicine in Youngstown and Mahoning Valley, Ohio.* Youngstown, Ohio, 1973.

26. "A Giant Thermometer," *Youngstown Vindicator,* March 26, 1912.

27. *Youngstown Telegram,* April 18, 1912.

28. John C. Melnick, "St. Elizabeth Hospital." *Bulletin of the Mahoning County Medical Society,* vol. XLII (August 1972): 219; *Youngstown Vindicator,* April 24, 25, 1912.

29. *Youngstown Vindicator,* April 25, 1912.

30. "Rousing Opening Of Big Hospital Campaign Is Held," *Youngstown Telegram,* April 18, 1912.

31. Butler, "Competition—Its Uses and Abuses." *Iron Age,* vol. 89, no. 21 (May 23, 1912):1270.

32. Arthur M. Schlesinger, Jr., *Almanac of American History,* 422, and Nathan Miller, *Theodore Roosevelt, A Life,* 531, and Lewis L. Goud, *Four Hats in The Ring, The 1912 Election and the Birth of Modern American Politics,* (Lawrence Kansas, University Press of Kansas, 2008).

33. "The Steel Corporation Dissolution Suit," *Iron Age,* vol. 90, no. 19 (November 7, 1912): 1131.

34. Arthur M. Schlesinger, Jr., *Almanac of American History,* 423, see also Brands, *Woodrow Wilson,* 30–37 for Wilson on business.

35. Butler to *New York Herald,* April 8, 1913. MVHS Scrapbook, 70–51.27.

36. Brands, *Woodrow Wilson,* 33.

37. Butler, *Recollections,* 64–65.

38. *Youngstown, The City of Progress, A Natural Center of Manufacture and Distribution,* (Youngstown Chamber of Commerce: Youngstown, 1913).

39. Mark C. Peyko, *Understanding the Downtown: Architecture, Downtown Directory, Historic Preservation,* 1991; Another useful guide to the origins and architecture of central Youngstown is William Brenner's *Downtown and the University* published by the author in 1976, revised 2006. See also Blue et.al, *Mahoning Memories,* 72, 114.

40. *Youngstown, The City of Progress.* The statement about "men in charge" is on page 41; the comment on labor is on page 19.

41. Quoted in, "Impromptu Addresses in Response to the Call of Judge Gary," *Yearbook of the American Iron and Steel Institute,* October 1913: 463.

42. Kendrick Clements, and Eric Cheezum, *Woodrow Wilson.* (Washington, D.C.: CQ Press, 2003), 138.

43. "Impromptu Addresses in Response to the Call of Judge Gary," *Yearbook of the American Iron and Steel Institute,* October 1913: 463.

44. Butler, *Recollections,* 225.

45. New Hotel Opens Doors To Public," *Youngstown Telegram,* September 29, 1913; "Hotel Is Greeted With Open Arms By Youngstown," *Youngstown Telegram,* September 30, 1913; "Youngstown's New Hotel" (editorial), *Youngstown Telegram,* September 30, 1913; "Regrets Sent By Absent Friends," *Youngstown Telegram,* September 30, 1913.

Chapter Thirteen

1. Butler, *Recollections,* 90.
2. Butler, *Recollections,* 89, 91.
3. *Joseph G. Butler, Jr. Testimonial Banquet, December 21, 1910,* 33.
4. *Niles Daily News,* August 2, 1915.
5. The National McKinley Birthplace Memorial and The McKinley Birthplace Home & Research Center brochure; Butler to Captain W.L. Curry, March 13, 1924, MVHS.
6. *Niles Daily Times,* August 2, 1915. The full text of the bill may be found in Butler, *Life of McKinley and History of the National McKinley Birthplace Memorial,* 25–30.
7. *Niles Daily Times,* August 2, 1915; Butler, *Recollections,* 91; *New York Times,* May 23, 1914.
8. Butler, *Recollections,* 90–91.
9. *New York Times,* May 19, 1911; *Niles Daily Times,* August 2, 1915; a check for $5,000.00 dated May 17, 1911, from Butler to the McKinley Memorial Trustees. This first subscription is in the National McKinley Birthplace Memorial Archives. *Youngstown Telegram,* February 5, 1910.

10. Butler, *Life of McKinley and History of the National McKinley Birthplace Memorial*, 21; Butler, *Recollections*, 90.

11. *Niles Daily News*, June 13 and 27, 1912.

12. *New York Times*, July 28, 1912; *Niles Daily News*, August 2, 1915.

13. "Impromptu Addresses in Response to the Call of Judge Gary," *Year Book of The American Iron and Steel Institute* (New York: AISI, October 1913).

14. Butler to Grace Butler McGraw, January 29, 1913, MVHS. 70.51.32:133.

15. Butler to Captain W.L. Curry, March 13, 1924, MVHS.

16. "William McKinley Memorial, Niles, Ohio" *Architectural Forum*, vol. 31, no. 6 (December 1919): 205.

17. *Youngstown Telegram*, October 17, 1914. The six architectural firms that were the finalists in the competition to design the McKinley Memorial were: Henry Bacon; Cass Gilbert; McKim, Mead & White, H. Van Buren Magonigle; Palmer, Hornbostel & Jones and J.L. Decker, Associated—all from New York; and Zantzinger, Borie & Medary from Philadelphia.

18. *Leland M. Roth, The Architecture of McKim, Mead, & White, 1870–1920 a Building List*, ix. Roth's claim that the firm was the largest in the world by 1900 is found on page xxxv.

19. "William McKinley Memorial, Niles, Ohio" *Architectural Forum*, vol. 31, no. 6 (December 1919): 205.

20. Wayne Craven, *Sculpture in America (From the Colonial Period to the Present)*, (New York: Thomas Y. Crowell Co., 1968), 486–488.

21. Butler, *Recollections*, 248–49.

22. Letter from William Howard Taft to Butler, August 10, 1915, McKinley Memorial Archives, Niles, Ohio. Taft notes the selection on August 7, 1915, of John H. Parker Co. of New York as the builder of the McKinley Memorial.

23. Butler, *Recollections*, 274; the September 30, 1915, check for $50,000 ($1.24 million in 2018 dollars) from Henry C. Frick to the McKinley Memorial Trustees is in the McKinley Memorial Museum.

24. *Youngstown Vindicator*, November 20, 1915.

25. Progress of the memorial's exterior construction is recorded in a series of dated photographs on display at the McKinley Memorial Library.

26. Paul H. Rohrbaugh, Jr., "Friendship Memorialized: Joseph G. Butler and the McKinley National Birthplace Memorial," Master's thesis, (Youngstown State University, 2001), 62.

27. *Nashville Tennessean*, October 6, 1917, MVHS, 70.51.32: 23; A press release from the National McKinley Birthplace Memorial Association dated August 22, 1916, provides the pricing and includes the text of the authorization law approved by President Wilson on February 23, 1916. "McKinley Memorial Gold dollar," *The CoinSite,* https://coinsite.com/mckinley-memorial-gold-dollar/ (accessed November 10, 2018). The web site contains a highly critical review of the McKinley coin: "After suffering protracted arguments with the Commission of Fine Arts over the recent Panama-pacific coinage, the U.S. Mint evidently wanted to streamline the design process for the McKinley coin, as it assigned the preparation of models to its own staff. Chief Engraver Charles E. Barber, then in his final year of life, sculpted the obverse, a mediocre profile bust of the late president that scarcely resembled him. Several numismatic authors have commented that Barber seemed to be avoiding any comparison with his earlier portrait of McKinley that appeared on one of the Louisiana Purchase Exposition dollars in 1903. Barber's advanced age (76) is a more plausible explanation. His Assistant Engraver, George T. Morgan, created the reverse, a facing view of the McKinley Birthplace Memorial structure. This model was even worse than Barber's, architecturally inaccurate and crudely rendered. When combined with the fact that these coins, aside from a handful of proofs, are often seen weakly struck, the whole makes for an aesthetically poor creation. Objections tendered by the Commission of Fine Arts were simply ignored. The worst was still to come, however, when the Association attempted to market these mediocre coins to the public at $3 apiece."

28. Rohrbaugh, "Friendship Memorialized," 73.

29. *Youngstown Vindicator*, June 13, 1926.

30. Butler, *Life of William McKinley*, 17–18; *Youngstown Vindicator*, October 6, 1917; "In Remembrance of William McKinley," *National Magazine*, June 17, 1923.

31. *Youngstown Vindicator*, July 11, 1920. Butler would later finance additional busts and bronze tablets honoring such men as Butler's own father and grandfather and other prominent local citizens

32. *Youngstown Telegram*, October 5, 1917.

33. *Youngstown Telegram*, October 5, 1917.

34. Butler, *Recollections*, 95-96. The full text of his address at the Memorial dedication is on pages 94-95.

35. *Warren Chronicle*, October 5, 1917.

36. *Youngstown Vindicator*, October 6, 1917; Rohrbaugh, "Friendship Memorialized," 65; Myron T. Herrick to Butler, July 6, 1917, MVHS.

37. "Dedication Marked by Ideal Day," *Niles Daily Times*, October 5, 1917; "In Remembrance of William McKinley," *National Magazine*, June 17, 1923.

38. Butler, *Recollections*, 94.

Chapter Fourteen

1. "The New Pig Iron Association," *Iron Age*, vol. 93, no. 3 (January 15, 1914): 213-14.

2. Butler, "The Country's Steel Business Needs To Be Let Alone," *Iron Age*, vol. 95, no. (January 7, 1915):29. See also H.W. Brand's, *Woodrow Wilson, The American Presidents*, (New York: Henry Hold and Company, 2003), 46-39.

3. *Youngstown Telegram*, November 24, 1915.

4. Public Library of Youngstown and Mahoning County, Library History 1910-29, unmounted. Joseph G. Butler, Jr., served as a trustee of the Reuben McMillan Free Library from 1915 until his death in 1927. Henry A. Butler was elected to replace his father on the board and served until 1932. Butler's grandson John Willard Ford was elected in 1933 to replace his Uncle Henry and served until 1954. After his death the volumes from his personal library, many of them still identifiable by his signature under the *ex libris* heading, were donated to public libraries. Butler's bookplate symbolized his life's interests. The heading is supported on the left side by smokestacks and on the right by the mast and sail of a ship. Across the bottom from left to right is a stack of pig iron, an Indian head in the center looking right, and on the right, an artist's paint brushes and palette. In the center is a woven Indian rug. The Reuben McMillan Free Library holds in its collection today many of the iron and steel trade volumes that once graced the shelves of Butler's library.

5. Butler, *Recollections*, 63; *Youngstown Telegram*, January 10, 1916. The inscription on the front of the Loving Cup was: "Presented to Mr. and Mrs. Joseph G. Butler, Jr., on the occasion of the 50th anniversary of their marriage, Jan. 10, 1916." On the back were inscribed the names of the friends who had given the gift: "H.H. Stambaugh, John Stambaugh, John Tod, David Tod, R.C. Steese, W.A. Thomas, E.L. Ford, Paul Jones, Robert Bentley, J.A. Campbell, W.G. Pollock, H.M. Garlick, C.D. Hine, Frank Billings, Harry Bonnell."

6. Blue, et.al., *Mahoning Memories*, writes that the strike was not over working conditions but living conditions where residences were overcrowded and unsanitary. Butler "Observed that alcohol had caused the rioting when local authorities ailed to close down the saloons as advised. On the other hand, findings of a 1916 investigation concluded that the IWW had caused the rioting," 106, 131. See also Raymond Boryczka and Lorin Lee Cary's *No Strength Without Union, An Illustrated History of Ohio Workers, 1803-1980*, (Columbus, Ohio: Ohio Historical Society, 1982), "the strikes idled over 16,000 workers, the bulk of them unorganized and foreign-born. Economic conditions lay at the heart of these strikes," 139.

7. Butler, *History of Youngstown*, vol. 1: 242-43.

8. *Youngstown Telegram*, January 5, 1916.

9. *Youngstown Telegram*, January 6, 1916.

10. *Youngstown Telegram*, January 7, 1916.

11. Sherry Lee Linkon and John Russo, *Steeltown U.S.A.: Work and Memory in Youngstown* (Lawrence, KS: University Press of Kansas, 2002), 26-27.

12. *New York Times*, January 8, 1916.

13. Butler, *History of Youngstown*, vol. 1: 243.

14. *Youngstown Telegram*, January 8, 1916.

15. "Grand Jury Indicts Big Steel Companies," *Youngstown Vindicator*, March 8, 1916, quoted in Linkon and Russo, 29.

16. Butler, *History of Youngstown*, vol. 1: 84.

17. Robert H. Wiebe, *The Search for Order, 1877-1920* (NY: Hill and Wang, 1967), 288.

18. Butler, "The Small Museum." Transcript of a speech Butler gave at the 7th Annual Convention of the American Federation of Art on May 17, 1916, at the New Willard Hotel in Washington, D.C. Courtesy of the Butler Institute of American Art.

19. *Official Report of the Proceedings of the Sixteenth Republican National Convention*, reported by George L. Hart. (NY: Tenny Press, 1916). Butler is listed as a delegate on page 58. The other delegate from Ohio's 19th district was Hiram E. Starkey of Jefferson. The first and second roll calls for the presidential nomination are on pages 181–85. The third roll call is on pages 197–202.

20. Joseph G. Butler, Jr., to Hon. Chas. E. Hughes (telegram), June 10, 1916; Joseph G. Butler, Jr., to Theodore Roosevelt (telegram), June 10, 1916. Joseph Butler Scrapbooks, vol. 4: 104. MVHS.

21. *New York Times*, August 5, 1916.

22. Butler, *A Journey Through France in War Time* (Cleveland: Penton Press, 1917), 14–15. This and other quotes are all taken from *Journey to France in War Time*. The records of the American Industrial Commission to France in 1916 are housed in the New York Public Library. They consist of the official printed report and William Wallace Nichols's scrapbook containing letters, reports, and photographs.

23. Butler, *Journey*. Butler's observation of Youngstown steel on the Bordeaux docks is on page 27; his visit to the American Ambulance is on pages 33–34, and the visit to the dressmaking establishment is on page 36. His conversation with David Lloyd George is on page 39. The cheering crowds in Marseilles are described on page 93.

24. Butler, *Journey*, 128.

25. Butler, *Journey*, 170.

26. Butler, "The French Steel Industry in War Time," *Iron Age*, vol. 98, 18 (November 2, 1916): 1009.

27. The always meticulous Butler made a typed list of his souvenirs from France. The complete list is as follows: "Tapestry painting Joffre, Porcelain portrait of Joffre, 5 Rings made in the trenches by soldiers—buttons from soldiers uniforms, 2 bracelets made in the trenches from exploded shells, 1 Cigarette holder for use in trenches, 2 Cigarette cases—Red Cross, 1 piece Zeppelin, 2 paper cutters made in trenches from exploded shells, 5 pieces Glass from Reims cathedral, 2 cigar lighters—shape of projectiles, Key of Archbishop's Palace, bone from Tomb, 12 pairs gloves, 2 boxes candy, 3 hat pins soldiers buttons, 500 Postal cards, 20 Postal cards painted in trenches." Butler Scrapbooks, vol. 37: 115, MVHS.

28. Butler, "The French Steel Industry in War Time," *Iron Age*, vol. 98, 18 (November 2, 1916): 1008.

29. A card advertising the amenities of the Red Cross Canteen is in the Butler Scrapbooks, vol. 37: 119, MVHS.

30. Butler, *History of Youngstown*, vol. 1: 784–88.

31. "Lowest Output in Relation to Capacity," *Iron Age*, vol. 109, no. 1 (January 5, 1922): 59.

32. "Intense patriotism at Institute Meeting," *Iron Age*, vol. 100, no. 18 (November 1, 1917): 1035–37.

33. Butler, "Wonderful Development of the Iron Business," *Iron Age*, vol. 100, no. 18 (November 1, 1917): 1041–45. Butler's account of his career in iron and steel from 1857 to 1917 coincides with the existence of the trade paper, *The Iron Age*, which began publication in 1855. In the January 6, 1916, issue (vol. 97, no. 1) the editors ran a feature titled "Industrial Progress of Sixty Years—The Lifetime of *The Iron Age*" that is an interesting companion piece to Butler's reminiscences.

34. *Iron Trade Review* (February 14, 1918), Butler Scrapbooks, vol. 4: 13, MVHS.

35. Henry A. Butler, *Overseas Sketches* (1921) 16–18, 47, 54.

36. Henry A. Butler, *Overseas Sketches* (1921) 140–41; Butler, *History of Youngstown*, vol. 3: 705.

37. "Obituary—Henry H. Stambaugh," *Iron Age*, vol. 103, no. 2 (January 9, 1919): 157; Butler, *Recollections*, 86.

38. Joseph G. Butler, Jr., "Record of American Steel in World War," *Iron Age*, vol. 103, no. 22 (May 29, 1919): 1436–39.

Chapter Fifteen

1. *Youngstown Vindicator*, April 25, 1911.

2. *Youngstown Vindicator*, October 23, 1914.

3. *Youngstown Vindicator*, November 9, 1914.

4. The 15 trustees of the Youngstown Museum of Art were: Sara O. Baker, Robert Bentley, Joseph G. Butler Jr., Dr. Ida Clarke, Edward L. Ford, Grace J Hitchcock, Rev. Edward Mears, Helene Strouss Meyer, Charles F. Owsley, James W Porter, John Stambaugh, Alice Wood Tod, Jonathan Warner, Caroline H. B Wick, and Mellicent Wick. The *Youngstown Vindicator*, November 9, 1914, lists the names of the incorporators and Articles of Incorporation, and dues. See the *Youngstown Vindicator*, November 24, 1914, for a list the Trustees' names and addresses.

5. Joseph G. Butler Jr., to Nina Spalding Stevens, March 27, 1915.

6. Joseph G. Butler Jr., to Nina Spalding Stevens, March 27, 1915.

7. *American Painting*, Mahoning Institute of Art catalog, May 1915, BIAA.

8. *Youngstown Telegram*, December 7, 8, 10, 1917.

9. *Youngstown Telegram*, December 13, 1917.

10. "Joseph G. Butler, Jr., Loses Art Collection," *Iron Age*, vol. 100, no. 25 (December 20, 1917): 1504.

11. *Youngstown Telegram*, December 12, 1917.

12. YDH to JGB (telegram), December 11, 1917, MVHS. (YDH is apparently Henry A. Butler, *Your Devoted Henry?*)

13. *Youngstown Vindicator*, December 12, 1917.

14. Butler, *Recollections*, 99. Clyde Singer, a noted painter, who later became a curator and the associate director of the Butler Institute of American Art wrote in 1950 that after the fire Butler "immediately planned an art gallery" across from his partially destroyed house. *Youngstown Vindicator*, January 29, 1950; Grandson, Joseph G. Butler III repeated in 1975 that his grandfather "immediately began to plan" for the museum as a result of the fire. (Butler III interviewed by Bick, Youngstown State University, December 10, 1975); McClelland, "Butler's Gift to Youngstown, *Western Reserve Magazine*, August/September 1985, states that the fire "triggered the idea" of a "public gallery where his art would be safe."; Seely, "Joseph Green Butler, Jr., "*Iron and Steel Industry Encyclopedia*, 1994, concluded that Butler "decided to build a museum" after the fire struck. Countless newspaper articles over the years perpetuated the misinformation. One of the few reports that accurately described the Butler museum's creation was a 1974 study by the Youngstown City Planning Commission.

15. *Youngstown Telegram*, December 12, 1917; "Joseph G. Butler, Jr., Loses Art Collection," *Iron Age*, Vol. 100, no. 25 (1917): 1504.

16. Arthur McGraw to Butler, December 12, 1917, MVHS; John W. Ford to Butler, December 13, 1917, MVHS; John A. Penton to Butler, December 12, 1917, MVHS.

17. Willis L. King to Butler, December 17, 1917, MVHS; Butler to J.J. Turner, December 17, 1917, Butlermuseum.org bf1917 244.

18. Butler, Joseph G. Jr., "The Small Museum." BIAA. Henry K. Wick's bequest is also mentioned in the *Youngstown Vindicator*, March 27, 1938. The 1938 article notes that Mellicent Wick is still alive and that "the claims of creditors have virtually annihilated the estate, left to maintain and endow the gallery."

19. Butler to Henry M. Garlick, January 8, 1917, Butlermuseum.ort.bf1917003.

20. Youngstown Planning Commission Historic Preservation, June 1974, and William Mitchell Kendall to Butler December 13 and September 13, 1916, Butlermuseum.org.

21. McKim to Butler, December 13, 1916.

22. *Youngstown Vindicator*, June 14, 1917; Kendall to Butler, December 13, 1916, Butlermuseum.org.

23. Arthur McGraw to Butler, May 14, 1917, Butlermuseum.org., bf1917066a.

24. Butler to McKim, Mead & White, March 22, 1917.

25. *Youngstown Vindicator*, June 14, 1917.

26. Undated article about J. Massey Rhind, *Carnegie Magazine*, Butler museum.org.

27. J. Massey Rhind to Butler, June 12, 1917, Butlermuseum.org.

28. Butler to Rhind, June 29, 1917, Butlermuseum.org.

29. Alexander Anderson to E.L. Ford, May 10, 1017. Butlermuseum.org. bf1917 058a.

Notes—Chapter Sixteen

30. John H. Parker Company to Butler, November 22, 1917, butlermuseum.org bf1917235.

31. Lindsey Watson to United Electric Construction Co., January 4, 1918, butlermuseum.org. bf1918003.

32. McKim, Mead & White to Butler, March 15, 1919, Butlermuseum.org. bf1919 006.

33. Sweetkind, *Master Paintings*, 9, 7, 138, 206.

34. Rhind to Butler, October 8, 1918; Rhind to Butler, November 6, 1919; Rhind to Butler, December 22, 1919, all from Butlermuseum.org.

35. *American Association of Museums Directory*, Reed Elsevier, 2002

36. Butler, *Recollections*, 293, 249.

37. Butler, III interviewed by Bick, Youngstown State University, December 10, 1975; McClelland, "Butler's Gift to Youngstown." *Western Reserve Magazine*, August/September 1985.

38. Butler to McKim, Mead & White, October 29, 1918, Butlermuseum.org, bf1918 047; Ethel Quinton Mason to Rhind, February 6, 1919, butlermuseum.org.

39. *Youngstown Vindicator*, March 27, 1938, and Butler's *History of Youngstown*, 3 vols., I: 380.

40. Butler to Rhind, October 17, 1919, Butlermuseum.org.; "Memorandum of Agreement between John W. Young and Joseph G. Butler, Jr., January 26, 1918, for the purchase of *Tragedy at Sea*, by George Inness. Butler paid $25,000 for the painting. Butler Museum Collection; *Youngstown Vindicator*, October 16, 1919; for Henry H. Stambaugh's obituary, see *Iron Age*, vol. 103, no. 2 (January 9, 1919): 157.

41. *Youngstown Vindicator*, October 16, 1919; Butler to Rhind, October 17, 1919, butlermuseum.org.

42. *Youngstown Vindicator*, October 15, 16, 1919.

43. Butler, *History*, vol. 1:382. Butler, *Recollections*, 99. Clyde Singer, a noted painter, who later became a curator and the associate director of the Butler Institute of American Art wrote in 1950 that after the fire Butler "immediately planned an art gallery" across from his partially destroyed house. *Youngstown Vindicator*, January 29, 1950; Grandson, Joseph G. Butler III repeated in 1975 that his grandfather "immediately began to plan" for the museum as a result of the fire. (Butler III interviewed by Bick, Youngstown State University, December 10, 1975); McClelland, "Butler's Gift to Youngstown, *Western Reserve Magazine*, August/September 1985, states that the fire "triggered the idea" of a "public gallery where his art would be safe."; Seely, "Joseph Green Butler, Jr., "*Iron and Steel Industry Encyclopedia*, 1994, concluded that Butler "decided to build a museum" after the fire struck. Countless newspaper articles over the years perpetuated the misinformation. One of the few reports that accurately described the Butler museum's creation was a 1974 study by the Youngstown City Planning Commission. On December 27, 1919, he incorporated the Butler Art Institute. In addition to Butler himself, the other incorporators were his son Henry A. Butler, grandson John W. Ford, and two longtime friends and business associates, John Stambaugh and Jonathan Warner (whose house stood adjacent to the new gallery)

Chapter Sixteen

1. "H.C. Frick's First Visit," Framed handwritten list of names of H.C. Frick party on his first visit to the McKinley Memorial including J.G. Butler, October 29, 1919, McKinley National Birthplace Museum Archives, Niles, Ohio, accession # 95.1.96; *Youngstown Vindicator*, December 5, 1919; "Death of Henry Clay Frick," *Iron Age*, vol. 104, no. 23 (December 4, 1919): 1144–45.

2. *Youngstown Vindicator*, December 6, 1919; *Youngstown Telegram*, Dec. 6, 1919.

3. W. Booth to Butler, December 16, 1919, MVHS.

4. *Youngstown Vindicator*, October 16, 1914; Butler, *Recollections*, 253.

5. Butler, *Fifty Years of Iron and Steel*, 7th ed. (Cleveland: Penton Press, 1923): 103; *United States v. United States Steel Corporation et al.*, 251 U.S. 417 (1920).

6. Butler, *Recollections*, 333.

7. Doris Kearns Goodwin, *Team of Rivals*, 244.

8. *Youngstown Telegram*, June 14, 1920; Butler, *Recollections*, 310.

9. Butler to Hugh A. Crawford, April 24, 1924, MVHS; Butler's *Recollections*, 334.

10. *Youngstown Telegram*, June 14, 1920; Francis Russell, *The Shadow of Blooming Grove, Warren G. Harding and His Times* (New York: McGraw-Hill Book Company, 1968), 355–96. In Chapter 15 "The Dark Convention," Russell provides a detailed story of the 1920 Republican Convention that is somewhat at odds with Joseph Butler's version of events.

11. *Youngstown Telegram*, June 14, 1920; Butler, *Recollections* 334–35. Also, see Russell, *The Shadow of Blooming Grove*, 228–230.

12. *Youngstown Telegram*, June 14, 1920.

13. Butler, *Recollections*, 311; Butler to William H. Taft, May 31, 1921.

14. Butler to Kendall, September 17, 1920, butlermuseum.org, bf1920 007; *Youngstown Vindicator*, September 11, 1920; *Youngstown Telegram*, September 11, 1920. Butler believed, incorrectly as it would turn out, that $200,000 would be enough to cover the operating costs of the gallery in perpetuity. His donation of $700,000 would be the equivalent of $8.8 million in 2018 dollars.

15. Butler, *History of Youngstown*, vol. 1: 382, and *Youngstown Telegram*, Sept.11, 1920.

16. "J.G. Butler, Jr., Honored," *Iron Trade Review*, October 28, 1920, 1219.

17. Butler to Taft, May 31, 1921, MVHS.

18. *Youngstown Telegram*, April 27, 1921.

19. *Youngstown Telegram*, April 27, 1921; *Youngstown Vindicator*, April 27, 1921, and December 22, 1927; Butler, *Recollections*, 61.

20. *Niles Daily News*, June 18, 1921.

21. *Youngstown Vindicator*, April 17, 1933.

22. Butler, *Recollections*, 254.

23. Butler to President Warren G. Harding, August 28, 1921, MVHS. At the time of Butler's visit, the Hotel Traymore, an architectural wonder, was six years old and the tallest building in Atlantic City.

24. "Sketch of Career of Joseph G. Butler, Jr." *The Blast Furnace & Steel Plant*, January 1922: 60–62.

25. Butler, *Recollections*, 279–81.

26. Butler, *Recollections*, 127, 285.

27. Butler, *Recollections*, 314.

28. *Youngstown Vindicator*, September 4, 1923.

29. Butler, *Recollections*, 68.

30. Butler, Memorandum for Mr. R.J. Kaylor, October 11, 1924.

31. Andrew B. Humphrey, secretary of the Sulgrave Institution, to Joseph G. Butler, Jr., January 16, 1921. The letterhead stationery carries the list of the Board of Governors. MVHS, Butler Scrapbooks, vol. 46:63. Butler reprinted his essay "A Day in Washington's Country" as the final chapter of *My First Trip Abroad* (1921). Two websites are worth examining. The official website of the Glessner House Museum has a useful description of Sulgrave Manor. It contains photos and a lengthy quote from a Chicago *Tribune* article "Rejoice in 100 Years of Peace." https://www.glessnerhouse.org/story-of-a-house/2017/2/19/sulgrave-manor-ancestral-home-of-george-washington (accessed July 29, 2018). For another history of Sulgrave Manor, see: https://www.geni.com/projects/Sulgrave-Manor-Northamptonshire-Now-Oxfordshire-England/25510 (accessed July 29, 2018).

32. W. Lanier Washington to Butler, February 22, 1925, Butler Scrapbooks, vol. 46:63; Charles Stewart Davison to Messrs. Norton, Rose & Co., August 5, 1925, MVHS, Butler Scrapbooks, vol. 46: 34.

33. *Ohio History Quarterly*, vol. 34, 428–433, July 1925, 39; Butler to John Penton, January 11, 1927, MVHS, Butler Scrapbooks, vol. 23:90.

34. *Youngstown Vindicator*, June 14, 1925.

35. The Archives of the Mahoning Valley Historical Society, Youngstown, Ohio, has in its collection 52 large Butler scrapbooks. They vary in length, but many exceed one hundred pages.

36. Butler, *Autographed Portraits*, Butler Art Institute, 1927: foreword and preface, n. p.; *Youngstown Vindicator*, April 11, 1927; Joseph G. Butler, Jr., to Justice John H. Clarke, November 4, 1926. MVHS Butler Scrapbooks, vol. 23: 74.

37. David Tod, Butler's partner in the Tod-Stambaugh Company, was the son of William Tod and grandson of his namesake, Ohio's former governor David Tod. Howard Melville Hanna, Jr., was the nephew of Mark Hanna, whom Butler had befriended for nearly 50 years. H.M. Hanna to Butler, May 14, 1926, MVHS Butler Scrapbooks, vol. 30:37.

38. *Youngstown Vindicator*, December 22, 1926.

39. *Youngstown Telegram*, July 5, 1927;

Youngstown Vindicator, July 5, 1927. E.L. Ford's estate was appraised at $3,487,651.67, one of the largest ever filed in Mahoning County. *Youngstown Vindicator*, July 21, 1927. For a lengthy obituary and editorial, see *Iron Age*, vol. 120 (August 8, 1927): 415–17, 420, 422.

40. E.A.S. Clarke to Butler, November 1, 1927, MVHS; Charles Schwab to Butler, January 31, 1921, MVHS; *Youngstown Vindicator*, November 11, 1927.

41. *Youngstown Vindicator*, December 20, 1927; *Youngstown Telegram*, December 20, 1927.

42. *Youngstown Telegram*, December 22, 1927.

43. *Youngstown Vindicator*, December 22, 1927. Rev. William Andrew Leonard, who delivered Butler's eulogy, served as the fourth Episcopal Bishop of Ohio from 1889 to 1930.

Epilogue

1. Linkon and Russo, 29.

Bibliography

MVHS is the abbreviation for Mahoning Valley Historical Society Archives.
BIAA is the abbreviation for Butler Institute of American Art Archives.

Articles

"Against Lower Duties on Iron and Steel." [Testimony of Joseph G. Butler Jr.]. *Iron Age* 89, no. 9 (February 29, 1912): 532.

Bining, Arthur Cecil. "The Rise of Iron Manufacture in Western Pennsylvania," *Western Pennsylvania Historical Magazine* 16, no. 4 (November 1933): 235.

Butler, Joseph G., Jr. "Against Lower Duties," *Iron Age* 89, no. 9 (February 29, 1912): 532.

Butler, Joseph G., Jr. "Competition—Its Uses and Abuses," *Iron Age* 89, no. 21 (May 23, 1912): 1270.

Butler, Joseph G., Jr. "The Country's Steel Business Needs to Be Let Alone," *Iron Age* 95, no. 1 (January 7, 1915): 29.

Butler, Joseph G., Jr. "The French Steel Industry in War Time," *Iron Age* 98, no. 18 (November 2, 1916): 1008.

Butler, Joseph G., Jr. "Record of American Steel in World War," *Iron Age* 103, no. 22 (May 29, 1919): 1436–39.

Butler, Joseph G., Jr. "Wonderful Development of the Iron Business," *Iron Age* 100, no. 18 (November 1, 1917): 1041–45.

Bryan, William Jennings. "The Election of 1900," *North American Review* 171, no. 529 (December 1900): 788–801.

"Death of Henry Clay Frick," *Iron Age* 104, no. 23 (December 4, 1919): 1144.

"In Remembrance of William McKinley," *National Magazine*, June 17, 1923.

"Intense Patriotism at Institute Meeting," *Iron Age* 100, no. 18 (November 1, 1917): 1035–37.

"Iron and Steel Prices for Twenty-One Years," *Iron Age* 109, no. 1 (January 5, 1922): 59–68.

"J.G. Butler, Jr., Honored," *Iron Trade Review*, October 28, 1920, 1219.

"Joseph Green Butler, Jr.," *Iron Trade Review*, December 22, 1927.

"Joseph G. Butler, Jr., Loses Art Collection," *Iron Age* 100, no. 25 (December 20, 1917): 1504.

"Labor Strikes," *Manufacturer and Builder* 21, no. 6 (June 1889): 129.

"Life Chairmanship Given J.G. Butler, Jr., by Pig Iron Men," *Iron Trade Review*, February 14, 1918.

McClelland, Elizabeth. "Joseph Green Butler's Gift to Youngstown," *Western Reserve Magazine*, August/September 1985.

Melnick, John C. "St. Elizabeth Hospital," *Bulletin of the Mahoning County Medical Society*, 42 (August 1972): 219.

"Mr. Butler Discontinues Collection of Pig-Iron Statistics," *Iron Age* 103, no. 3. (January 16, 1919): 195.

"Nestor of the Iron Trade Honored," *Iron Trade Review*, November 9, 1905.

"The New Pig Iron Association," *Iron Age* 93, no. 3 (January 15, 1914): 213–14.

"Obituary—Henry H. Stambaugh," *Iron Age* 103, no. 2 (January 9, 1919): 157.

Page, William H. "The Gary Dinners and the Meaning of Concerted Action," *SMU Law Review* 62, no. 2 (Spring 2009): 597–620.

"Pig Iron Makers Organize," *Iron Age* 93, no. 3 (January 15, 1914): 215.

"Sketch of Career of Joseph G. Butler, Jr.,"

The Blast Furnace & Steel Plant, January 1922.

"The Steel Corporation Dissolution Suit," *Iron Age* 90, no. 19 (November 7, 1912): 1131.

"The Tariff, English and American interests. Rejoicing in England. English iron masters jubilant over the downfall of American iron industry. The treason of Congress to American interests," *Miners' Journal*, May 14, 1870, *An American Time Capsule: Three Centuries of Broadsides and Other Printed Ephemera*.

"Trusts and Public Policy," *The Atlantic Monthly: A Magazine of Literature, Science, Art, and Politics* 87, no. 524, June 1901, Cornell University Making of America.

Books

Aley, Howard. *A Heritage to Share: The Bicentennial History of Youngstown and Mahoning County, Ohio*. Youngstown, Ohio: Bicentennial Commission, 1975.

Ambrose, Stephen E. *Nothing Like It in the World: The Men Who Built the Transcontinental Railroad, 1863–1869*. New York: Simon & Schuster, 2000.

American Association of Museums Directory, Reed Elsevier, 2002.

American Iron and Steel Association. *Directory to the Iron and Steel Works of the United States: Embracing the Blast Furnaces, Rolling Mills, Steel Works, Forges, and Bloomaries in Every State and Territory*. Philadelphia: No. 265 South Fourth Street, 1880.

Bicentennial History Book, Warren, Ohio: Warren-Trumbull County Bicentennial Commission, 1976.

Bining, Arthur Cecil. *Pennsylvania Iron Manufacture in the Eighteenth Century*. Harrisburg: Pennsylvania Historical Commission, 1938.

Biographical History of Northeastern Ohio, Embracing the Counties of Ashtabula, Trumbull, and Mahoning. Chicago: The Lewis Publishing Company, 1893.

Blue, Frederick J., William D. Jenkins, H. William Lawson, Joan M. Reedy. *Mahoning Memories: A History of Youngstown and Mahoning County*. Virginia Beach, VA: Donning Company, 1995.

Bodnar, John E. *The Transplanted: A History of Immigrants in Urban America*. Bloomington, IN: Indiana University Press, 1985.

Boryczka, Raymond, and Lorin Lee Cary. *No Strength Without Union, an Illustrated History of Ohio Workers, 1803–1980*. Columbus: The Ohio Historical Society, 1982.

Brand, H.W. *Woodrow Wilson, the American Presidents*, edited by Arthur M. Schlesinger, Jr., New York: Henry Holt and Company, 2003.

Brown, Ryan C. *Pittsburgh and the Great Steel Strike of 1919*. Charleston, SC: The History Press, 2019.

Butler, Henry A. *Overseas Sketches: Being a Journal of My Experiences in Service with the American Red Cross in France*. (n. p., 1921).

Butler, Joseph G., Jr., ed. *Autographed Portraits*. Youngstown, OH: Butler Art Institute, 1927.

Butler, Joseph G., Jr. *Fifty Years of Iron and Steel*. 7th edition. Cleveland: Penton Press, 1923.

Butler, Joseph G., Jr. *A Journey Through France in War Time*. Cleveland: Penton Press, 1917.

Butler, Joseph G., Jr. *History of Youngstown and the Mahoning Valley, Ohio*. Chicago: American Historical Society, 1921.

Butler, Joseph G., Jr. *Life of William McKinley and History of the National McKinley Birthplace Memorial*. Cleveland, 1924.

Butler, Joseph G., Jr. *My First Trip Abroad*. Youngstown: Joseph G. Butler Jr., 1921; Cleveland: Penton Press, 1922.

Butler, Joseph G., Jr. *Presidents I Have Seen and Known, Lincoln to Taft and A Day in Washington's Country*. Cleveland: Penton Press, 1910.

Butler, Joseph G., Jr. *Recollections of Men and Events, An Autobiography*. Cleveland, OH: Penton Press, 1925; New York: G.P. Putnam's Sons, 1927.

Butler, Joseph Green, III. *A Venerable Vessel. A Short Story of the Bulk Carrier Joseph G. Butler, Jr., 1905–1971*. Poland, OH: Joseph Green Butler III, 1972.

Butler, William David, John Cromwell Butler, Joseph Marion Butler. *Butler Family in America*. St. Louis, MO: Shallcross Printing Co., 1909.

Calhoun, Charles William. *The Gilded Age: Perspectives on the Origins of Modern*

Bibliography

America. Washington, D.C.: Rowman & Lifflefield, 2007.

Camp, J.M., and C.B. Francis. *The Making, Shaping and Treating of Steel*, 4th edition. Pittsburgh: Carnegie Steel Company, 1925.

Cart, Sarah, Paul Jagnow, Robert McFerren. *These Hundred Years: A Chronicle of the Twentieth Century*. Youngstown, Ohio: Vindicator Printing Company, 2000.

Cashman, Sean Dennis. *America in the Gilded Age: From the Death of Lincoln to the Rise of Theodore Roosevelt*, New York: New York University, 1984.

Chernow, Ron. *The House of Morgan, An American Banking Dynasty and The Rise of Modern Finance*. New York: Atlantic Monthly Press, 1990.

Clark, Victor S. *History of Manufactures in the United States*. New York: McGraw-Hill, 1929.

Clements, Kendrick, and Eric Cheezum. *Woodrow Wilson*. Washington, D.C.: CQ Press, 2003.

Combination Atlas of the County of Mercer and the State of Pennsylvania, From Actual Surveys and Official Records. Philadelphia: G.M. Hopkins and Company, 1873.

Cotter, Arundel. *The Authentic History of the United States Steel Corporation*. New York: Moody Magazine and Book Company, 1916.

Cotter, Arundel. *The Gary I Knew*. Boston: The Stratford Company, 1928.

Craven, Wayne. *Sculpture in America (From the Colonial Period to the Present)*, New York: Thomas Y. Crowell Co., 1968.

Directory to the Iron and Steel Works of the United States, Vol. II (1901), 256–259.

Egan, Timothy. *Short Nights of the Shadow Catcher, The Epic Life and Immortal Photographs of Edward Curtis*. New York: Houghton Mifflin Harcourt, 2012.

Fleming, James S. "Oscar W. Underwood: The First Modern House Leader, 1911–1915." In *Masters of the House: Congressional Leaders Over Two Centuries*, edited by Roger H. Davidson, Susan Webb Hammond, and Raymond W. Smock. Boulder, Colorado: Westview Press, 1998: 96.

Foner, Eric, and John A. Garraty, ed. *The Reader's Companion to American History*. Boston: Houghton Mifflin, 1991.

Fraser, Steve. *The Age of Acquiescence: The Life and Death of American Resistance to Organized Wealth and Power*. Boston: Little, Brown and Company, 2015.

Goodwin, Doris Kearns. *Team of Rivals: The Political Genius of Abraham Lincoln*. New York: Simon & Schuster, 2005.

Gould, Lewis L. *Four Hats in the Ring, The 1912 Election and the Birth of Modern American Politics*. Lawrence, Kansas: University Press of Kansas, 2008.

Grant, H. Roger. *Self-Help in the 1890s Depression*. Ames, IA: Iowa State University Press, 1983.

Green, Hardy. *The Company Town: The Industrial Edens and Satanic Mills That Shaped the American Economy*. New York: Basic Books, 2010.

Hartzell, Frank. *The Nation's Memorial to William McKinley, Erected at Canton*. Canton, Ohio: The McKinley National Memorial Association, 1913.

Hatcher, Harlan. *The Western Reserve: The Story of New Connecticut in Ohio*. New York: Bobbs-Merrill, 1949.

Hessen, Robert. *Steel Titan: The Life of Charles M. Schwab*. New York: Oxford University Press, 1975.

Higham, John. *Strangers in the Land*. New York: Rutgers University, 2002.

Higley, George. *Youngstown, An Intimate History*. Youngstown, Ohio: n.p., 1953.

Hiltzik, Michael. *Iron Empires, Robber Barons, Railroads, and the Making of Modern America*. New York: Houghton, Mifflin, Harcourt, 2020.

History of Mercer County, Pennsylvania with Illustrations Descriptive of its Scenery. Philadelphia: L.H. Everts & Company, 1877.

History of Trumbull and Mahoning Counties with Illustrations. Cleveland, Ohio: H.Z. Williams & Bro., 1882.

Hoerr, John P. *And the Wolf Finally Came, The Decline of the American Steel Industry*. Pittsburgh: University of Pittsburgh Press, 1988.

Hoffman, Charles. *The Depression of the Nineties: An Economic History*. Westport, CT: Greenwood Press, 1970.

Hogan, William T. *Economic History of the Iron and Steel Industry in the United States*. New York: Lexington Books, 1971.

Horwitz, Lester V. *The Longest Raid of the Civil War, Little-Known & Untold Stories of Morgan's Raid into Kentucky,*

Indiana & Ohio. Cincinnati, OH: Farmcourt Publishing, Inc., 2001.
Hunt, George D. *History of Salem and the Immediate Vicinity: Columbiana County, Ohio*. Salem, O.: Author, 1898.
Ingham, John N. *The Iron Barons, A Social Analysis of an American Urban Elite, 1874–1965*. Westport, Connecticut: Greenwood Press, 1978.
Keeler, P.E. "Nye County," in *The History of Nevada*, Vol. 2. edited by Sam P. Davis. Reno, NV: Elms Publishing, 1913.
Korom, Joseph J. *The American Skyscraper, 1850–1940: A Celebration of Height*. Braden Books, 2008.
Krass, Peter. *Carnegie*. Hoboken, NJ: John Wiley & Sons, 2002: 366.
Lamoreaux, Naomi R. *The Great Merger Movement in American Business, 1895–1904*. Cambridge: Cambridge University Press, 1985.
Leech, Margaret. *In the Days of McKinley*. New York: Harper, 1959.
Lesley, J. *The Iron Manufacturer's Guide to the Furnaces, Forges and Rolling Mills of the United States with Discussion of Iron as A Chemical Element, An American Ore, and A Manufactured Article, in Commerce and in History*. New York: John Wiley, 1859.
Linkon, Sherry Lee, and John Russo. *Steeltown U.S.A.: Work and Memory in Youngstown*. Lawrence, KS: University Press of Kansas, 2002.
Martin, Steve. *A Native of Immigrants*. New York: Cambridge University Press, 2011.
McKnight, William James. *A Pioneer Outline History of Northwestern Pennsylvania*. Philadelphia: J.B. Lippincott Company, 1905.
Merry, Robert W. *President McKinley, Architect of the American Century*. New York: Simon & Schuster, 2017.
Miller, Nathan. *Theodore Roosevelt, A Life*. New York: William Morrow and Company, Inc., 1992.
Misa, Thomas J. *A Nation of Steel: The Making of Modern America, 1865–1925*. Baltimore: Johns Hopkins Press, 1995.
Morgan, H. Wayne. *William McKinley and His America*. Kent, OH: Kent State Press, 2003.
Morris, Edmund. *The Rise of Theodore Roosevelt*. New York: Coward, McCann & Geoghegan, Inc., 1979.
Mulkearn, Lois and Edwin V. Pugh. *A Traveler's Guide to Historic Western Pennsylvania*. Pittsburgh: University of Pittsburgh Press, 1954.
Nasaw, David. *Andrew Carnegie*. New York: The Penguin Press, 2006.
National McKinley Birthplace Memorial Association. *Proposal to Build a Monument and Memorial to William McKinley at Niles, Ohio, the place of his birth*. Cleveland: Penton Press, 1911.
The Nation's Memorial to William McKinley Erected at Canton, Ohio. Canton, Ohio: The McKinley National Memorial Association, 1918.
N.H. Burch & Co. *Youngstown City Directory*. Youngstown, OH, 1886-7.
Niles Bicentennial History Committee. *A Pictorial History of Niles, Ohio: Bicentennial Edition*. Niles Historical Society, 1976.
Olcott, Charles S. *William McKinley*. Boston: Houghton Mifflin Company, 1916.
Palmquist, Peter E., and Thomas R. Kailbourn. *Pioneer Photographers of the Far West, A Biographical Dictionary, 1840–1865*. Stanford, California: Stanford University Press, 2000.
Pearse, John B. *A Concise History of the Iron Manufacture of the American Colonies up to the Revolution, and of Pennsylvania until the Present Time*. Philadelphia: Allen, Lane and Scott, 1876.
Reifsnider & Gardner. *Reifsnider & Gardner's Youngstown Directory*. Youngstown, OH: Courier Steam Print, 1872.
Riesenman, Joseph, Jr. *History of Northwestern Pennsylvania, Comprising the Counties of Erie, Crawford, Mercer, Venango, Warren, Forest, Clarion, McKean, Elk, Jefferson, Cameron and Clearfield*. New York: Lewis Historical Publishing Company, 1943.
Roth, Leland M. *The Architecture of McKim, Mead, & White, 1870–1920 a Building List*. New York: Garland Publishing, 1978.
Ruminski, Clayton J. *Iron Valley: The Transformation of the Iron Industry in Ohio's Mahoning Valley, 1802–1913*. Columbus, Ohio: Trillium, 2017.
Russell, Francis. *Shadow of Blooming Grove: Warren G. Harding and His Times*. New York: McGraw-Hill, 1968.
Schlesinger, Arthur M., Jr., ed. *Almanac of American History, Revised and Updated*. New York: Barnes & Noble Books, 1993.

Shafer, Dale E. *Salem, A Quaker City History, The Making of America Series.* Charleston, SC: Arcadia Publishing, 2002.
Skardon, Alvin W. *Steel Valley University, The Origin of Youngstown State.* Cincinnati: C.J. Krehbiel Co., 1983.
Smith, Theodore Clarke. *The Life and Letters of James Abram Garfield.* Hamden, CT: Archon Books, 1968.
Standiford, Les. *Meet You in Hell: Andrew Carnegie, Henry Clay Frick, and The Bitter Partnership That Transformed America.* New York: Three Rivers Press, 2005.
Stewart, John Struthers. *History of Northeastern Ohio*, Vols. 1, 2. Indianapolis: Historical Publishing Company, 1935.
Swank, James M. *History of the Manufacture of Iron in All Ages, and Particularly in the United States for Three Hundred years from 1585 to 1885.* Philadelphia: Allen, Lane and Scott, 1884.
Sweetkind, Irene S., ed. *Master Paintings from the Butler Institute of American Art.* New York: Harry N. Abrams, 1994.
Upton, Harriet Taylor. *History of the Western Reserve.* Chicago-New York: The Lewis Publishing Co., 1910.
Walker, Joseph E. *Hopewell Village, A Social and Economic History of an Iron-Making Community.* Philadelphia: University of Pennsylvania Press, 1966.
Wall, Joseph Frazier. *Andrew Carnegie.* New York: Oxford University Press, 1970.
Warren, Kenneth. *The American Steel Industry, 1850-1970. A Geographical Interpretation.* Oxford: Clarendon Press, 1973.
Warren, Kenneth. *Triumphant Capitalism: Henry Clay Frick and the Industrial Transformation of America.* Pittsburgh: The University of Pittsburgh Press, 2000.
White, J.G. *A Twentieth Century History of Mercer County, Pennsylvania*, vol. 1. Chicago: Lewis Publishing Company, 1909.
Wiebe, Robert H. *The Search for Order, 1877-1920.* New York: Hill and Wang, 1967.
Youngstown, The City of Progress, A Natural Center of Manufacture and Distribution. Youngstown, Ohio: Youngstown Chamber of Commerce, 1913.

Newspapers

Detroit Free Press
Mahoning Courier(Ohio)
Nashville Tennessean
New York Herald
New York Times
Niles Daily News (Ohio)
Niles Daily Times (Ohio)
Toledo Review
Warren Chronicle (Ohio)
Washington Post
Western Reserve Chronicle (Ohio)
Youngstown Sheet & Tube Bulletin
Youngstown Telegram
Youngstown Vindicator
Youngstown Weekly News and Register

Other Sources

Abbott, Carl. "Lewis and Clark Exposition." *The Oregon Encyclopedia*, Oregon Historical Society, accessed October 27, 2018, https://oregonencyclopedia.org/articles/lewis_clark_exposition/.
American Painting, Mahoning Institute of Art catalog, May 1915, Butler Institute of American Art Archives.
Announcement on Joseph Pennell's availability for lectures, The American Federation of Arts, August 9, 1917, Washington, D.C.
Bulletin of the American Iron and Steel Association, vol. 42, no. 12 (Philadelphia, September 1, 1908): 90.
Butler, Joseph G., III, interviewed by Paul Bick, December 10, 1975. Youngstown State University Oral History Program, Youngstown, Ohio.
Butler, Joseph G., Jr. "Impressions of the World's Fair, 1904," 4, MVHS.
Butler, Joseph G., Jr. "Impressions of the World's Fair, 1904," 9, MVHS.
Butler, Joseph G., Jr. "Memorandum for Mr. R.J. Kaylor," October 11, 1924.
Butler, Joseph G., Jr. "Mr. Butler's Report of His Southern Trip in October, A.D. 1890." Accession no. 66.56.01.09, MVHS.
Butler, Joseph G., Jr. "Notes of a Third Trip to the Pacific Coast—The Lewis & Clark Centennial Exposition and Oriental Fair, 1905," Collection #209, Box 2, Joseph Green.
Butler, Joseph G., Jr. "Notes of a Third Trip to the Pacific Coast, 1905," 8, MVHS.
Butler, Joseph G., Jr. "Opposition to Roosevelt." Undated typed draft. Butler Scrapbook 70.51.27. MVHS.
Butler, Joseph G., Jr. "Opposition to Roo-

sevelt." Undated typed draft. Joseph G. Butler Jr., files. MVHS.

Butler, Joseph G., Jr. "Pig Iron During 1904." Bessemer Pig Iron Association, Typed draft, 3. MVHS.

Butler, Joseph G., Jr. "Raw Materials," *Congratulatory Addresses Delivered at a Complimentary Dinner Tendered to Judge Elbert H. Gary*, Waldorf-Astoria, New York, October 15, 1909.

Butler, Joseph G., Jr. "The Small Museum." Transcript of lecture, 7th Annual American Federation of Art Convention, New Willard Hotel in Washington, D.C., May 17, 1916, Butler Institute of American Art Archives.

Butler, Joseph G., Jr. "Weekly Letter to the Members of the Bessemer Pig Iron Association." October 26, 1904. MVHS.

Butler, Joseph G., Jr., to R.J. Kaylor, memorandum, October 11, 1924. Vertical Files on David Tod, Public Library of Youngstown and Mahoning County, Ohio.

Butler Jr. Papers, Accession no. 66.56.01.12, MVHS.

Duff's Business Institute file, Pennsylvania Department, Carnegie Library, Pittsburgh, PA. *50 Years in Steel, the Story of The Youngstown Sheet and Tube Company, This is America*. Youngstown, Ohio: The Youngstown Sheet & Tube Company, 1950.

Gillespie, P. Ann. "Wick Avenue 1940–1967: Millionaire's Row and Youngstown State University," Master's thesis, Youngstown State University, December 2006.

"H.C. Frick's First Visit," October 29, 1919, National McKinley Birthplace Museum Archives, Niles, Ohio, Accession no. 95.1.96.

Harper's New Monthly Magazine (March 1894) Vol. 88, No. 526: 587–602.

Harris, Marc. "James Ward," *Encyclopedia of American Business History and Biography, Iron and Steel in the Nineteenth Century*. Edited by Paul F. Paskoff. (New York: Bruccoli Clark Layman, Inc., and Facts on File, 1989).

Hessen, Robert. "Charles M. Schwab," in *Encyclopedia of American Business History and Biography: Iron and Steel in the Twentieth Century*, Edited by Bruce E. Seely. (New York: Bruccoli Clark Layman and Facts on File, 1994).

Hughes, George W. "The Pioneer Iron Industry in Western Pennsylvania," *Western Pennsylvania Historical Magazine*, vol. 14, 1931, 207–224.

"Impromptu Addresses in Response to the Call of Judge Gary," *Year Book of The American Iron and Steel Institute* (New York: AISI, October 1913).

"J. Massey Rhind," Undated article. *Carnegie Magazine*, Butler Institute of American Art Archives.

"Joseph G. Butler, Jr. Testimonial Banquet," held at The Union Club, Cleveland, Ohio, "Joseph G. Butler, Jr., 1854," file, MVHS.

Kaylor, *In Thirty Years*, Unpublished draft. Joseph G. Butler, Jr., Papers, MVHS.

Kennon, Donald, and Rebecca M. Rogers. *The Committee on Ways and Means: A Bicentennial History 1789–1989, House Documents* no. *100–244*, 197, Washington, D.C.: U.S. Government Publishing Office, 1989.

Lown, Marilyn R. *The Pennsylvania and Ohio Canal, A Brief History*, unpublished Commemorative Publication, 2000.

"Mahoning Valley Historical Society," Dorothy Welsh interview conducted by Hugh G. Earnhart in Youngstown, Ohio, 1975-11-04. Youngstown State University Oral History program.

"McKinley Memorial Gold Dollar," *The CoinSite*, accessed November 10, 2018, https://coinsite.com/mckinley-memorial-gold-dollar/.

Memorandum from Butler to Kaylor, October 11, 1924, 22.

Memorandum of Agreement between John W. Young and Joseph G. Butler, Jr., January 26, 1918, for the purchase of *Tragedy at Sea*, by George Inness.

National McKinley Birthplace Memorial and The McKinley Birthplace Home & Research Center brochure.

National Society of the Daughters of the American Revolution, vol. 39, 251, Dar.htm.

Official Report of the Proceedings of the Sixteenth Republican National Convention, reported by George L. Hart. New York: Tenny Press, 1916.

Ohio Historical Society Fundamental Documents, David Tod. resources.ohiohistory.org/governors.

Ohio History Quarterly 34 (July 1925): 428–433.

Bibliography

Pennsylvania Historical Magazine 16:4 (Nov. 1933), 238. August 9, 1942.

Peyko, Mark Christopher. *Understanding the Downtown: Architecture, Downtown Directory, Historic Preservation.* Public Library of Youngstown and Mahoning County.

Popenoe/Popnoe/Poppino & Allied Families. Genealogy-Sylvanus Seely's Family, www.popenoe.com/Diary/Seely Diary2htm.

Rohrbaugh, Paul H., Jr. "Friendship Memorialized: Joseph G. Butler and the McKinley National Birthplace Memorial," Master's thesis, Youngstown State University, 2001.

Rowfant Club: Printed Ephemera and Associated Items, 1901–1997. www.grolierclub.org/Libraryamc.rowfantclub.htm.

Rutherford, Roy. "Rollin C. Steese, Key Man in Valley's Growth," *Youngstown Vindicator*, April 20, 1947.

Rutherford, Roy. "Rollin C. Steese Rose to Superintendency of Brier Hill Iron & Coal in Six Months," *Youngstown Vindicator*, April 13, 1947.

Seely, Bruce E. "Joseph Green Butler, Jr." *Iron and Steel in the Twentieth Century, Encyclopedia of American History and Business.* 1994.

Stockholders Meeting of Brier Hill Iron and Coal Company including contract between Brier Hill Iron and Coal Company and Joseph G. Butler Jr., and Thomas H. Pollock, May 9, 1878," MVHS.

Sypolt, Larry. "James Anson Campbell," *Encyclopedia of American Business History and Biography.* Edited by Bruce Seely.

Sypolt, Larry N., and Bruce E. Seely, "Youngstown Sheet and Tube Company," *Encyclopedia of American Business History and Biography: Iron and Steel in the Twentieth Century*, ed. Bruce E. Seely (New York: Bruccoli Clark Layman and Facts On File, 1994).

"Trustees Through the Years." Library History 1910–29, unmounted. Public Library of Youngstown and Mahoning County, Ohio.

United States v. United States Steel Corporation et al., 251 U.S. 417 (1920).

Western Pennsylvania Historical Magazine 16:4 (November 1933).

"William McKinley Memorial, Niles, Ohio" *Architectural Forum* 31, no. 6 (December 1919): 205.

William McKinley papers, circa 1847–1935.

Youngstown Planning Commission Historic Preservation, June 1974. 100th Anniversary Gala Program, October 19, 2019, Butler Institute of American Art Archives.

Index

Numbers in ***bold italics*** indicate pages with illustrations

Adams, Asael 99, 100
African Americans, as laborers 6, 55
Agler, Benjamin 155, 191
Agler, Josephine Ford 107, 115, 155, 163, 191, 192
Akron, Ohio 16
Albany and Rensselaer Iron and Steel Company 60
Albright Gallery (Buffalo) 176
Aldrich, Nelson W. 122
Allegheny Valley 44
Alnwick 172
Althorp House 125
A.M. Byers Company 42, ***48***
Amalgamated Association of Iron and Steel Workers 55, 71, 72, 73, 75, 76
American Association of Museum Directory 176
American Federation of Arts 158
American Historical Society 184
American Industrial Commission ***161***, 160-162
American Institute of Architects 146
American Institute of Mining Engineers 110
American Iron and Steel Institute (AISI) 31, 71, 131, 132, 156, 165, 180, 188, 189; Belgium 131; British industrialists in Chicago 126; Butler 137, 140, 158, 160; Elbert Gary 117; and James Swank 130; support for McKinley memorial 142, 145
American Manufacturer 65, 76
American Manufacturers' Export Association of New York 159
American Pig Iron Association 154; Butler retires as president of 164
American Renaissance movement 174
American Scotch pig iron 57, 66
American Sheet Steel Company 85

American Shipbuilding Company 115
American Steel and Wire Company 98
American Steel Hoop Company 85
American Tin Plate Company 98
Americanization 157, 193
Amerika 112
Andrew, Chauncey 39, 40
Andrews & Hitchcock Company 53
Andrews Bros. 53, 56, 71
Anna Furnace 44
anthracite 41
Apollo 178
Appalachian Mountains, and iron industry 12
The Architecture of McKim, Mead & White 1870-1920 a Building List see Roth, Leland M.
Arms, Freeman O. 41
Art Institute (Buffalo) 176
Atchison, Topeka, and Santa Fe Railroad 80
Atlantic City, New Jersey 179, 184, 185
The Atlantic Monthly 102
Autographed Portraits 188
Ayer, John 30-31

Baker, Sara 168
Baldwin, William H. 85
Ballymoney, County Antrim, Ireland 113
Baltimore, Maryland 17, 49
Baltimore and Ohio Railroad 58
Barclay, William 39
Barnum, P.T. 19
Barnum and Bailey Circus 19
Battle of Gettysburg 29
Beaver and Erie Canal, construction 13
beehive coke ovens 41
Bell, Sir Isaac Lowthian 38
Bellefonte, Pennsylvania 10

Index

Belmont Park Cemetery (Youngstown, Ohio) 183, 190
Bentley, Robert 130
Berlin, Germany 64, 112
Besancon, France 161, 162
Bessemer Furnace association 96
Bessemer, Sir Henry 151
Bessemer Limestone Company 62, 106, 165
Bessemer Limestone Company of Pennsylvania 60, 61
Bessemer Limestone Company of West Virginia 60, 61
Bessemer Pig Iron Association (Mahoning Valley Iron Manufacturers' Association) 63, 81, 103, 105, 106
Bessemer process 59, 82
Bethlehem Steel 128
Beveridge, Albert 120
Birmingham, Alabama 66, 72
Biwabik Mining Company 134
black-band ore 24, 25, 48, 57
The Blast Furnace & Steel Plant 184
blast furnace, construction 14, 15
Blue Ridge Marble Company 174
Bodnar, John 55
Bonnell, Henry O. 71, 72, 78; Bessemer Pig Iron Association 63; death 63
Bonnell, William 118
Boucherle, Paul 172
Boyle, James 144, 145
Brier Hill (coal) 33, 39, 41, 42, 44, 47
Brier Hill Iron and Coal Company 44, 53, 56, 57, 58, 123, 165; Butler 34, 52; furnace explosion 54; name change 59; *see also* Grace furnace
Brier Hill Iron Company 62, 64, 69, 71, 74, 85, 78, 106, 110; company lab 66; competition 103; manufacture steel 134; New York capitalists 77; Ohio Steel Company 84; reliance on pig iron production 105; reorganized 59; spiegeleisen 60; use of science 81
Brier Hill Limestone Company 60
Brier Hill Steel Company 134, 156, 161, 165, 185
British American Peace Committee 126
British Iron and Steel Institute 66, 107, 112
Brown, Joseph 31
Brown, Richard 31, 39, 40, 118
Brown, Thomas 31
Brown, Bonnell and Company 53, 71, 84, 99 and Hale & Ayer 31; strike breaking 56
Brussels, Belgium 131
Bryan, William Jennings 89, 90, 93, 94, 95
Buchanan, James 130
Buckeye Iron Company 106

Buffalo, New York 96, 110, 144
Buhl, Frank 151
Bull Moose Party 138
Bullock, Charles 102, 103
Burbank, Elbridge Ayer 175
Burns, Robert 147
Burton, Theodore 120, 159
Butler, Alice 18
Butler, Ann 10
Butler Art Institute 5, 167–178, **177**, 182, 191; American art 176; American Renaissance movement 174; architect (McKim, Mead, and White 172; William Mitchell Kendall) 172, 174; art acquisitions 175, 176, 177, 182; Butler's will 191; concept 171; construction 171, 173, 174–175; cost 173, 178; dedication 177; design 173, 174; dimensions 173; director 176; endowment 182; expansion 173, 182; exterior 173, 177; fireproof 173; gifted to city of Youngstown 182; HVAC 173; J. Massey Rhind 174, 175, 176, 177, 178; John H. Parker company 174, 175; landscape 172, 173; Owsley and Boucherle, local architect 172; style 172, 173; transfer to city of Youngstown 182; Wick property 173
Butler, Edward Steven 18, 28
Butler, Emma Eliza 18
Butler, Grace Heath 107
Butler, Harriet (Voorhees Ingersoll) 7, 34, **35**, 64, 68, 110–112, 139, 155, 177, 183, 189, 190; birth 34; death 183; funeral 183; health 155; house fire 170–171; marriage 35; parents 34
Butler, Henry Audubon 7, 115, 155, **159**, 171, 179, 182, **183**, 185, 187, 189, 191, 192; birth 36; death 192; education 64, 68, 112; family 107; and Mahoning Valley Mortgage Company 165; and Red Cross 163, 164, 165; Squirrel Island 165
Butler, Irvin *see* Butler, James Irwin
Butler, Ithamar 12, 18
Butler, James (brother of Joseph G. Butler, Sr.) 10
Butler, James Irwin "Irvin" 18, **20**, 28, 31; Best Man for Butler 35; owned furnace in Tennessee and death 41
Butler, James Ward 18, 189, 191
Butler, Joseph (first) 10, 67–68
Butler, Joseph G., III 107, 115, 155, **159**, **164**, 176, 191;as art institute director 192; education 111
Butler, Beadling and Wick *see* Butler Wick 192
Butler Day (Niles, Ohio) 182
The Butler Family in America 10

Butler, Joseph G., Jr. *32*, *70*, *124*, *125*, *138*, *159*, *160*, *178*; American Federation of Arts 156; American Historical Society's request of Butler 184; and American Industrial Commission 160–162, *161*; and American Iron and Steel Institute, (A.I.S.I.) 31, 117, 131, 137, 140, 142, 145, 158, 163; and A.M. Byers 42, 43, 47, 51, 52; American Pig Iron Association 154; and Andrew Carnegie and Butler's pursuit of a donation for Ruben McMillan Library 118, 122, 124, 147, 148; art collection 8, 69, 112, 113, 167, 170, 171, 172, 175; Atlantic City, New Jersey health retreat 179, 184, 185; auto accident 179; *Autographed Portraits* 188; baptism 185; Belgium 131; Bessemer Limestone Companies 60, 61, 62, 106, 165; Bessemer Pig Iron Association president 63, 81; birth at Temperance Furnace 9, 15; books 9, 28, 80, 99, 123, 129, 130, 162, 180, 184, 186, 187, 188; and Brier Hill Iron and Coal Company 34, 51–52, 55–56, 59; Buckeye Iron Company stockholder 106; business philosophy 6, 26, 31, 39, 40, 56, 59, 87, 118, 137; Butler Art Institute 5, 167–178, 182, 191; Butler Day 182; candidacy for U.S. Senate 120; character traits 62, 67, 68, 100; and Charles Schwab 129, 189; childhood 16, 18, 19, *19*, *20*, 67; children *see* Blanche Butler Ford, Grace Butler McGraw, and Henry Audubon Butler; and Civil War 28, 29; congressional testimony 44, 87, 128, 133, 135, 139; and David Tod 33, 34, 39, 52, 53, 56, 62; death 189; desire to be Ironmaster 26; Duff's Commercial College 26–27, 67; East Youngstown Riot 156–158; education 19, 20, 22, 26–27, 67; and Elbridge Ayer Burbank artwork 175; Frick funeral 179; friendship with Henry Stambaugh 53, 108, 165; death 165; funeral 8, 189–190; and Gary Dinners 115–118; and Girard Iron Company 34, 37; grandchildren *see* Josephine Ford Agler, Joseph G. Butler, III, Mary Grace Butler, John; Willard Ford, Arthur Butler McGraw; and Hale & Ayer 30–31; health 107, 124, 182–183, 184, 187; *History of Youngstown and the Mahoning Valley* 9, 80, 99, 184; home life in Niles 18; Hotel Ohio 141; house fire 170–172, 174; Ireland 113; and J. Massey Rhind 172, 174–178; and James Swank 132; James Ward 22–28, 30, 32, 40, 67; and John Stambaugh, Jr. 128–129; and John Stambaugh, Sr. 51–53, 62; *A Journey Through France in War Time* 162; Lake Superior Nut and Washer Company 31; last will 182, 191; and Liberty Bell 154–155; Mahoning County Republican Executive Committee 94; Mahoning Institute of Art president 169; Mahoning Iron Company 48; Mahoning Valley Historical Society 122, 123, 130; and Mark Hanna 89, 94; marriage 35; and Merchant Marine League 119, 131, 180; *My First Trip Abroad* 186; National McKinley Birthplace Memorial (Association) 143–152; and Native American culture 107, 111; at New Wilmington, Pa. 21; night school for Ward Company employees 24; and Ohio Steel 74–78, 138; Ohio-Tonopah Mining Company 108, 109; opinion of Charles Owsley 169; parents 11; patriotism 111, 154, 187; politics 25, 28, 45, 87 (*see* Harding; McKinley; Republican Conventions; Republican Party; Roosevelt; Taft); Portage Silica Company president 165; *Presidents I Have Seen and Known* 129–130; pursuit of John Hunt Morgan 29; on railroad rates 69–70; *Recollections of Men and Events* 187; religion 26, 68, 185; and Republican Conventions 93, 94, 138, 159, 180; residence at Rayen Avenue and Phelps St. 36, 68–69; Reuben McMillan Library 122, 148; book donation 155; and St. Elizabeth Hospital 136, 137, 145; saved from drowning 91; seventieth birthday gathering 128–129; siblings 12, 18, 28, 31, 35, 41, 189, 191; *A Small Museum and Its Value to a Community* 156; and Soldiers' Monument 178; and Sulgrave Manor 125, 126, 186, 193; tariffs, view on 40, 44, 45, 87–88, 90, 120, 128, 132, 133, 135, 142; and Theodore Roosevelt 94, 105, 106, 123, 159; and Thomas McDonald 78–79; Tod House 127; Tod-Stambaugh Company 188; and Tom Scott 49; Tonopah Mines 108–109; "The Town Beautiful" 124, 142; travels 107–114; at Tremont Furnace 21; Uncle Joe 5, 8, 9, 128, 135; Underwood Tariff 135; and Warren G. Harding 149, 180; William Howard Taft 120, 138, 143, 145, 146, 151, 152; and William McKinley 5, 18, 21, 78, 87–96, 123, 124, 130, 142, 152; and William "Uncle Billie" Pollock 33, 51, 54; and William Ward 34; witnesses first steel rolled in the United States 31; World's fairs 76, 110, 153, 154; and Youngstown Art Association 167; Youngstown Board of Health 130; and Youngstown Chamber of Commerce 123, 124, 130; and Youngstown City Council 39, 60, 68, 130; Youngstown Humane Society 130–131; Youngstown Iron and Mining Company 59; and Youngstown (Iron) Sheet & Tube

228　Index

Co. 100, 106, 127, 185; Youngstown Museum of Art 168, 169; and Youngstown Savings and Loan Association 40
Butler, Joseph G. Sr. (also referred to as Green Butler) *11*, 67–68; Abraham Lincoln 25; birth 10; blast furnace manager 11; death 92; elected sheriff 28; marriage 11; move to Mercer County 12, 13; Niles 15; physical description 10; Quaker 10; religion 10; Temperance Furnace 15; Tremont Furnace 21; Ward Company store manager 16, 18, 22, 23; and William McKinley, Sr. 14
Butler, Joseph Marion 17
Butler, Mary Grace 191
Butler, Miles 12, 18, 28
Butler, Nicholas Murray 180
Butler, Sarah Grace Heath 155, 163
Butler, Temperance Orwig *12*, 18; birth 11; death 92; marriage 11; Quaker 11
Butler, Thomas 10
Butler, William 18
Byers, Alexander M. 42, 43, 47, 51, 52

Caldwell, James 78
Calhoun, John C. 147
Cambria Iron Company 60
Cambridge 186
Campbell, James A. 7, 128, 129, 133, 136, 163, 185; biographical sketch 101; Youngstown Iron and Sheet and Tube 100
Canfield, Ohio 29
Cannon, Joseph 119
Canton, Ohio 89, 90, 92, 96, 97, 110, 143
Capitol News Bureau, Columbus, Ohio 153
Captains of Industry 7, 102
Carbon Limestone Company 60
Carnegie, Andrew 5–7, 9, 67, 84, 98, *119*, 128; business philosophy 56, 121; bust at McKinley memorial 151; and Captain Bill Jones 58; influence on politicians 87; and J.P. Morgan 101, 102; and Julian Kennedy 60; Library 118, 122, 124, 147, 148; on organized labor 72
Carnegie Steel 72, 73, 85, 101, 102, 103, 104
Case School of Applied Sciences 66
Centennial Exhibition, 1876 176
Centre County (Pennsylvania) 10, 11
Centre Furnace 15
Chase, William Merritt 169, 171
Chemical Phenomena of Iron Smelting 38
Chicago, Illinois 30–31, 49, 66, 69, 70, 76, 95, 110, 126, 138, 140, 154
Chief Joseph 175
Chinese pig iron 134
Christ Mission 191

Churchill 39
Cincinnati, Ohio 134
Cincinnati Commercial Gazette 144
Civil War 9, 28–29, 32–33, 36, 37, 40, 46, 48, 49, 84, 87
Clark, James "Champ" 163
Clark, Victor 80
Clarke, E.A.S., member of A.I.S.I. 131
Clarke, Emma Butler 18, 190, 191
Clarke, John H. 188
Clayton Anti-Trust Act 154
Cleveland, Ohio 16, 17, 23, 30, 43, 59, 66, 88, 92, 96, 97, 119, 120, 121, 133
Cleveland and Mahoning Railroad 58
Cleveland Catholic Diocese 136, 137
Cleveland Herald 46
Cleveland Leader 46
Cochran, L.E. 127
Cogswell, William 31
coke 41, 42, 47
Colorado Springs 107
Columbia River 111
Columbia University 176
Columbian Exposition *see* World's Fair Chicago 1893
Columbiana County Ohio 14, 29, 88
Columbus, Ohio 133, 153
"Competition—Its Uses and Abuses" 137
Comstock Lode 108
Concricote, Delia 189
Connellsville, Pennsylvania (coke) 42, 47, 57
U.S.S. *Constitution* 34
Coolidge, Calvin 180, 181, 184
Cooper, Evelyn 112
Corns, Joseph 54
Corns Iron Company *see* Girard Rolling Mill
Cortelyou, George 94, 95, 96
Cotter, Arundel 102, 103
Cox, James 151
Crab Creek 46
Craig, Charles 107
Craven, Wayne 147
Credit Mobilier Bridge 74
Crooked Creek 14
Curtis, Edward Sheriff 111
Cuxhaven, Germany 112
Czolgosz, Leon 97

Dalrymple, Ann 10
Dalrymple, Thomas 10
Darwin, Charles 112
Davison, Charles Stewart 186
"A Day in Washington's Country" 125, 186
Della Rovere, Giuliano 172
de Medici, Cosimo (patron of Brunelleschi and Donatello) 172

Index

de Santa Anna, Antonio Lopez *see* Santa Anna
Detroit, Michigan 107
Diamond Match Company 85
Dick, Charles 121
Dickens, Charles 113
Dollar Savings and Trust Company 99
Dollar Savings Bank of Niles 124
Duff, Peter 27
Duff's Commercial (Mercantile) College 26–27, 67
Dulton, C. Seymour 64

Eagle Furnace 53
The Earle of Spencer 125
East Youngstown, Ohio 156, 157; riot 156–158, 192
Ecton, England 125
Edgar Thompson Works 76
Empire Steel and Iron Company 133, 134
Eph Woodworth's Tavern 25
Erie Extension Canal *see* Beaver and Erie Canal
Erie Railroad 58
The Eton Boy see Chase, William Merritt
Evans, Margaret 176, 177, 192
Evans, Richard 188
Evans, Roger 90

Farrell, James 131, 132, 159, 160
Farrelly, Bishop J. 137
Federal Reserve Act 141
Federal Steel 101, 103
Federal Trade Commission 154
Fellowship of the Pennsylvania Academy of the Fine Arts 167
Fifty Years of Iron and Steel 164, 180, 184, 186
first steel rolled in the United States, Butler witnesses 31
Follansbee, William 132, 133
Foraker, Joseph 119, 120
Ford, Blanche Butler 68, 112, 115, 155, 188; birth 36; death 139; marriage 60, 64; relationship with father 68, 185
Ford, Edward L. 100, 107, 110, 155, 173; Brier Hill Iron Co. 71; Brier Hill training 66; Butler Art Institute 173; Butler house fire 170; death 188; early career 60; education 60; marriage to Blanche Butler 60, 64; spiegeleisen 122; and Youngstown Steel Company 71
Ford, John Willard 107, 171, 192; attorney 155; Butler Art Institute trustee 182; Butler's will 191; captain in the U.S. Air Service 163, 164; at St. Louis fair Butler 109, 110; travels to Europe with Butler 112, 113

Ford, Tod 108
Fordyce, George L. 100
Fort Pitt Foundry 28
Franco-British Exposition 113
Franklin, Benjamin 125
Franklin, Josiah 125
Fremont, John C. 25
French Trade Commission 159
Frick, Henry Clay 5–7, 9, 56, 67, 128, 148, *149*, 151; coke transaction 42; funeral 179; influence on politicians 87; and National McKinley Birthplace Memorial 148, 179; on organized labor 72; personal art collection 148

Gallinger, Jacob 119
Gallinger Bill *see* Ocean Mail Act
Garfield, James A. 44, 47, 130; death 45; on tariff reduction 45
Garfield, Lucretia, on *Presidents I Have Seen and Known* 130
Garlick, Richard 127
Gary, Elbert 103, *117*, 126, 129, 151, 156, 180; and A.I.S.I. 115–118; death 188; Doctrine of Competition 103, 104, 115–116, 117, 118; supports Butler 163, 188, 189; supports McKinley memorial project 144; "Uncle Joe" 135
Gary dinners 115–118, 188, 189
Geronimo 175
Gilbert, E.A. 151
Gilded Age, the 6, 9
Girard, Ohio 34, 36, 38, 74, 79
Girard Iron Company 36, *43*, 47, 48, 49, 50, 51, 52, 54, 59; furnace construction 38–39; Tod organizes 33–34
Girard Rolling Mill 54
The Golden Wood see Murphy, Francis
Goldfield 108, 109
Gompers, Samuel 126
Goose Island 74
Goulder, Harvey D. 119
G.P. Putnam's Sons 187
Grace, Mary 155
Grace Furnace 53, 59, 76
Grand Army of the Republic, Canton post 146, 151
Grand Canyon 108
Grand Hotel 112
The Grand Opera House 46
Grant, H. Roger 80
Grant, Ulysses S. 29, 47
The Great Merger Movement in American Business, 1895–1904 81
Great War *see* World War I
Greeley, Horace 25

Index

Green, Esther 10
Green, Hanna 10
Green, Hardy 23
Guild's Lake 111

Haldeman, Horace 133
Hale, Samuel 30
Hale & Ayer Iron Company 30–33
Hall, W.B. 127
Hamburg, Germany 112
Hamilton, Homer 39
Hanna, Howard M., Jr. 188
Hanna, Mark 88–89, 94, 146
Harding, Warren G. 149, 180, 184; death 185
Harper's New Monthly Magazine 82
Harris, Andrew H. 120
Hartenstein, Fred 140
Hassam, Childe 169
Hatcher, Harlan 58
Hawkins Farm 74–77
Hay, John 151
Hays, Will H. 181
Heaton, James 17, 151
Heaton's Furnace 17
Henry the Second 10
Herrick, Myron T. 94, 129; and Merchant Marine League 120, 180; National McKinley Birthplace Memorial Association 143, 149, 152; and participation at 1920 Republican convention 181
Hessen, Robert 98, 101, 103, 104
Hickory Creek Valley 60
Higley, George 74
Hillsville, Pennsylvania 60
Himrod Furnace Company 53
History of Mercer County 15
History of Northwestern Pennsylvania 13
History of Youngstown and the Mahoning Valley 9, 80, 99, 184
Hobart, Garret 93
Hoboken, New Jersey 112
Hoffman, Charles 79
Hogan, William T. 32
Homer, Winslow: *Snap the Whip* 176, 177
Homestead Strike 72, 73
Honesdale, Pennsylvania 35
Hoover, Herbert 126
Hotel Ohio 141
Hoyt, James 128
Hubbard, Ohio 77
Hughes, Charles Evans 120, 126, 159
Hughes, George W. 13
Huntingdon County, Pennsylvania 10
Hutchinson and Company 115

Illinois Steel Company 85
immigrants, European, as laborers 6, 41, 55, 93, 157–158
In Flanders Field see Robert Vonnoh
Independence Hall 154
Indian Scout (J. Massey Rhind) 175, 176
Ingersoll, Catherine Seely 34, 35
Ingersoll, Charles 34
Ingersoll, Jonathan 34
Inness, George; (*Tragedy at Sea*) 177
The Iron Age 66, 69, 138, 164, 171, 188; Butler's observations on France 162
Iron Trade Review 120, 162
Italian Renaissance 172, 173

James Ward & Company 21–24, **25**, 26, 30–32, 42; American Scotch pig iron 57; and Butler 67; Butler, Sr. 15, 17, 18; company scrip 22–23
Jay Cooke & Company 46
Jefferson, Joe 171
Jefferson Memorial 143
John H. Parker Company 148, 149, 174, 175
Johnson, Hiram 180
Joliet Steel Company 60
Jones, Captain Bill 58, 59
Jones, Jenkins 66, 112
Jones & Laughlin Steel Company 135, 143
Joseph G. Butler, Jr. 115
The Joseph G. Butler, Jr. Testimonial Banquet 129
A Journey Through France in War Time 162
Juniata Valley, iron industry 11, 12, 44

Kahn, Albert 139
Kaylor, Raymond J. 184, 186
Kelley, William 48, 65, 130
Kendall, William Mitchell 172, 173, 174
Kennedy, Julian 60, 66, 76, 77, 78, 82, 83
Kennedy, T.W. 58
King, Singleton 77
King Edward VII 113
King, Willis, and A.I.S.I 131; Butler house fire 171–172; National McKinley Birthplace Memorial 142–143; Underwood Tariff 135
Kirk, Frank M. 108, 109
Kitson, Hilda 112
Kitson, Sir James (former Lord Airedale) 66, 112
Kline, Peter 39
Knights Templar 149
Krass, Peter 85, 88
Krause, Paul 73
Kyle, Maria 145

labor strikes 49, 51, 52, 55–56, 71–72, 76, 77, 156–158
Lafayette 160
Lafayette, Gilbert du Motier, Marquis de 162
Lake Carriers Association 119
Lake Erie 13, 115
Lake Shore & Eastern Railroad 58
Lake Superior Nut & Washer Company 31
Lake Superior Ore Region 9, 22, 39, 43, 48, 57, 135
Lamoreaux, Naomi 77, 81
Lee, Robert E. 29
Leech, Margaret 88
Le Havre, England 162
Lenroot, Irvine 181
Leonard, the Rev. W.A. 190
Lewis, John 24
Lewis and Clark Centennial and American Pacific Exposition and Oriental Fair 110
Lewis and Clark Expedition 110
Liberty Bell 154–155
Liberty Bonds 153, 163
Liberty Township, Ohio 39, 44
Lincoln, Abraham 25, 28, 123, 180
Lincoln-Douglas Debates 25
Lincoln Memorial 143
Lind, Jenny 19, 112
Linkon, Sherry Lee 157
Lisbon, Ohio 16, 17, 88
Little Alice Furnace 104
Liverpool, England 162
Lloyd George, David 161
London, England 113, 126, 162, 164
The London Mining Journal on tariff reductions 45
Long, John D. 94
Lorain, Ohio 115
Lord Airedale *see* Kitson, Sir James
Louisiana Purchase Exposition 110
Lowden, Frank 180, 181
Lowellville, Ohio 36, 39, 44, 48
Luce's Press Clipping Bureau 153

M.A. Hanna Company 188
MacArthur, J.R. 162
Macbeth Gallery (New York) 176
Mahoning County (Ohio) 96, 118
Mahoning County Committee of the Women's Council of National Defense 163
Mahoning County Courthouse 139, 169
Mahoning County Republican Executive Committee, and McKinley presidential campaign 94
Mahoning Golf Club 122
Mahoning Institute of Art 158, 169, 172
Mahoning Iron Company 48

Mahoning National Bank 139
Mahoning (Ohio) *Courier* 38
Mahoning (Ohio) *Register* 46
Mahoning (Ohio) *Vindicator* 46
Mahoning River 17, 18, 36, 44, 74, 79, 99
Mahoning Valley Historical Society 122, 123, 130
Mahoning Valley Iron Company 71, 101
Mahoning Valley Iron Manufacturers' Association *see* Bessemer Pig Iron Association 63, 69, 70
Mahoning Valley Mortgage Company 165
U.S.S. *Maine* 91, 92
Manhattan Insurance Company 79
Maria Furnace 17
Marquette County (Michigan) 57, 59
Mason, Ethel Quinton 176, 177
Martinsburg, West Virginia 49
Mather, Samuel 103, 128
McDonald, Ohio 79
McDonald, Thomas, Brier Hill 66, 78–79; and Frick 78; and Ohio Steel 80, 82, 83; village named for 79
McElhaney, Margaret 19
McGraw, Arthur 129, 130, 171; Butler Art Institute 173; family 107, 155; marriage 68; medical treatment and death 185
McGraw, Arthur Butler 107, 155, 189, 191
McGraw, Grace Butler 185; birth 136; education in Berlin 64, 112; family 107; father's death 189; father's will 191; letter from her father 130; marriage 68; parents' fiftieth wedding anniversary 155
McGuffey Readers 24
McIntyre, Robert 176
McKim, Charles Follen 147
McKim, Mead & White 146, 147, 172, 174, 175, 176
McKinley, Helen 21, 152
McKinley, William 87–97, 130; ancestral home 113; biographical sketch 87; birth house 124; childhood in Niles 5, 18, 21; elected president 86; friendship with Butler 123; political career 19; saved from drowning 91; soldiers' monument 78; tariff proponent 142; train car to Buffalo 110
McKinley, William, Sr. 16, 88; in iron industry 14; and Joseph G. Butler, Sr. 14; moves family
to Poland, Ohio 21; and Tremont Furnace 21
McKinley coin 150
McKinley mausoleum (William McKinley Tomb in Canton) 143
McKinley Tariff of 1890 *see* Tariff of 1890
McKnight, William 13
McMaster brickyard 74

Index

McMillan, Reuben 35–36, 118
Mead, William Rutherford 147
Meadville, Pennsylvania 170
Meissner, C.A. 66
Melchers, Gari 112
Mellon, Andrew 6, 7
Menominee Range 57, 59
Mercer County (Pennsylvania) 12, 13, 14, 23, 57
Mercer Luminary 14
Merchant Marine League 119, 131, 180
Mesabi Iron Range 109
Meyer Robertson's Band 151
Michelangelo 172
Milburn, John 143, 144, 146
Mill Creek Park 140
Milwaukee, Wisconsin 47
Mineral Ridge, Ohio 22, 24, 57
Miners' Journal 45
Minerva 178
Minneapolis Institute of Art 174
Misa, Thomas 72
Mississippi River 38, 98
Monongahela River 72
Moore, William H. 85, 101
Morgan, John Hunt 29
Morgan, J.P. 5, 7, 84, 128; Federal Steel 101, 103; Gary Dinner 116
Morris, Evan 39
Morris County (New Jersey) 35
Morse, Anna 119, 124
Mosquito Creek 17
Murphy, Francis: *The Golden Wood* 171
My First Trip Abroad 184, 186

A Nation of Steel: The Making of Modern America, A 1865–1925, 72
National Biscuit Company 85
National Cordage Company 79
National Gallery (Berlin) 112
National Gallery (London) 113
National McKinley Birthplace Memorial Association 5, 130, 132, 142–153, **152**, 159, 163, 169, 172, 174, 179, 184, 186, 189, 191, 193; A.I.S.I. support 142, 143, 145; artifacts 150; Association created 143; B.F. Perry 149; busts 151, 152, 153; charter 143, 144; cornerstone 144, 148; cost 144, 146; Dedication Day 151; design 146; donations 144, 148; E.A. Gilbert 151; Elbert Gary donation 144; federal funding 143; fundraising campaign 145; Governor Frank Willis 149; Governor James Cox 151; Governor Myron Herrick 149, 152; Henry Clay Frick 148; J. Massey Rhind 147, 148, 150, 152; James Boyle 144, 145; John H. Parker Company 148, 149; Mahoning Valley support 143, 145, 149, 151; McKim, Mead, and White 146, 147; McKinley coin 150; Meyer Robertson 151; Niles Board of Trade 142, 146; President William Howard Taft's support 126, 143, 145, 150, 152; President Woodrow Wilson 148–149; trustee 143, 144, 150–151; U.S. Senator Warren G. Harding 149; W. Aubrey Thomas 143, 151
National Museum (Florence) 172
National Society of the Colonial Dames of America 186
National Steel Company 85, 98, 101, 103
Native Americans 107, 111, 170, 175, 177
Neilson, James 71
Nelson, Georgia 174
New Castle, Pennsylvania 124
New Dudley Gallery 113
New Wilmington, Pennsylvania 21
New York Central Railroad 58, 185
New York City 35, 59, 101, 112, 116, 119, 126, 137, 145, 146, 153, 154, 156, 158, 162, 164
New York Herald 139
New Lisbon, Ohio *see* Lisbon, Ohio
New York State Library 119
New York Stock Exchange 46
New York Times 131, 157, 160
New York Tribune 25
Newbury, Truman Handy 119
Niagara Falls 106
Nichols, William Wallace 160, 162
Niles, Hezekiah 17
Niles, Ohio 5, 14–16, 20–24, 28–30, 36, 42, 45, 57, 75, 87, 89, 124, 143, 144, 151, 155; Butler family life 16, 18, 19
Niles (Ohio) Board of Trade 124, 142, 146
Niles (Ohio) Chamber of Commerce 182
Niles (Ohio) Daily News 143, 145, 153
Niles (Ohio) Weekly Register 17
North Chicago Rolling Mill 31
Northamptonshire, England 186
Nye County (Nevada) 109

O'Brien, Ann 187
Ocean Mail Act 120
Ogden, Utah 107
Oglebay, E.W. 116
Ohio Federation of Women's Club 167
Ohio History Quarterly 187
Ohio National Guard 157
Ohio River 13, 29, 39
Ohio Steel Company 74–78, 80–85, 98, 101, 103, 138
Ohio-Tonopah Mining Company 108, 109
Olcott, Charles 14
The Old Homestead see Jefferson, Joe

Index 233

Old White Schoolhouse 19, 146, 176
Olinsky, Ivan 177
Oliver Iron and Steel 80
Orwig, Jacob 11
Orwig, Rebecca Mains 11
Ottawa, Canada 126
Owsley, Charles F. 139; designs Reuben McMillan Library 118; other building credits 169; Youngstown Museum of Art 168
Owsley and Boucherle 172
"Ox and Sheep" 112
Oyster Bay, New York 105, 106

Page, William 116
Palace Hotel 109
Pan-American Exposition 96, 97
Panama Canal 131, 134, 140
Panama-Pacific International Exposition 154, 155
Panic of 1837 13, 40
Panic of 1857 40
Panic of 1873 46, 53, 55
Panic of 1893 80, 81, 83
Panic of 1907 115–117
Paris, France 113, 164, 176
Park Theater 120
Parker, Rachel Gould 10
Pasadena, California 108
Passavant, Henry E. 84
Payne, Sereno 122
Payne-Aldrich Act 122, 132, 133, 135
Peckitt, Leonard 133
Pennsylvania and Ohio (P&O) Canal 16–19, 25, 36–37, 40–41, 48
Pennsylvania National Guard 72
Pennsylvania Railroad Company 49, 58, 163
Penrose, Boies 135
Penton, John 123, 162, 171, 187; Butler's funeral 190; Merchant Marine League 120, 131
Penton Press 162, 164, 184, 187
Perry, B.F. 149
Philadelphia, Pennsylvania 154, 155
Philadelphia and Reading Railroad 79
Philadelphia Centennial 1876, 109
Philadelphia Mint 150
Phillips Exeter Academy 155
Pickands Mather and Company 104
Pierce, Franklin 130
Pig Iron During 1904, 104
Pike's Peak 107
Pinkerton National Detective Agency 72
Pioneer Steamship Company 115
Pittsburgh, Pennsylvania 11, 12, 16, 17, 26, 41–43, 47, 49, 51, 53, 58, 73, 72, 76, 78, 90, 133, 138

Pittsburgh and Lake Erie Railroad 58
Pocono Mountains 35
Poland, Ohio 21, 60
Pollock, Porter 127
Pollock, Thomas 51–54, 56
Pollock, William "Uncle Billie" 33, 51, 54
Pope Julius II 172
Portage Silica Company 165
Porter, James 168
Portland, Oregon 110, 111
Presidents I Have Seen and Known—Lincoln to Taft 123, 129, 130
Pro Bono Publico 178
Progressive Party 159
Protestant Episcopal Diocese of Ohio 190
puddling 18, 71–72
Pulaski Iron Company 133
pull up boys 18, 24

Queen Alexandra 113

Ration Day at the Reservation see Sharp, Joseph Henry
The Rayen School 139
Rayner, Isidor 121
Recollections of Men and Events, Being Some Account of Activities, Experiences, Observations and Personal Impressions During a Long and Busy Life 28, 187
Red Cross 153, 63–165
Reid, Whitelaw 126
Reilly, Albert A. 184
Reno, Nevada 109
Republic Iron & Steel Company 99–101, 154–156
Republican National Conventions 93, 94, 138, 159, 180
Republican Party 25, 45, 89, 120
Reuben McMillan Free Library 122, 124, 139, 147, 148, 155, 192; and Andrew Carnegie 118, 122, 124, 147, 148; art displays 167, 169, 170, 175
Revolutionary War 10, 35
Rhind, J. Massey, biographical sketch 147; busts of Taft and Butler, Jr. 152; Carnegie bust 125, 147, 148; discusses with Butler the idea of an art museum 172; family plot 183, 190; McKinley statue 147, 148, 150; statues and assistance with Butler Art Institute 174–178; statutes at Butler
Richards, William 34, 38, 42, 43
Robber Barons 7
Robertson, Meyer 151
Robinson, Thomas L. 127
Rockefeller, John D. 6, 7
Rogers, William 134, 176

Index

Rogers-Brown Iron Company 134
Roosevelt, Theodore 93, 120; bust at National McKinley Birthplace Memorial 146, 151; Butler and Vice Presidency nomination on McKinley ticket 94; Butler visits at White House and Oyster Bay 105, 106; election results of 1912 138; and Merchant Marine 119; relations with Butler 123, 159; and U.S. Steel merger 103; visits World's Fair, 1904 110
Root, Elihu 151
Rosser, Benjamin, Mrs. 22
Roth, Leland M. 147
The Rowfant Club 123
Russell, Thomas 17
Russell, William 18
Russo, John 157

Sagamore Hill 105
Sage, Cornelia 176
St. Elizabeth Hospital 136, 137, 145, 191, 193; groundbreaking *138*
St. John's Episcopal Church 183, 185, 189, 190
St. Louis, Missouri 89, 154
St. Patrick's Church 136
Salineville, Ohio 29
Sallie Furnace 53
San Francisco, California 108, 109, 155
Sandy Creek Township (Mercer County) Pennsylvania 53
Sanford, Alva 20
Santa Anna 20
Schiller, William B. 60
Schlesinger, Arthur M., Jr. 122
Schmidlapp, J.G. 143
Schwab, Charles 9, *102*, 189; A.I.S.I. speech 163; and Belgium 131; Bethlehem Steel 128; business deal 81; friendship with Butler 129, 189; and United States Steel 101–104
Scotch pig iron 66
Scott, Tom 49
scrip 22, 23, 47
Sculpture in America 147
The Search for Order see Wiebe, Robert
Seely, Henry W. 35
Seely, Sylvanus 35
Self-help in the 1890's Depression 80
Shakespeare, William 113
Sharon, Pennsylvania 121
Sharon Iron Company 121
Sharp, Joseph Henry 175
Sharpsville, Pennsylvania 104
Shelar, Jacob 91
Shenango Canal 14
Shenango River Valley 12, 57

Simonds, George, and Lake Superior Nut & Washer Company 31
Simonds, Gustavus, and Lake Superior Nut & Washer Company 31
Singer Sargent, John 169
"A Small Museum and Its Value to a Community" 158
Snap the Whip see Homer, Winslow
Social Darwinism 56
Soldiers' Monument 78
Sons of the American Revolution 154
South Chicago Steel 76
South High School, Youngstown, Ohio 169
Southampton, England 162
Spanish-American War 86, 91, 93
Spencer, Herbert 56
spiegeleisen 60
Springfield, Illinois 25
Springfield Iron Company 60
Squirrel Island, Maine *164*, 165
Staffordshire, England 17
Stambaugh, Henry *70*, *165*, 169, 177; death 165; elected director of Youngstown Sheet & Tube 127; friendship with Butler, Jr. 53, 165; travels to the West with Butler 108
Stambaugh, John, Jr. 128; Butler Art Institute trustee 182; and launching of the *Joseph G. Butler, Jr.* 115; praise of Butler 129; and Tod-Stambaugh Company 188
Stambaugh, John, Sr. 51–53, 62; charity 62; death 62; partnership with David Tod 44; Youngstown Savings and Loan 40
Stambaugh Building 139
Standard Oil Trust 117
Standiford, Les 72, 73
Steel and Tube Company of America 104, 185
Steeltown, U.S.A. 157
Steese, Rollin 66, *70*, 85
Stevens, Nina 167, 169
Stratford-on-Avon 113
Struthers, Thomas 44
Struthers, Ohio 36, 75
Struthers Furnace 39, 58
Struthers Iron Company 53, 58
Stryker, the Rev. L.W.S. 190
Sulgrave Institution 186
Sulgrave Manor 125, 126, 186, 193
Swank, James Moore 130, 132

Taft, William Howard 123, 135, 181; Butler at White House 143; campaign of 1908 120; and McKinley memorial 145, 146, 151, 152; Payne-Aldrich 122; Republican Convention 1912 138; and Sulgrave Institute 126

Index

Tariff Act of 1890 (McKinley Bill) 88, 90
Tariff Commission 87–88, 120, 133
Tariff of 1842 40
Tate Gallery, London 113
Tayler, Robert Walker 94–96
Taylor, Zachary 130
Temperance Furnace 15, 16, 18
Thomas, Aubrey 143
Thomas, W.A. 134
Thomas Steel Company 134
Tiergarten 112
Tin Plate Company 85
Titanic 136, 137
Tod, Gov. David 36, 38–40, 43, 44, 46, 56, 67, 151, 186; biographical sketch 33–34; Butler 41, 52, 53, 62; Girard Iron Company 34, 39; and John Hunt Morgan 29; Soldier's Monument 46; Youngstown Savings & Loan 40
Tod, Sen. David 136, 188
Tod, George 58; Brier Hill Iron Company president 62; impression 62, **70**
Tod, Henry 58, 60, **70**
Tod, John 39
Tod, Butler & Company 60
Tod Furnace 53, 59
Tod House 126, 127
Tod-Stambaugh Company 39; creation 188
Toensmeier, Rev. E.S. 151
Toledo Museum of Art 167, 168
Toledo Review 49
Tonopah, Nevada 108, 109
Topping, John 154
"The Town Beautiful" 124, 142
Tragedy at Sea see Inness, George
Tremont Furnace 21
Trenton, New Jersey 118
Trumbull County (Ohio) 14, 28, 101
Trumbull Iron Company 101
Turner, J.J. 172
Twachtman, J.H. 169
Tyrolean Alps Café 110

Underwood Bill (Underwood-Simmons Tariff) 132, 135, 140, 141
Underwood, Oscar 128, 131, 132, 133
Union Club (Cleveland) 89, 128, 143
Union Iron and Steel Company 71
Union Pacific Railroad 80
United States Steel 79, 84, 102–104, 106, 115–118, 121, 128, 132, 138, 144, 156, 159, 180, 189
United States v. United States Steel Corporation 180
Universalism 10
University of Chicago 176

Valley Forge 10
Van Buren Magonigle, H. 146
Vanderbilt, Cornelius 5
Veterans of Foreign Wars 187
Vicksburg, Mississippi 29
Vienna Township, Ohio 44
Vonnoh, Robert: *In Flanders Field* 177
Von Zugel, Heinrich 112

Waldorf-Astoria Hotel 116, 117
Walker, Joseph 15
Wall, Joseph Frazier 121
Walter, Thebold 10
War of 1812 126
Ward, Eliza 21, 28
Ward, James, Jr. **20**, 28, 30, 42
Ward, James, Sr. birth 17; childhood 17; death 32; influence on Butler's life 23, 26, 28, 30, 32, 40, 67; and John Lewis's slate 24; at Lisbon 17; at McKinley Birthplace Memorial 151; move to Niles 15, 17; politics 25; rehires Butler, Sr. 21; steel production 65; tariff 40
Ward, William 15, 17, 18, 28, 34, 42, 43
Warner, Jonathan 168, 182
Warren, Kenneth 44, 63
Warren, Ohio 28, 34, 36, 65, 101, 124
Warren (Ohio) Chronicle 152
Warren Township, Ohio 28
Washington, George 10, 125, 147, 186
Washington, Lawrence 125
Washington, W. Lanier 186
Washington, D.C. 86, 92, 119, 126, 128, 140, 142, 143, 145, 154, 158
Washington Manor *see* Sulgrave Manor
Washington Monument 143
Watson, Lindsay 174, 175
Wayne County (Pennsylvania) 35
Weathersfield Township, Ohio 28, 146
Weeks, Joseph 65
Welsh, Dorothy 122
Welsh immigrants 22
Western Reserve 58, 95
Western Reserve Chronicle (Warren, Ohio) 130
Western Reserve Steel Company 134
Western Union 96
Westminster Abbey 112
Wheeling, West Virginia 53, 61
Whig party 25
White, J.G. 15
White, Standford 147
Wick, Caleb 24, 173
Wick, George D.: death 135–137; health 101; influence on steel plant construction 70–71; residence 68; Youngstown Hotel

Company 127; and Youngstown Iron Sheet and Tube Co. 100
Wick, Henry K. 75–78, 138, 172, 192
Wick, Mellicent 168
Wick, Myron 71
Wick, Phillip 192
Wick Ave. 68–69
Wickersham, George 118
Wiebe, Robert 39, 40, 44, 50, 89, 158
Wilkoff, William 100
William Macbeth Company 176
William the Conqueror 10
William Tod & Company 56, 64
William Ward & Company 42
Willis, Frank 149
Wilson, Woodrow, Butler and Underwood Tariff 141; Federal Trade Commission 154; Inaugural Address 138–139; and National McKinley Birthplace Memorial 148, 149; policy of neutrality during World War I 162; tariff reform 140
Windsor Castle 113
Winfield, H.H. 179
Wood Furnace 38
Wood, Leonard 180, 181
Wool and Woolens Act of 1867, 44
Wolverine Manufacturing Company 68
World's Fair Chicago 1893, 76, 110, 153, 154; St. Louis 1904, 110, 154
World War I 152, 153; and American steel industry 156, 160, 163, 164, 193
Wulf, W.H. 191
Wyandotte, Michigan 31

Youghiogheny River 42
Youngstown and Austintown Railroad 58
Youngstown Art Association 167
Youngstown Bessemer Steel Company 58
Youngstown Board of Health, Butler's service 130
Youngstown Chamber of Commerce 7, 123, 124, 130, 131, 139, 180
Youngstown City Council 39, 60, 68, 130
Youngstown City Hall 169
Youngstown City Hospital 136, 191
Youngstown, The City of Progress 139
Youngstown Club 120
Youngstown Country Club 122
Youngstown Defense Day 187
Youngstown Hotel Company 127, 136
Youngstown Humane Society 130
Youngstown Iron and Mining Company 59
Youngstown Iron Sheet and Tube Company, Inc. 100, 101, 103, 104
Youngstown Library Association 118
Youngstown Museum of Art 168, 169
Youngstown, Ohio 23, 36, 39, 45–47, 49, 64, 75, 76, 92, 120, 139, 154, 155, 162, 163, 167
Youngstown (Ohio) Courier 46
Youngstown (Ohio) Telegram 91, 95, 98, 99, 124, 151, 155, 156, 157, 170, 181, 184, 192
Youngstown (Ohio) Vindicator 49, 53, 54, 56, 65, 75, 76, 77, 79, 80, 90, 93, 94, 95, 123, 126, 137, 167, 170, 171, 173, 177
Youngstown Opera House Company 62
Youngstown Rolling Mill Company 55
Youngstown Savings and Loan Association 40
Youngstown Sheet and Tube Company 104, 106, 127, 128, 133, 136, 156, 161, 164, 165, 184, 185
Youngstown Steel Company 71, 134

Zantsinger, Borie & Medary 146
Zimmerman, William W. 182

www.ingramcontent.com/pod-product-compliance
Lightning Source LLC
Chambersburg PA
CBHW052059300426
44117CB00013B/2199